# GREATS *of the* GAME

*The Players, Games, Teams, and Managers That Made Baseball History*

RAY ROBINSON AND CHRISTOPHER JENNISON

# GREATS *of the* GAME

*The Players, Games, Teams, and Managers That Made Baseball History*

HARRY N. ABRAMS, INC., PUBLISHERS

FRONTISPIECE
Pitching for the Texas Rangers in 1991, Nolan Ryan
achieved his seventh no-hitter on May 1, at the age of
forty-four. The game was not televised, and fans listening
to radios started to line up at the ballpark as the seventh
inning began. *Dallas Times Herald* columnist Skip Bayless
wrote, "He wasn't just no-hitting the Toronto Blue Jays;
he was no-hoping them. He was overpowering and over-
matching the best-hitting team in the American League."

Project Manager: Christopher Sweet
Editor: Richard Slovak
Editorial Assistant: Isa Loundon
Designer: Darilyn Lowe Carnes
Production Manager: Jane Searle

Library of Congress Cataloging-in-Publication Data

Robinson, Ray, 1920 Dec. 4-
Greats of the game : the players, games, teams, and
managers that made baseball history/ Ray Robinson and
Christopher Jennison.
      p. cm.
  Includes bibliographical references and index.
  ISBN 0–8109–5882–1 (hardcover : alk. paper)
  1.  Baseball.  I. Jennison, Christopher.  II. Title.

  GV867.R543 2005
  796.357—dc22

                                  2004021400

Printed and bound in China
10 9 8 7 6 5 4 3 2 1

Harry N. Abrams, Inc.
100 Fifth Avenue
New York, N.Y. 10011
www.abramsbooks.com

Abrams is a subsidiary of

LA MARTINIÈRE
GROUPE

# Contents

*To Phyllis, who somewhat defensively "took up" baseball, then learned to agonize over it.*

R. R.

*To Nancy, my cheerleader and splendid companion.*

C. J.

# Acknowledgments

WE WOULD LIKE TO ACKNOWLEDGE AND THANK several people who helped us complete this book. At Abrams, Christopher Sweet, who has worked with us on two previous books, was a constant source of encouragement and good advice, and Isa Loundon worked efficiently and cheerfully in making sure all the details were seen to. A tip of the cap as well to Darilyn Lowe Carnes, for her creative talents in design, and Richard Slovak, who provided invaluable editorial work. Our good friend Andy Jurinko provided some splendid photographs of ballparks. Others who assisted in the picture research were Elvis Brathwaite at AP/Wide World, Carol Butler at Brown Brothers, Mark Rucker at Transcendental Graphics, Jim O'Leary at Sport Media Enterprises, Inc., and Jan Grenci, Mary Ison, and Khadija Camp at the Library of Congress. Lew Lipset kindly granted permission to use a photograph of Ebbets Field.

OPPOSITE
Sandy Koufax of the Los Angeles Dodgers. See pages 28, 29.

# Introduction

by Ray Robinson

MY FASCINATION WITH BASEBALL—some might unkindly call it an obsession—began more than seventy years ago. My next-door neighbor on the Upper West Side of Manhattan, a stoutish man named Mr. Prinz, invited me to join him in his box seats at the Polo Grounds. Previously I had rooted for two members of the New York Yankees, the unforgettable Iron Horse, Lou Gehrig, and a southpaw pitcher, Herb Pennock. Mind you, I rooted for Gehrig and Pennock, but not for their team! In fact, while the name of Babe Ruth was practically a religious mantra to the other little kids on the block, I didn't much care for him.

Then, for a while, I found myself much taken with the Philadelphia Athletics, though at the time I didn't have the slightest notion where Philadelphia was on the map. The fact that the Athletics had registered a preposterous ten runs in one inning of the 1929 World Series against the Chicago Cubs, when they had trailed 8–0 in the seventh inning, was obviously the factor that had drawn my youthful attention to the Athletics.

Back to Mr. Prinz. He was a German-born former bootlegger, with a pleasant wife, Maria. They were both in their sixties, which seemed incredibly old to me then, and they had no children. I think they took a fondness to me because I was quiet a good deal of the time and didn't get under their legs. As a passionate follower of baseball, Mr. Prinz spent many hours talking about the game with the doorman in our building, a wiry Irishman named Bill Fitzpatrick. Bill insisted that he had played minor-league baseball someplace or other, and I believed it. Years later I learned that Mr. Prinz had been an occasional drinking buddy of John McGraw's, the autocratic manager of the New York Giants.

My father had been a classmate at Columbia of the great Eddie Collins, the Hall of Fame second baseman. But that didn't make my dad into much of a baseball fan. I suspect he became demoralized about the game because the year before I was born, some sleazy gamblers had "played with the faith of 50 million people" (as F. Scott Fitzgerald wrote in *The Great Gatsby*) and fixed the 1919 World Series between the Chicago White Sox and the Cincinnati Reds. Thereafter, the White Sox transmuted into the Black Sox. Although Collins was a part of that White Sox team, he was not implicated in the fix. Nevertheless, the whole scenario saddened my father, and, I'm certain, any others who cherished the game.

So it was that Mr. Prinz, and not my father, introduced me to the wonders, romance, mystery, and timelessness of baseball. In the process, I turned into a Giants fan. It was fitting that an ex-bootlegger was the catalyst for my early conversion, for the major part of the Giants clientele in those years consisted of taxi drivers, down-on-their-luck actors, bookies, hooky players, Tammany ward heelers, theatrical celebrities, and, of course, ex-bootleggers.

In the interest of full disclosure, I should tell you that my fellow conspirator and collaborator on this book, picture man Chris Jennison, also started out in life as a Giants fan. "I was about eight years old, living in Rockland County," Chris recalls, "when my dad drove past the Polo Grounds one day. I was struck by the enormity of the place, compared to the sandlots I had been playing on, and from that time on I became a Giants fan." That is, until he saw an even bigger place: Yankee Stadium. That made him a Yankee fan. "I guess I also liked winning," Chris adds, thoughtfully. What long-suffering baseball fan would hold that against him? Chris and I remain mesmerized by the charm and endless promise of baseball, warts and all. I must admit, however, that we both stopped collecting bubble-gum cards a long time ago.

The late Yale president, Renaissance scholar, and commissioner of baseball, A. Bartlett Giamatti, once wrote, in a seeming moment of melancholy, that "baseball can break your heart." No truer words have ever been spoken about the sport; think, for instance, about those bedeviled Boston Red Sox, at least until 2004, and Chicago Cubs fans in 2003—and then the monumental collapse of the Yankees against those same Red Sox in the post-season of 2004.

But after baseball manages to break certain partisan hearts each long season, these same people often comfort themselves with the knowledge that there is always next year. That continues to be an essential part of the game's singular appeal, a kind of roseate, incalculable hope that exists from one season to the next. That's just another reason that baseball commands our attention, year in and year out. That is why we appreciate the game's climaxes, its anticlimaxes, its unexpected and serendipitous moments. Even the periods of languor in almost every baseball contest give us time to pause, to take a long breath, to gnaw on our hot dogs, to gulp our beers, to consult our scorecards, and to chat with our neighbors, whom we may never have seen before in our lives, and will never see again.

Baseball is seemingly a simple and primitive pastime—a stick-and-ball game—but it has more nuances, wrinkles, and complexities than even Euclid might ever have envisioned. Maybe it disturbs some people that many of the early heroes of baseball were fellows you wouldn't care to invite into your parlor. In the order of their social acceptance, these types rated about as high as circus clowns or train robbers. Even among many of today's overpaid and overweight athletes, there are those you would not want as role models for your children. But can you name any occupation, profession, or pursuit that doesn't encompass its own reprobates and recidivists? Perhaps we should transpose historian Jacques Barzun's oft-quoted statement—"Whoever wants to know the heart and mind of America had better learn baseball"—and, instead, have it read, "Whoever wants to know the heart and mind of baseball had better learn America."

It might make some baseball addicts squirm, but the outspoken actress Susan Sarandon has come closest to articulating what baseball still means to many millions. In the entertaining movie *Bull Durham*, she says, thanks to her screenwriter, the following: "I believe in the Church of Baseball. I've tried all of the major religions and most of the minor ones. And the only church that feeds the soul, day in and day out, is the Church of Baseball."

Amen.

# 1. The IMMORTALS

# "I swing big, I hit big, I miss big," SAID RUTH. "I live as big as I can."

**BASEBALL WAS WITH US**, in various modes, even before President Abraham Lincoln, pressed by stalwart abolitionists, fought to keep the Union intact. Of course, he didn't pursue this course to promote "the national pastime," as one addlebrained broadcaster of the 1940s once suggested. However, it has been reported on good authority that Honest Abe did take to the game, even as much as he loved rail-splitting. He "brought a baseball background to the White House," according to one imaginative publicist, who in 1939 was helping to celebrate baseball's purported centennial year.

A by-product of the fratricidal Civil War was that baseball *did* keep going—before and after the bloody business—and does to this day. Many young men relished playing the grand game from morning till night on front yards, on sandlots, and on pastures that were often festooned with cow deposits representing each base. Town ball, an early version of the game, marked the social culture of those times. Historian Carl Sandburg wrote that as a youth his "head seemed empty of everything except baseball names and figures." But Sandburg was not alone in such mental exercises, and in the ensuing years other generations of youngsters have followed the same engaging pastime.

Still another intriguing aspect of baseball is that it has produced hundreds of heroes and icons, from one generation to the next. You can set off a whale of an argument anytime as to who exactly qualifies for consideration as baseball royalty—or, to use a more tumescent phrase, baseball immortality. No other sport seems to have collected such worthies, and in such numbers. These so-called immortals have evolved from all backgrounds, humble and grand. Sometimes the word *immortal* has been used more loosely than it should be. The human fireplug, Hack Wilson of the Chicago Cubs, who pounded out fifty-six home runs in 1930, as well as a National League record of 190 RBIs, died in a Baltimore gutter in 1948. He had a spotty career, cut short by his excesses in the barrooms of whatever town he was playing in. An inscription over his grave in Martinsburg, West Virginia, reads: "One of baseball's

immortals, Louis R. 'Hack' Wilson rests here." But baseball quite never embraced the unfortunate Hack, so it is clear that the lapidary tribute to him remains a sentimental exaggeration. Immortals have come in all shapes, sizes, hues, predispositions, temperaments, and attitudes. They have hailed from all geographic sections and represent every religious persuasion that you can think of. They have been Irish-American, German-American, Italian-American, Polish-American, Backwoods-American, Big City–American. Some have been well educated, while others didn't even finish public school. Some have lived tumultuous lives; others have specialized in tranquillity. One, a great pitcher named Dizzy Dean, insisted he was born in three different states. Another, Ty Cobb, the masterful hitter, was always in one state—of anger.

All of these factors have contributed to the role baseball has played—and will play—in attracting fans, young and old, wise and foolish. Incoming groups to the United States, eager to assimilate, as they have always been; become "Americanized" by an attachment to baseball. Others who have been here longer "continue to love baseball so much because the past casts an important shadow on the present," David Halberstam has written. "Players are measured not just against those whom they play today, but against those who have gone before them."

Thus, we cherish looking back at our most accomplished players. And as we mull over the candidates for immortality, it is inevitable that we start with one glowing figure: George Herman "Babe" Ruth.

It's easy to refer to **BABE RUTH** as larger than life, for that is the way he always regarded himself. "I swing big, I hit big, I miss big," said Ruth. "I live as big as I can." He was certainly the biggest—and most implausible—personality the game has ever produced.

Though gone since 1948, when he died in New York City at the age of fifty-three, if Ruth suddenly appeared today, just about everyone in the world would know exactly who he was. How could anyone not be able to recognize that

Babe sitting in the Griffith Stadium locker room on September 30, 1934, his last day in a Yankee uniform. Before the game, he was presented with a parchment scroll bearing the signatures of ten thousand admirers. The first signer was Franklin D. Roosevelt. The presentation followed a performance by a fifty-piece band from St. Mary's Industrial School of Baltimore, where Babe had lived for several years.

pumpkin face with the Santa Claus cheeks? And who among all of these people would not know that he was a more prolific hitter of higher-than-heaven home runs than any other player who ever lived? Yes, pure and simple, Ruth's thundering melody lingers on.

Everyone loved the Babe, outside of enemy pitchers and, of course, those Red Sox fans, who once professed that there was a Curse of the Bambino that accounted for their team's dismal fortunes ever since he was sold to the Yankees. Babe broke all of the rules. He ate like a wolf, drank Prohibition booze without restraint, and did his share of womanizing. He could be uncouth and had a hard time remembering anybody's name. He quipped that Depression-era president Herbert Hoover deserved to receive a smaller salary, because "I had a better year than he did." He never became a manager, because the conventional wisdom said he couldn't manage himself.

But for all of his imperfections, Babe Ruth captured the fancy of millions of post–World War I fans, only bowing out in 1935, when be was fatigued, fat, and about forty. When he hung up his spikes, with his then record 714 lifetime home runs (and 15 in World Series play), the Ruthian myths were constantly written about and argued over. Did he really eat ten hot dogs and wash them down with ten soda pops before a game? Did Babe really point to Wrigley Field's center-field bleachers in the 1932 World Series, signaling to all the world that he was about to hit a homer there? Did Babe really ever hold manager Miller Huggins by the legs out of the last car of a speeding train? Did Leo Durocher, as a devilish rookie, really steal Babe's watch when both men were with the Yankees? Did Babe really try to commit suicide when no team would hire him as a manager?

The answer to all of these questions is probably not, or at least not proven, as Scottish law would have it. But it keeps reminding us about the ongoing, compelling Ruthian legend—more myth than history, or more history than myth?

Babe Ruth started life in Baltimore in February 1894, or February 1895 (the exact date

has long been in dispute). But there is little dispute about the dismal circumstances of his childhood. Another Ruth myth paints him as an orphan. That wasn't so. Babe himself always denied that portrayal. However, his bartender father didn't have much time for him, and his mother died when he was thirteen years old. Always candid about his roots, Babe admitted he was nothing but "a bum" in his early years. That he avoided school with a passion was common knowledge.

At the age of seven, Ruth was consigned to a Baltimore school for boys, where he was suppos-edly training to become a tailor or shirtmaker. Brother Matthias, taking an interest in him, realized the boy wasn't cut out to be either. What he did notice was Ruth's singular baseball talent. In Ruth's late teens, Jack Dunn, a for-mer journeyman pitcher now running the Balti-more Orioles, became the boy's "guardian" by agreement with Brother Matthias. It is worth noting that Ruth would be paid $600 for the whole season, about $100 a month.

"You'll make it," Brother Matthias assured his protégé. As it turned out, no truer words had ever been uttered about a ballplayer's prospects. Dunn also did Ruth another favor. His young pupil would soon be known as "Dunn's baby," a reference that was inevitably altered to "Babe." In those days, Babe was a common nickname, shorthand for any kid player who wasn't yet shaving.

In mid-season of 1914, Baltimore, needing money, sold Babe, who had become a southpaw pitcher, to Boston for $2,900. It was as a pitcher that Babe first drew attention to his potential as a player of varied and immense talents. By 1916 and 1917, Babe was winning more than twenty games each year. In two World Series, against the Brooklyn Dodgers and the Chicago Cubs, he rang up twenty-nine and two-thirds straight innings of scoreless pitching, a mark that held up until another future Yankee lefty, Whitey Ford, broke it four decades later.

But by 1919, manager Ed Barrow had moved Ruth to the outfield; he had been encouraged to do so by Red Sox outfielder

PREVIOUS
**Babe Ruth has just clouted his first home run of the 1932 season. The Tigers' Mickey Cochrane can only watch, if not admire. A month later, a** *Boston Evening American* **headline read, "Ruth to Head New Red Sox." The article claimed that the sale of the team was contingent on Ruth's agreeing to assume the manager's job in 1933, and that the source of the story was "unimpeachable." When asked about it, Babe said, "It's news to me."**

Harry Hooper, who appeared to be the first to recognize that Babe would be more valuable as a full-time player. After the season ended, the financially pressed Red Sox moved Ruth to the New York Yankees. (Barrow followed him a year later, as general manager of the New York team.) The move literally transformed the game of baseball, as well as transforming the Yankees into the mightiest team in the sport. Many have suggested that Babe's arrival with the Yankees saved baseball from self-destruction, lifting the profession out of the ashes of the recent Black Sox scandal.

With his bat and his personality, Babe also became the catalyst that propelled the Yankees ahead of John McGraw's Giants in the affections of thousands of New York fans. As the homers boomed off his bat—fifty-four in 1920, fifty-nine the next year—Babe became the dominant figure in New York baseball, causing Mr. McGraw unending heartache.

By 1923, the Yankees' owner, Colonel Jacob Ruppert, who had brought Babe to the Bronx in a move of transcendent prescience, also supplied his star with a new ballpark: the dramatic Yankee Stadium. From the first moment Babe placed his celery-stick legs on stadium turf, he fell in love with the place. As he helped to lure fans into the stadium, almost doubling home-game attendance (as well as becoming a mammoth attraction out of town), it became inevitable that the secular cathedral would be dubbed "the House That Ruth Built." Waite Hoyt, a fine pitcher and a teammate of Babe's in the 1920s, said, "He was the greatest crowd-pleaser of them all."

In 1927, Babe hit his landmark sixty home runs—often called "the sacrosanct sixty." Power hitters of later eras may have punched holes in that mark, but that has failed to diminish the Ruthian achievement—he got there first, long before anyone else. Ruth's blasts helped to get the Yankees into seven World Series. His club, known as Murderers' Row, won four straight in three of those Series, in 1927, 1928, and 1932. His name became synonymous with home-run slugging, but that didn't prevent him from compiling a lifetime batting average of .342, which

was solid evidence that he could reach base without homers.

Babe was a law unto himself, in a rowdy, noisy, undisciplined era of flagpole sitters, stock-market manipulators, bathtub gin, English Channel swimmers, gangsters in white fedoras, Lindy Hoppers, and some laughable presidents. He was the icon to end all icons, surpassing Jack Dempsey, Bobby Jones, Red Grange, Bill Tilden, Knute Rockne, and the non-sports-page hero of the day, Charles A. Lindbergh.

Yes, some of Ruth's records have gone the way of all flesh. But Babe was Babe. "The Ruth is mighty and shall prevail," wrote columnist Heywood Broun in 1923. Indeed, Babe has prevailed—and still does.

Well-earned immortality for **TYRUS RAYMOND COBB** does not imply that he was a man of impeccable character or equable disposition. To the contrary, Ty Cobb was probably the meanest and most despised ballplayer of his time (1905–28). He was a reptilian person and a certifiable racist and bigot, who thought the South hadn't lost the Civil War. Despite all of these flaws, Cobb, who played with Detroit and the Athletics, may have been the most talented, dedicated hitter who ever played the game for money. Some have said he would have played even if he had been charged something for the privilege.

There wasn't any phase of the game that Ty Cobb couldn't execute—and well. He always said he didn't care to hit home runs. But when Babe Ruth came along, Cobb, in 1921, at the age of thirty-five, hit twelve of them, more than he'd ever hit before. He wanted to demonstrate that he could do it, if he chose to. No player of Cobb's time could bunt as well as he did, or steal bases as successfully, and with as much ferocity, as he did. With a lifetime batting average of .367, the highest of any player in history, he led the American League in batting twelve times, including nine times consecutively. He led in stolen bases six times, frequently precipitating fights as his spikes came in high on intimidated infielders. His total number of hits in his career was eventually surpassed only by

Pete Rose, who edged out Cobb's 4,191 hits fifty-seven years after Cobb left the game.

In Cobb's final year, when he was forty-two, he stole home one last time, giving him thirty-five such swipes in his career. His final batting average in that valedictory season was .323. When he was past seventy, he was still convinced he could hit over .300. Shockingly, there were those who agreed with him.

Cobb played with a constant rage that may have accounted, in part, for his brilliance. He possessed no humor, and jokes made about his temper and personality were rewarded on the field by punches and spikings. On one memorable occasion, he jumped into the stands at Hilltop Park in New York and beat up a fan who had presumably been razzing him. It turned out that the victim of his assault had no hands. Known as the Georgia Peach, in honor of his home state, he was regarded sourly by those who played against him. But many of his teammates also loathed him. One called him "a rotten skunk"; another described him as "a really hateful guy." Such antipathy, which would have diminished another, less combative man, did not deter him on the diamond.

"My batting average has been increased by at least fifty points by qualities that I'd call purely mental," said Cobb, in one of his many self-assessments. Certainly Cobb would have picked himself as the greatest player of all time. But he had little use for modern-day players. In his mind, they were either fakers or malingerers, a harsh judgment from a harsh man.

Many explanations have been offered for Cobb's behavior. A sports columnist who covered Cobb, Paul Gallico, said he was a mental case. Al Stump, Cobb's biographer, who spent a good deal of time with him in the last years of the player's life, was disgusted by Cobb's "vile temper and mistreatment of others." Not being a psychiatrist, Stump did not offer a psychological profile; he left that to others. To outside observers, and by any fair standard, Cobb could have been a psychopathic personality. Possibly the best clue to his psyche may reside in the murder of his father, whom Cobb revered, by his mother in 1905, when Cobb was nineteen

Even in batting practice, Ty Cobb wore an embattled expression. His characteristic grip enabled him to achieve masterly bat control, and he rarely stood still in the batter's box, preferring to position himself as advantageously as he could. Fred Haney, who played with Cobb for four seasons, told a reporter, "Cobb was the first man who really put psychology into baseball. . . . He worked along entirely original lines."

OPPOSITE
By 1913, when this picture was taken, Cobb had played for the Tigers for eight seasons, and he had accumulated nearly four hundred stolen bases. Branch Rickey, who managed the St. Louis Browns when Cobb was at the peak of his career, said, "He has brains in his feet."

One called [Cobb] *"a rotten skunk"*; another described him as "A REALLY HATEFUL GUY."

years old. His mother insisted that the killing was a ghastly mistake, and she was exonerated in a trial. Many feel that the deed could have implanted the seeds of hatred and paranoia in her son.

Whatever the truth happens to be, Ty Cobb is a baseball immortal, whether we like it or not.

"God gets you to the plate," said **TED WILLIAMS**, "but from there on, you're on your own." Has any player ever known as much about the art of hitting as Theodore Samuel Williams, a man who spent most of his waking hours thinking about hitting a baseball? He may even have dreamt about it.

It was not uncommon throughout Williams's career with the Boston Red Sox (1939–60, with time out for military service in 1943–45 and parts of 1952–53) for him to stand in front of a mirror in his hotel room and swing his south-paw bat. On one occasion, it is reported, he inadvertently smashed a bedpost into splinters. "What power!" he said, exultantly.

The Williams legend, supported by his life-time batting mark of .344 (better than those of Joe DiMaggio, Willie Mays, Mickey Mantle, and Stan Musial), owes much to the afternoon of September 28, 1941, the final day of that season. Ted came into that doubleheader at Philadelphia's Shibe Park with a batting average of .3996 (which would be rounded up to .400). His manager, Joe Cronin, informed him that he could sit down that day and still join with pride the exclusive circle of .400 hitters. But in his moment of truth, Williams had stubbornly made up his mind. He had only one impulse, and that was to play.

"I don't want anyone to say that I walked through the back door," he said. "A man is a .400 hitter or he isn't. He's got to prove it."

Prove it he did. In the first game, he banged out four hits in five trips to the plate. In the second game, he went two for three. The end result of such a commitment: a final batting average of .406 and entry into the ranks of the .400 immortals. The last player to have climbed that mountain had been Bill Terry of the New York Giants, who finished at .401 in 1930. Since

Ted did it, no other player has gotten there. "With the fading of the Babe, the totemic bats-man was Williams," wrote Donald Honig.

There would be other signal achievements in Ted's career, all of which added considerably to his luster. He compiled 521 home runs, won six American League batting titles, and was voted his league's Most Valuable Player twice. In the 1941 All-Star Game at Detroit, Ted hit a game winner against pitcher Claude Passeau with two men on base in the ninth inning, when his team trailed by a run. "Boy, wasn't that a pip of a homer!" he exclaimed in the clubhouse after the game. He hit another truly amazing All-Star Game home run in 1946, playing in his own backyard at Fenway Park. The blow came off the "eephus pitch" delivery of hurler Rip Sewell. It was a junk pitch thrown so high that a trailer truck could have been driven under it. But Ted propelled the almost unpropellable ball some 380 feet.

As a fitting valedictory to his career, Ted hit a home run in his last at bat in 1960, off pitcher Jack Fisher of Baltimore. Only ten thousand fans were on hand to see Ted bid good-bye in such a fitting fashion. But writer John Updike provided a literary gem on the subject: "He ran as he always ran out his homers, hurriedly, unsmiling, head down, as if praise were a storm of rain to get out of."

The Williams temperament, abrasive and volcanic at times, and at other times rude and impatient, caused some Red Sox fans to regard him with distaste. You don't spit at fans, as he once did, and win friends either in the stands or in the press box. He wasn't too good defen-sively in the outfield either, but that phase of the game never appeared to interest him.

"When I'm an old man I want to walk down the street and have people say, 'There goes the game's greatest hitter,'" he once said. The remark belongs on his plaque at Cooperstown.

Off the field, the Splendid Splinter (he was six-foot-three and weighed about 190 pounds) served as a Marine pilot in World War II and in Korea. He was the *real* John Wayne (whom he was said to resemble) of his time; Wayne never served in any war, anywhere. In fact, Ted was

OPPOSITE

"Get a good ball to hit," Rogers Hornsby told Ted Williams in 1939, Ted's rookie sea-son. The advice was followed obsessively. In 1957, he walked 119 times in 132 games. "I'd never pitch to him in a close game if there was a base open," Bob Feller said. But genius can exact a price. In 1946, Bob Considine wrote, "He is a bed of assorted neuroses as are all artists from painters to adept street cleaners."

Ted Williams was not an easy man to interview. In 1956, Les Woodcock, a *Sports Illustrated* reporter, approached Williams as he left the batting-practice cage at Yankee Stadium. Williams scowled and walked toward Woodcock, waving his bat menacingly in front of him. Woodcock was reasonably certain that Williams would stop short of hitting him, but he didn't wait to find out.

PAGES 22–23
Yankee catcher Bill Dickey once conducted a pregame discussion of the Red Sox lineup. He reviewed the strengths and weaknesses of the Boston hitters, and when he got to Ted Williams, he looked up, shrugged, and said, "Boys, he's just a damned good hitter."

OPPOSITE
After 2,130 consecutive games, Lou Gehrig took himself out of the lineup in Detroit on May 2, 1939. His replacement, Babe Dahlgren, was stunned by the news, and he needed some encouragement from Lou. The Yankees won that afternoon, 22–2, but no one celebrated.

handsome as hell, even better looking than the movie star.

Born in San Diego in August 1918, Ted was the product of what has come to be called a dysfunctional family. "A terrible home," David Halberstam wrote about Ted's roots. His father was an alcoholic, and his mother was a neurotic Salvation Army worker who had little time for her son. Such a relationship caused him deep hurt and probably was the catalyst for both his anger and his compulsion for excellence as a batter.

The fact that his mother was half Mexican must have weighed heavily in making him a person who tried to treat all kinds of people fairly. When he was inducted into the Hall of Fame in 1966, he lobbied strongly for previously shunned Negro Leagues stars such as Satchel Paige and Josh Gibson to be admitted to baseball's sanctum.

Have you ever heard of any baseball fan—past or present, partisan or nonpartisan—who hasn't chosen **LOU GEHRIG** as the all-time first baseman? No, you haven't. There's no contest.

Yet Gehrig is remembered today for much more than his prodigious slugging, his Iron Horse commitment (a record 2,130 consecutive games, until Cal Ripken Jr. came along), and his symbiotic relationship with teammate Babe Ruth. To those in the world who suffer from ALS (now also called Lou Gehrig's disease), Lou is a symbol and an icon in the search to find a cure for the still-incurable disease that killed him in 1941. One female ALS advocate, whose mother has the disease, said of Lou that "he is a beloved figure, a man of strength and consistency."

The witty rhymer Ogden Nash once penned this little four-line tribute to Gehrig:

G is for Gehrig
The Pride of the Stadium
His record pure gold
His courage, pure radium

While Gehrig has become an inspiration to Nash and millions of others for his character

and stamina, we must never forget his remarkable overall record. As he followed Babe in the Yankee lineup (wearing number 4, a numeral now retired by the Yankees), he amassed a lifetime batting average of .340, only a few points lower than Ruth's. Of his 493 home runs, 23 were hit with the bases loaded, still the all-time high in that department. His runs batted in each year included the all-time American League mark of 184 in 1931. In four other seasons, he also led his league in RBIs, marking him as one of the most productive batters in history.

Lou's luck reached a new high—and low—on the afternoon of June 3, 1932, in Philadelphia. That day he hit four home runs in the first seven innings and barely missed a fifth homer in the ninth inning. The four blows in four consecutive times at bat marked the first time any player in the twentieth century had performed such a feat. Yet, once again, Lou had to settle as a runner-up. That same day, John McGraw resigned after thirty years as the manager of the New York Giants, robbing Lou of the headlines that he so richly deserved.

First it had been Babe Ruth, whose silhouette had overshadowed Lou's own profile; then came McGraw. And then, in 1936, came the elegant center fielder Joe DiMaggio to take attention away from the Yankee captain.

However, there was nothing to reduce Lou to secondary status on July 4, 1939, when he spoke his short, emotional farewell to baseball. His memorable words—the game's Gettysburg Address—have found their way into many anthologies of the world's greatest speeches. I was at Yankee Stadium that day and feel privileged to have heard his valedictory.

After Gehrig ceased being such a dynamic force on the diamond, he had behaved with such grace that he was at once elected to Baseball's Hall of Fame. In time, he would become a figure who transcended his sport.

Lou was born in 1903 in New York City into a lower-middle-class family, for whom money was often hard to come by. He went to Commerce High School, then to Columbia University, where he starred in baseball and football. When

On July 4, 1939, a galaxy of former teammates and rivals, as well as politicians and celebrities, gathered at Yankee Stadium to honor Gehrig. New York Mayor Fiorello LaGuardia is seen here shaking hands with Lou, and Babe Ruth, in a white suit, is applauding. Before the game, Lou told a friend, "There hasn't been a day since I came up that I wasn't anxious to get into uniform and out on the field. But today I wish I was anywhere but in this stadium."

OPPOSITE
Lou Gehrig was one of the most powerful hitters in baseball history, and this picture displays where a lot of the power resided. Pitcher Sam Jones, a teammate of Gehrig's for four seasons, said, "Lou was the kind of boy if you had a son, he's the kind of person you'd like your son to be."

*G is for Gehrig*
*The Pride of the Stadium*
*His record pure gold*
*His courage, pure radium*

the Yankees came along, he dropped out of Columbia, after only one year of college baseball. Yet Columbia now honors him as one of its Living Legacies, the only athlete so honored among a covey of distinguished poets, scholars, scientists, and world figures.

A boy, then a man, of the city, Lou chose to spend the last two years of his life serving on Mayor Fiorello LaGuardia's Parole Board. Eleanor Gehrig, Lou's wife since 1933, said Lou wanted to give something back to the city that had nurtured and inspired him.

On June 2, 1941, Lou died at home. He was not yet thirty-eight years old. His ashes rest in Kensico Cemetery, near White Plains, New York, only a few miles from where Babe Ruth is buried.

In the first game of the 1963 World Series between the Los Angeles Dodgers and the New York Yankees, at Yankee Stadium, **SANDY KOUFAX** struck out a record-tying fifteen Yankees, in a demonstration of blazing consistency. I sat next to the former major-league pitcher Jim Hearn that afternoon and listened to him say, rather enigmatically, that Sandy's artistry had been "boring."

Koufax struck out the first three Yankee batters on twelve pitches. He struck out Bobby Richardson three times, after Bobby had whiffed only twenty-two times in more than six hundred at bats during the regular season. He fooled Mickey Mantle twice on strikeouts. This was "boring"? Had Hearn really meant to say soaring instead of boring?

Four days later in that Series, Sandy beat the Yankees, 2–1, to clinch a four-game sweep for the Los Angeles Dodgers.

Sandy's career started in 1955 with the Brooklyn Dodgers. Until 1961, when he won eighteen games, he had never won more than eleven games in a season. After six years in a wilderness of wildness, Sandy suddenly emerged as the best pitcher of his generation. In the next six years, through 1966, he was almost unhittable. He was feared, admired, and appreciated by friend and foe alike. "I start every game with the hope of pitching a no-hitter," Sandy said, without braggadocio, "and after

that first hit, I'm trying for a one-hitter. If I lose a shutout, then I try to pitch a one-run game."

Koufax had been transformed from a journeyman flinger into a true pitching giant of his time. Perhaps no great pitcher had ever taken so long to incubate as Koufax, but when he finally achieved his pitching maturity he was simply devastating. The turnaround featured some amazing achievements. Witness: 129–47 win-loss record; four no-hitters, including one perfect game; a record five straight earned-run-average titles; more than three hundred strikeouts in each of three different years.

Then, just as suddenly as Koufax had become the preeminent southpaw of his time, and of any time (with possible apologies to Warren Spahn and Lefty Grove), it all ended for him at age thirty-one. One day he announced he didn't care to pitch any longer, because he had degenerative arthritis that caused him to devour painkilling pills and bathe his shoulder in ice after each game. He had never let on before that he was in such discomfort. He had been stoic about it, and he had often pitched after only two days' rest. But doctors had told him he could be crippled if he kept pitching. The baseball world was shocked by his retirement. But to Koufax it was the prudent thing to do, even in an age of increasingly high salaries for ballplayers.

Before World War II, Hank Greenberg, the Detroit Tigers' slugger, had played a singular role for many in America's Jewish community. He became a beacon of hope and pride for them in a dark world in which Europe's Jews were being murdered by Hitler's thugs. In the postwar 1950s and especially the 1960s, it was the handsome, reserved Koufax, the kid from Brooklyn, who took over Greenberg's legacy among many of his fellow Jews. Neither man had sought such an anointment, but when it was thrust upon them they acted with grace. It was a bit much to rate Koufax as the greatest Jew since Einstein or Freud; a more apt description was one newspaper assessment that "he was a cross between a Greek god and Gregory Peck."

It was ironic that Sandy Koufax started out as a basketball player at the University of

At the peak of his career, Sandy Koufax was a frightening mound presence. In the Dodgers' sweep of the Yankees in the 1963 World Series, he won two complete games, struck out twenty-three batters, walked three, and gave up only three earned runs. "I see how he won twenty-five games," Yogi Berra said of Koufax's regular-season totals. "What I don't understand is how he lost five."

RIGHT
In early June 2004, Bob Feller was asked to name the best pitcher he ever saw, a question that encompassed several decades of expertise. "Sandy Koufax" was Feller's unhesitating reply. Koufax is seen here early in his Los Angeles tenure, as he was still developing into a dominant pitcher. "I became a good pitcher," he said, "when I stopped trying to make them miss the ball, and started trying to make them hit it."

"*I start every game with the hope of pitching a no-hitter,*" SANDY said, *without braggadocio, "and after that first hit, I'm trying for a one-hitter. If I lose a shutout, then I try to pitch a one-run game.*"

When Willie Mays reported to military service in May 1952, the Giants lost their next
eight out of ten games, and dropped out of first place. In 1954, when Willie returned,
the Giants won a world championship. He especially enjoyed playing against the
Dodgers. From 1954 through 1960, Willie played against them in 153 games, just
about a full season in those days, and he batted .376 and hit fifty-seven homers.

Cincinnati in 1953, but he soon shifted to baseball. In 1954, when he was nineteen years old, he signed with the Dodgers for a $20,000 bonus, a lot of money for those times. The fact that he threw nothing but balls in his beginning years antagonized some of his teammates. His manager, Walter Alston, was mystified by his chronic wildness. "What the hell have we got here?" he asked himself. In a few years, Alston and the other doubters wouldn't have any more rancorous questions.

In the early 1960s, when Koufax emerged as such an icon, I had a bright, lively secretary who begged me to get Sandy's autograph for her. I enlisted Ed Linn, a biographer of Koufax, to obtain the signature. When I presented the autograph to her, she was beside herself with joy. She told me recently that the autograph, inside Linn's book, still occupies a place of honor in her Maryland house.

There aren't many players—immortals or otherwise—who would rate being described as charismatic. But that's what **WILLIE MAYS** was, in every sense of the word. Preceded by an avalanche of publicity and flummery before he joined the New York Giants in May 1951, the twenty-year-old's zestful, buoyant style of play immediately seized the imagination of slumbering Giants fans. But those fans had to suffer Willie's first twelve at bats, which produced twelve loud outs. It might have been expected that Willie's manager, Leo Durocher, would have cussed the young man out, for Leo was not noted for his soothing diplomacy. Instead, Durocher put his arm around the lad. "You're my center fielder," he assured Willie. The next day at the Polo Grounds, Willie connected for a home run in his first at bat against the redoubtable Warren Spahn of the Braves. The first to comment, exuberantly and poetically, was manager Durocher: "I never saw a fucking ball go out of a fucking ballpark so fucking fast in my fucking life."

Thus began the beautiful friendship between Willie and his Giants supporters. It's fair to say that they loved him unconditionally in New York, and although when Willie went

Willie Mays often appeared to play baseball just for the sheer fun of it. He told Roger Kahn in 1956, "You shouldn't fight about how much you're gonna get. You love the game and practice it and play it good, and you don't have to worry. The money, it'll come."

OPPOSITE
Willie, seen here in 1951, his rookie season, joined the Giants three weeks after his twentieth birthday. Manager Leo Durocher encouraged Willie through his first few uncertain games. "Willie has a contagious happiness," Durocher said.

*There aren't many players who would rate being described as* charismatic. *But that's what Willie Mays was.*

west to San Francisco in 1958 the fans there were somewhat less accepting (one columnist remarked that San Francisco was a city that booed Willie Mays and cheered Khrushchev), that was no sign that the talent of the world's greatest center fielder had depreciated in the least. In fact, he remained a hero for all time in New York after only six seasons there, even as he put together fifteen splendid seasons in Tony Bennett's favorite city.

"Willie's legend seems to spin upon an axis of stunning defensive plays," baseball historian Donald Honig has written. That is largely true, but it overlooks the fact that had Willie not spent part of the 1952 season and all of 1953 in military service, he most certainly would have overtaken Babe Ruth's sacrosanct home-run record. In addition, Willie may have been a better all-around base runner than Joe DiMaggio, who it was said never made a mistake on the base paths.

Nevertheless, it is hard to enumerate the number of defensive gems that Willie pulled off. He established his basket catch as a crowd-pleasing trademark and often followed that up with returns that were reminiscent of an expert javelin thrower. But when one of those defensive moments occurs in a World Series, "with the whole world watching," it automatically becomes more memorable. That particular episode even sparked an entire book by a friend of mine, Arnold Hano, who chose that moment to be in the Polo Grounds center-field bleachers, by far the best vantage point to observe Willie's deed. Suffice it to say that Willie decorated that first game of the 1954 World Series between the Giants and the heavily favored Cleveland Indians with an eighth-inning over-the-shoulder catch of Vic Wertz's sizzling, 470-foot drive. There were two men on base, with the score tied, and, following Willie's incredible grab, Al Rosen, who had been on first base, had to scramble back to first when Willie unleashed a throw that may have been even more remarkable than the catch.

That the Giants went on to win that game in the tenth inning may be beside the point. For many still believe that when Willie made his

audacious haul, Cleveland was pronounced dead on the spot. I don't concur with such a thought. But the record does show that the Indians lost the Series in four straight games, so you can draw your own conclusions about the effect of Willie's magic.

There are many who think that Willie was the consummate player, with a range of skill, brains, and uncanny reflexes that added to the innocence with which he played the game. They may have also noted that his temperament helped—intensely competitive without anger, never considered overtly troublesome to the white sensibility like the unrelenting Jackie Robinson (who paved the way for Willie's more benign disposition), and with a frivolous manner that belied his savvy.

What happened to those endearing characteristics after Willie finished his twenty-two-year career is another matter, for it has been suspected that Willie seethed at his lack of recognition, compared to the homage paid to such white contemporaries as Mantle, DiMaggio, and Williams. From an ebullient, lovable fellow, Mays had evolved into a surly, grouchy man, so unlike the exuberant figure of the playing field. But we will let it go at that.

Almost reduced to a footnote in Willie's career were the four home runs he hit in Milwaukee in a game in April 1961. That was icing on the cake for him. Take a look at these other accomplishments: 660 home runs, a .302 lifetime batting average, 1,903 RBIs (with ten seasons of more than 100 each), participation in four World Series, constant stardom in All-Star Games, two Most Valuable Player Awards, the National League batting championship in 1954, the National League stolen-bases leader four times, and the triples leader in his league three times.

Still another serendipitous footnote in Willie's career is that Charles Schulz, creator of the *Peanuts* comic strip, utilized Willie Mays's name more often than that of any other living person. Now that's what I call immortality!

Only a few prominent blacks chose to speak out in the 1950s about the most rancorous problem in the nation: the "race issue."

Instead, most behaved with defensive rectitude, as if they were walking through treacherous minefields. One exception was **JACKIE ROOSEVELT ROBINSON**.

Millions of words have been written and spoken about the role that Jackie Robinson played in finally integrating baseball in 1947, after years of dismal neglect and disregard. But it was the veteran baseball man Clyde Sukeforth, the former journeyman catcher and, as a scout, the eyes and ears of the Brooklyn Dodgers' owner Branch Rickey, who best summed up Robinson. "There was something about that man that just gripped you," he said. How right Sukeforth was.

Jackie survived incessant pressure—physical, mental, and psychological—to lead the Dodgers from 1947 through 1956. In those years, as the catalytic figure on the "Boys of Summer" club, Jackie batted .311, won the National League batting title in 1949 with a .342 mark, led his league twice in stolen bases, and was the Most Valuable Player in 1949. In this era, the Dodgers won six National League pennants and one World Series, against the Yankees. All the while, Jackie was the most galvanizing player in the game. Ralph Kiner, the great home-run slugger of the post–World War II period, remarked that Robinson was "the only player I've ever seen who could completely turn a game around by himself."

When Jackie first came to Brooklyn, it was rumored that he had promised Rickey he would turn the other cheek, for at least the first two years. Rachel Robinson, Jackie's bright and supportive wife, has denied that there was any such pact. It was a myth, she said, and it served only to misrepresent his strength of character. Considering that Jackie was a fiery competitor, it must have weighed heavily on him to resist confronting his tormentors, chief among them being manager Ben Chapman of the Philadelphia Phillies. Jackie once said that Chapman's viciousness, supported by a racist front office, almost caused him to lose his self-control. "To hell with Mr. Rickey's noble experiment," he said. "I could throw down my bat, go over to the Phillies dugout, grab one of those white sons of

OPPOSITE
Posing before the opening game of the 1947 season are third baseman Johnny "Spider" Jorgensen, shortstop Pee Wee Reese, second baseman Eddie Stanky, and a rookie first baseman named Jackie Robinson. Jackie's first season was marked by race-baiting and intentional injury to him, but he toughed it out, won the Rookie of the Year Award, and led the Dodgers to the World Series.

RALPH KINER *remarked that* Robinson *was "the only player*
*I've ever seen who could completely turn a game around by himself."*

bitches and smash his teeth in with my despised black fist." That Jackie managed to keep himself in check was a testament to his awareness of how much his behavior would mean to future generations of blacks aspiring to play big-league ball.

I got to know Jackie well enough to have great admiration for him. I also knew him well enough to argue with him about his politics. I exchanged letters with him about his endorsement of Richard Nixon over John F. Kennedy for the presidency in 1960. However, Jackie later regretted his support of Nixon—and told me so. He ended up backing Democrat Hubert Humphrey in 1968.

I would cast my own vote any day for Jackie Robinson as the most influential personality in baseball history. I would still put him on that pedestal even if he hadn't ever electrified crowds with his daring play, his volatility, his sudden steals of home, or his clutch base hits.

While he was on the diamond, either at Ebbets Field, where the Dodgers held forth, or on enemy fields, he took command, making himself almost impenetrable to bigoted remarks through the sheer brilliance of his efforts. But Jackie was able to show a forgiving side too. Pitcher Lew Burdette of Milwaukee, who had been known for hurling insults as well as occasional spitballs, called Jackie "a watermelon" one day. This slur was well known as a disparagement of African Americans. Jackie proceeded to challenge Burdette to a fight, but Burdette turned down the invitation. Instead, Burdette said he was only making reference to Jackie's waistline, which had, admittedly, grown ample. "I don't ride a man about his race," said Burdette. With every good reason to submit Burdette to a lie-detector test, Jackie felt that there was a veiled apology in the pitcher's remarks. "I think he's 100 percent honest," Jackie said. With that, the incident became history.

Some of Robinson's teammates, such as the Kentuckian Pee Wee Reese, who played short-stop alongside Jackie at second, reached out to him. On one occasion, after Jackie had been the target of the usual abuse from the opposition

dugout, Pee Wee walked over to him and put a friendly arm around him—in a conspicuous display of moral support. "He could be easy to dislike," Reese said later, "but he taught me more than I ever taught him." In another instance of support, Ralph Branca, also a teammate, prevented Jackie from tumbling into the dugout as he chased a foul ball.

Not long before he died at the age of fifty-three in 1972, I recall seeing Jackie Robinson standing with his back to a TV set at a New York cocktail party. The set was turned to a World Series game between Pittsburgh and Baltimore. Jackie's hair was completely white, his once-muscular body had turned hunched and frail, and he was nearly blind, the result of a long struggle with diabetes. Someone politely inquired of Jackie why he wasn't watching the game, since he had thrown out the first pitch of the Series only days before. "Baseball can go to hell!" Jackie snarled.

After all that he had accomplished for the game, and, for the country, Jackie was embittered because baseball had still failed to bring a black manager onto the field. It's worth noting, however, that the game Jackie had declined to watch featured a splendid black player, Roberto Clemente. He was there because two decades earlier, Jackie Robinson had staunchly withstood the taunts and threats that had been made against him. He had transformed the game and the way many Americans looked at blacks. Any less controversial a man, anyone less angry or abrupt, anyone less committed, might never have withstood the daily derision.

"Jackie Robinson did not let us down," wrote historian Roger Wilkins.

EDDIE COLLINS was a cocky little fellow, with loving-cup ears, who came off the Columbia University campus in 1907 to become one-half of an intriguing trivia question: which is the only school that has produced two Baseball Hall of Famers? Wouldn't you know that it's Columbia, where athletic fields have always taken a back-seat to study halls. Collins's eminent associatee in the Hall of Fame is, of course, Columbia Lou Gehrig.

On October 9, 1914, before the first game of the World Series, Eddie Collins was presented with a car, in recognition of being named the Athletics' most valuable player. A roadster this fancy was a genuine novelty in those days. Philadelphia was swept four games to none in the Series by the Boston Braves. Eddie had just three hits, and a few weeks later Connie Mack sold him to the White Sox.

OPPOSITE
A teammate of Eddie Collins called him "the smartest ballplayer who ever lived." Ted Lyons said, "He was a very intelligent guy. It was a pleasure to listen to him talk baseball." Collins played in six World Series, and he hit over .400 in three of them.

At Columbia, the slight, 140-pound Collins played quarterback on the football team, until the school abandoned the sport in 1905. After settling for baseball, Eddie came to the attention of Connie Mack, the manager of the Philadelphia Athletics. Under Mack, Eddie soon developed into one of the best second basemen of all time. By 1909, when he hit .346, he was an integral part of what was considered to be the game's most skillful infield combination. The foursome, with Stuffy McInnis on first base, Jack Barry at shortstop, Home Run Baker at third base, and Collins at second base, was awarded fulsome recognition as "the $100,000 Infield." Today the group would undoubtedly go for a few more pennies than that. Collins helped to lead the Athletics to pennant-winning seasons in 1910, 1911, 1913, and 1914. They won the World Series in the first three of those years.

Collins batted .429 in the 1910 Series, with nine hits and four stolen bases. During the regular season, he had swiped eighty-one bases, to lead the league. In the 1913 Series, he again batted over .400. In that decade, Collins was surpassed only by Ty Cobb as an all-around performer. Without Cobb's combustible presence, Eddie would have won more recognition. As it was, he could do more things well than probably any other player in baseball. Mack was fully appreciative of Eddie's skills. "He played the game the way it should be played," said the manager. "Eddie would be the captain of my all-time team."

However, after the debacle of the 1914 World Series, when the "miracle" Boston Braves wiped up the Athletics in four straight games, Mack decided to break up his team. That included Collins. He peddled Eddie to the Chicago White Sox for $65,000, an unheard-of wad of money in those days. Befuddled and dismayed by the deal, Collins proceeded to play his usual game for the White Sox. In 1917, the Sox won the World Series against the New York Giants, with Eddie batting .409 for a team that included the scarcely literate star ballplayer Shoeless Joe Jackson. It was in the 1917 Series that third baseman Heinie Zimmerman made the mistake of chasing Collins home in the last

"*He played the game the way it should be played,*" said THE MANAGER. "*Eddie would be the captain of my all-time team.*"

The close relationship between Christy Mathewson and the Giants' manager John McGraw is nowhere better described than in Eric Rolfe Greenberg's brilliant novel *The Celebrant.* They were, on the surface, an odd couple, but each admired the intelligence and gritty competitiveness of the other. When McGraw traded Matty to Cincinnati in 1916 so he could take over as the Reds' manager, Mathewson expressed his regrets at leaving McGraw, and his appreciation for the opportunity McGraw had made possible.

*Baseball historian*
HAROLD SEYMOUR
*wrote that* Matty *had*
*"elevated pitching to artistry."*

game. The play became part of baseball's folklore and was commemorated in a devilish poem paraphrasing Rudyard Kipling's "Gunga Din." "I'm faster than you, Heinie Zim," went the send-up.

In 1919, Eddie rejoined the White Sox, after a brief sojourn in the Marines during World War I. With a .319 batting average and thirty-three stolen bases, he helped the White Sox win the pennant and get into the World Series against the Cincinnati Reds. As things turned out, he probably wished that he had stayed in the Marines. For it was the Series of 1919 that scarred baseball's soul. Eight of the White Sox players allegedly fixed the outcome of the Series, and the Reds won, taking five games to three in the best-of-nine competition. Square shooter Collins was not part of the clique that engaged in the skulduggery. In the years to come, he was unforgiving toward the malefactors. But he also insisted that these Sox, forever after called the Black Sox, "were the greatest collection of players ever assembled."

Collins remained with the Sox until 1926, never batting lower than .324. He was named player-manager in 1925 and led the team with a .346 average. Finally, in 1927, he rejoined his admirer Connie Mack as a player-coach for Philadelphia, with the expectation that he would become manager when Mack stepped down. When it became clear that the unsinkable old man would be waving his scorecard forever, Collins decided to accept the post of general manager of the Boston Red Sox. It was in that job that he personally scouted Ted Williams and Bobby Doerr, two of the best players ever to wear Red Sox uniforms.

Eddie's brilliant and lengthy career was marred by his apparent role in failing to sign any black players for the Red Sox, at a time when other teams were pursuing such talent. It was never totally clear whether he was doing the bidding of owner Tom Yawkey or shared the racist philosophy of his intransigent employer.

Right-hander **CHRISTY MATHEWSON**—maybe the greatest of all right-handers—has often been taken for the heroic Frank Merriwell, and vice versa. In truth, Mathewson was the real thing, while Merriwell was the fictional beau ideal of writer Gilbert Patten. In the years when Matty rolled up his 373 career victories, against 188 defeats, from 1900 to 1916, he became a living legend of the New York Giants, an athlete who combined sharp intelligence with mechanical skills. Baseball historian Harold Seymour wrote that Matty had "elevated pitching to artistry." Who has ever contested such a description?

Matty may also qualify as the first bona fide hero of the game, for he came along at a time when many ballplayers were regarded as rowdies, drunkards, or otherwise disreputable characters, whom you wouldn't care to invite into your living room. Few players had college backgrounds, as Matty did, and many had not even finished high school. Matty was different in every respect, so much so that many mothers and fathers held him up to their children as role models, the first sports figure to be portrayed in such a manner.

The tiny town of Factoryville, Pennsylvania, was the birthplace of Matty in 1880. He was educated at Bucknell University, in Lewisburg, and while there he demonstrated his superb drop-kicking ability in football, as well as his aptitude as a pitcher. But when baseball beckoned, he didn't stick around for his degree; he became Bucknell's most celebrated dropout. Blessed with matinee-idol looks, a gentlemanly manner, and brains, Matty was also popularly known as "Big Six," presumably because he was more than six feet tall. He reached his peak in the 1905 World Series against the Philadelphia Athletics, when, in the course of six days, he defeated the A's three times, shutting out his foes in each game. He yielded only four, four, and six hits respectively in the three victories, walking only one batter and striking out eighteen. That Series performance marked him as the most accomplished pitcher of his era.

But it was only a beginning. He went on to pitch 79 shutouts, behind only those other masters Walter Johnson and Grover Cleveland Alexander. In 551 starts on the mound, he

In baseball's rowdy early years, polite, articulate, college-educated Christy Mathewson was an anomaly. His many endorsements included shirt collars, men's garters, and athletic equipment, but he piously turned down an offer to license his name to a pool hall and tavern. Matty's greatest season came in 1908, when he won thirty-seven games, pitched eleven shutouts, and recorded a 1.43 ERA. But he had a no decision in the Merkle tie game, and he lost to Mordecai "Three Finger" Brown of the Cubs in the pennant playoff game.

completed 435 games, an unheard-of ratio in today's game. His control was so good that he walked only an average of 1.57 men a game, and in some years he issued fewer bases on balls than the number of his victories. In 1913, Matty didn't permit a walk in 16 of his games, even as he didn't hit a single batter during that entire season. So impeccable was his control that he wagered in 1907 that he could throw the ball twenty consecutive times in exactly the same spot. He went on to perform the feat at West Point, winning his bet at odds of 12–1.

John McGraw, Matty's manager and close friend—and a man who was as bellicose and intemperate as Matty was gracious and diplomatic—said that "baseball would never see his like again." Even the irreverent writer Ring Lardner had only kind words to say about the pitcher, while *New York Times* columnist John Kieran said, "Matty was the greatest I ever saw. I don't care how good they were, Matty was the best."

One may argue that in Matty's years, conditions were highly favorable to pitchers. The ball, for instance, was not lively, and the horsehides were kept in use until they were as black as a threatening sky. Fans were even asked to throw back souvenir foul balls. The game was still being played in a minimalist fashion, with an accent on bunts, hit-and-run, stolen bases, and other plays to get one run at a time. On the other hand, the diamonds were poorly manicured, with balls behaving anarchically. Gloves were dainty and small, hardly as effective as today's defensive weapons. Matty and his fellow hurlers certainly did not benefit from those elements of diamond life.

While Matty served as a chemical-warfare officer in World War I, he was exposed to residual deposits of mustard gas, which may have had a long-term impact on his lungs. He later developed tuberculosis, and after a long battle succumbed at the age of forty-five. His death was followed by an outpouring of grief that was unprecedented for a baseball player. Even the usually sober editorial pages of newspapers paid tribute to "the best loved and most popular of all American athletes." In 1936, he was in the first group of five men elected to Baseball's Hall of Fame. The others were Ty Cobb, Babe Ruth, Honus Wagner, and Walter Johnson. In the voting, Matty finished ahead of Johnson.

There was a day at Yankee Stadium in 1968, the last year of **MICKEY MANTLE**'s eighteen-year odyssey with the New York Yankees, that dramatized for me the hold Mickey had on his admirers. I had a friend who was moving to England, perhaps never to return, and he wanted, more than anything else, to see Mickey play one last time. Not only did he see Mantle play, but, as fate would dictate, Mickey hit a long home run. "I knew he'd do it for me!" my friend exulted. He never did see Mickey play again.

Mickey Mantle wasn't ever certain why he was the object of so much adoration and worship from the fans. It had to be more than his remarkable talent, his Oklahoma innocence, and the fact that he insisted on playing through disabling injuries and pain. Was Mickey's appeal—and don't forget he was booed when he first arrived in New York in 1951—mainly based on the fact that he always played the game with an apparent love and commitment that few professionals of his time manifested?

The essence of Mantle, who surely would have lasted even longer in baseball had he taken better care of himself, was his pride in having played in more games—2,401—than any other Yankee in history. This always came first to Mickey, over and above his 536 home runs, his Triple Crown in 1956, his three MVP Awards before reaching the age of thirty-one, and his participation on twelve pennant-winning Yankee teams. Mickey wanted to be known as a team player, and those who had played alongside him knew him to be exactly that. "He plays with a dedication that is obsolete in the world," columnist Jimmy Cannon wrote, in only one of the many hymns inscribed for the young blond-haired man.

Mickey Charles Mantle was born in Spavinaw, Oklahoma, in 1931. His first name was a tip-off that his dad, known locally as Mutt, wanted him to be a ballplayer. Mutt's

OPPOSITE
**Mantle with his roommates in 1961: Bob Cerv (left), a left fielder, and Roger Maris, who played right field and broke Babe Ruth's single-season home-run record. Mickey had by then won over the New York fans, most of whom were rooting for him to break the record. He was in a hospital bed recovering from an infection when Maris hit his sixty-first homer. Mantle expressed his admiration for Maris, but he would have been forgiven for some wistfulness at reaching the fifty-four-homer mark and then being sidelined.**

*"We knew there was something poignant about MICKEY before we knew what poignant meant. You didn't just root for him, you felt for him."*

hero was Mickey Cochrane, the scrappy catcher, and his son derived his name from him. With a body weighing close to 209 pounds, and muscles bulging like inflated pillows, Mickey played every sport imaginable. Once he was kicked in the leg in a football game and developed a serious bone disease. Since both Mickey's father and grandfather died young of cancer, Mickey was morbidly haunted by their premature deaths and became convinced he'd also die before his time. Later in life, he mused, "If I thought I was going to live this long, I would have taken better care of myself."

When Mickey made his debut with the Yankees, writer Leonard Shecter said of him: "He has a face as open as the part of America that he came from." So there he was, a kid of nineteen, already heralded as the second coming of Babe Ruth, or at the very least the legitimate successor to Earle Combs and Joe DiMaggio, center fielders of previous Yankee dynasties. "When he hits the ball it even sounds different," they said about him. "He's got it iln his body to be great," added his grizzled manager Casey Stengel, who had been around long enough to qualify as an expert.

The advance publicity in behalf of Mickey may have hurt him, for he started with the Yankees at a slow pace. The fans reacted by expressing their displeasure, and Mickey found himself farmed out to Kansas City. After he told his dad that he didn't think he was up to playing in the big leagues, Mutt responded by telling his boy that he'd better stop complaining. Mutt challenged Mickey, who soon returned to the Yankees and, in time, responded to his dying father's words. The first few Mantle years were good, but hardly the kind of production one would expect from another Ruth. However, by the mid-1950s, when the tape-measure homers boomed off his bat and the RBIs and runs scored accumulated, Mickey had become the player his dad knew he could be.

Allen Barra, the perceptive baseball observer, commented about Mickey that "what he accomplished ranks him among the greatest players of his time. His record needs no apologies for what he might have been."

Mickey Mantle was just nineteen years old in 1951 when he hit .402 in spring training, bashed some Herculean homers, and made the opening-day lineup as the Yankees' right fielder. Not only was he playing where Babe Ruth had once played, but he was also the designated successor to center fielder Joe DiMaggio. Such an expectation, and the regular reminders by the press that he was destined for Hall of Fame greatness, made him uneasy. "I've still got so much to learn it scares me," he told a reporter.

OPPOSITE
In 1956, Mantle finally reached a level of performance that had been expected of him for five years. Fifty-two homers, 130 RBIs, a .353 batting average, and a .705 slugging average all led the majors, and earned him his first of three MVP Awards. He even exorcised the DiMaggio ghost. "I tried to do it, to live up to DiMaggio," he said. "It didn't work. I've quit trying now."

Hank Aaron is shown here in Yankee Stadium prior to the first game of the 1957 World Series. He hit forty-four homers that year, and his forty-third clinched the pennant for the Braves. New Yorkers might have seen a lot more of him, but for a penny-wise decision made by an unnamed New York Giants official. Aaron almost signed with the club in 1952, but he balked at the last minute over the salary offer. "They wanted to give me an A contract with a C salary," he said. Thus were Giants fans denied the chance to see Willie Mays and Hank Aaron in the same lineup.

BELOW
All eyes are on the flight of Hank Aaron's 715th career home run, the hit that broke what many thought was Babe Ruth's unassailable record. The date is April 8, 1974, and the opposing pitcher is the Dodgers' Al Downing. "I owed it to Jackie," Aaron said later, referring to Jackie Robinson. "I just wish he could have seen me do it. God, he would have been proud."

OVERLEAF
Hank Aaron was a slender infielder when he joined the Milwaukee Braves in 1954, and hit just thirteen home runs in 122 games that season. Still, he finished second to Wally Moon in the Rookie of the Year voting and displayed uncommon confidence in himself. Stan Musial said, "He thinks there's nothing he can't hit."

*After years of chasing the ghost of Ruth,* HANK SAID SIMPLY: *"Thank God, it's over. Now I can get some rest. And thank God I hit it in Atlanta."*

Was there ever a better switch-hitter or World Series player? Was there ever anyone who could entice more walks? Was there ever anyone who could negotiate the base paths faster than Mickey, despite his uncertain legs?

When Mickey died in 1995, not quite sixty-four, announcer Bob Costas eulogized him. "He exuded dynamism and excitement," said Costas, who had grown up idolizing Mantle. "But at the same time he touched your heart. We knew there was something poignant about Mickey before we knew what poignant meant. You didn't just root for him, you felt for him."

There are certain magic numerals in baseball's record books that elicit an immediate click in the fan's mind: Ruth's 714 home runs; DiMaggio's fifty-six-game hitting streak; Williams's .406 average in 1941; Gehrig's 2,130 straight games, now gone by the boards. The most productive home-run hitter of them all, **HENRY LOUIS "HANK" AARON**, ended up in 1976 with 755 home runs—41 more than Ruth—but how many pay such mesmerizing religious devotion to that number as they still do to Babe's total?

It seems fair to say that one can ascribe this outrageous situation to the fact that Hank Aaron was a black man who had the audacity to upend baseball's folk hero. And as he relentlessly pursued Ruth, Aaron found himself the target of abuse that probably wasn't even equaled when Jackie Robinson dared to break the color line. Hank faced daily hate mail, illiterate death threats, and obscene taunts that might have brought a lesser man to his knees. He was called "a black animal," one of the kinder felicitations he received; his children were threatened with kidnapping, and he was often forced to hire security guards for them and himself.

Then there were those who disparaged Hank because he didn't hit more than forty-seven homers in any one season. (He wore number 44 on his back and, ironically, hit forty-four homers in four different seasons.) These critics also charged that Hank never hit the ball as far, as high, or as hard as Babe had, and, they added,

it took Hank some four thousand more at bats to catch up with Ruth. These facts are essentially true, although there is no means of measuring just how hard these two men hit the ball.

We still think the lack of regard for Hank over the years was mainly due to his color. The fact that Aaron was a quiet, dignified, controlled fellow, as opposed to Ruth's outrageous flamboyance, also didn't help him gain the favor of the baseball public. Life can be unfair, John F. Kennedy once said, and Hank Aaron must know that in his heart.

A native of the South, born in Mobile, Alabama, home of so many ballplayers, in 1934, Hank came up through the Negro Leagues. He then joined the Sally League before spending the rest of his baseball life in Milwaukee and Atlanta.

After years of solid hitting (and fielding), Hank had amassed records that confounded many, who failed to comprehend how such an unobtrusive man could be that consistently good. He won two batting crowns and four **RBI** titles, had 2,297 RBIs, and played in twenty-four All-Star Games and fourteen World Series games. His lifetime total of 3,771 hits had him trailing only Ty Cobb and Pete Rose.

By 1973, it was surprisingly clear that this fellow (who once weighed only 140 pounds as a minor leaguer) had become a threat to Ruth's mark. As he made his assault on Babe, the avalanche of letters increased daily. Many of these "billets-doux" began with the salutation "Dear Nigger." Nonetheless, Hank stoically—at least on the surface—kept plugging away, as he reached 700, then 713, then a Babe-tying 714 in Cincinnati.

On the night of April 8, 1974, with the nation drawn to the event on TV, and, at long last, with millions of whites as well as blacks rooting him on, Hank delivered the coup de grâce. It happened in the fourth inning at Atlanta Stadium, on a pitch thrown plateward by southpaw Al Downing of the Dodgers. Afterward, with the pressure finally easing up on him, after years of chasing the ghost of Ruth, Hank said simply: "Thank God, it's over. Now I can get some rest. And thank God I hit it in Atlanta."

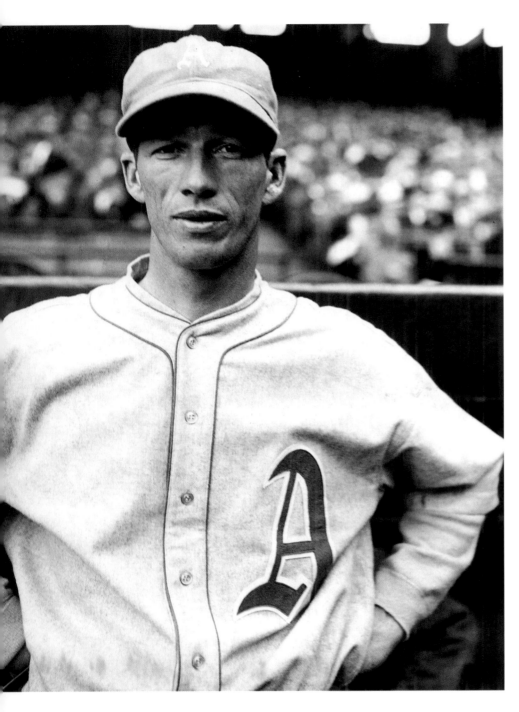

Pitching for the Athletics, Lefty Grove won 195 games in nine years, including seven successive years in which he won 20 or more. With money running low in Connie Mack's coffers, Grove was sold to the Red Sox in 1934. Despite this, he harbored no grudges against Mack, and once said of him, "He was just like a father to everyone."

One of the biggest problems Connie Mack had when he managed the Philadelphia Athletics was remembering the names of his players. LEFTY GROVE, his big southpaw, was always "Groves" to the old pilot. But to the many hundreds of American League batters who faced Grove in the 1920s and 1930s, there was no mistaking who he was or how he spelled his name. Robert Moses "Lefty" Grove had a fastball that could be thrown past a hungry wolf, as the columnist Bugs Baer once remarked, and an attitude that was even more assertive.

Winner of 300 games, while losing only 141, for a .680 winning percentage, Grove also had a Vesuvian temper that often erupted when he lost, or when he thought that he'd been done in by a poor fielding play. In 1931, while trying to extend a winning streak to 17 in a row (to put him past Walter Johnson and Joe Wood), Grove watched a brilliant effort go up in smoke when substitute outfielder Jimmy Moore misplayed a fly ball, giving the St. Louis Browns a 1–0 victory. In the clubhouse after the loss, Grove engaged in "the most complete clubhouse demolition in baseball history," reported author Jim Kaplan. Grove even attacked his own shirt, sending the buttons flying.

I can speak from my own boyhood experience about Lefty's explosive temper. In the lobby of New York's Alamac Motel in 1934, while scrambling for autographs from Red Sox players in town to face the Yankees, I approached Grove. He was decked out in an egg-white Panama suit and looked as if he could have been a dyspeptic master of a Southern plantation. I politely asked the big fellow for his autograph and turned to a page in my autograph book featuring several pictures of him. Then I handed my fountain pen to him. He took it and signed. But as he returned the book and my pen to me, I noticed a rivulet of dark blue ink dribbling its way down from his fly to his right knee. The pen—not a ballpoint, remember—had totally betrayed me. Ashen-faced, Grove grabbed me by the back of my thirteen-year-old neck. I thought he was going to throw me across the lobby at one hundred miles per hour, a smidgen faster than his famous fastball. Instead, he thought better of it.

"I don't ever want to see you again," he growled. I made certain he never did.

This wondrous pitcher was born in March 1900, in Lonaconing, Maryland, an area of soft-coal mines. After an early apprenticeship in the Blue Ridge League, Grove was signed by Jack Dunn, the man who sold Babe Ruth to the Red Sox. Lefty hurled for Dunn's Baltimore Orioles for several years, certainly long enough for Mr. Mack to appreciate how extraordinary he was. In the off-season of 1924, Mack bought Grove for $100,600, supposedly the largest sum ever doled out for a minor-league player.

Grove didn't disappoint anyone. By 1927, when he hung up a 20–13 mark, he began a streak of seven straight years of 20 or more triumphs. In the three dynastic years of 1929–31, when the A's ruled the baseball world, Grove put together a 79–15 record. In 1931, he went 31–4 and won the American League's Most Valuable Player Award. By 1933, still the most feared pitcher around, Grove came to Yankee Stadium and blanked the New Yorkers. What was so remarkable was that the Yankees hadn't been shut out in 308 games. That afternoon, Grove fanned Ruth three times and Gehrig twice.

As a reward for his continuing brilliance, Grove was sold to the Red Sox the following winter. Mr. Mack, like a lot of other folks during the Depression, needed money. The Red Sox handed over $125,000. Although he had a sore arm in his first season in Boston and finished at 8–8, Lefty was back in the 20-game circle in 1935. As hard as it was to contemplate, Lefty had added guile and a curveball to his repertoire, which kept him winning for a few more seasons. In all, he led his league in ERA nine times and in strikeouts seven times.

Perhaps the most unusual aspect of Grove's life in baseball was that even in his top years as a starter for Philadelphia, he also came in to relieve frequently. It is possible, as some admirers of Grove have pointed out, that he may have been a better man out of the bullpen than he was as a starter. Indeed, he had more saves

Lefty Grove's fastball earned the respect of every player who saw it, or tried to hit it. Red Sox teammate Wes Ferrell, who won twenty-five games in 1935, a year in which Grove won twenty, said, "Fastest pitcher I ever saw.... He'd throw the ball in there and you'd wonder where it went to. It would just *zing* and disappear."

WES FERRELL *said,*
        *"Fastest pitcher I ever saw....*
*[Lefty]'d throw the ball in there*
        *and you'd wonder where it went to.*
*It would just* zing *and* disappear."

than any Hall of Fame pitcher in the twentieth century. By 1975, when Grove died, the common consensus was that he was the best left-hander in history. You won't get any arguments from me—even if I never went back to him for another autograph.

In recent years, the halo that had once appeared to float permanently over JOSEPH PAUL DIMAGGIO's head has been knocked askew by some less-than-worshipful biographers. There has been an emphasis on DiMaggio's personality and character rather than on his enormous playing skills. His aloofness, his almost para-noid insistence on privacy, and his lack of generosity have been dwelt on by these writers. Richard Ben Cramer wrote in his biography of DiMaggio that Joe had "teammates but no mates . . . he was the loneliest hero we have ever had." Cramer also noted that DiMaggio hung around with mobsters and had a thick streak of suspiciousness toward almost everyone.

What ever happened to Joe's achievements on the field, his rivalry with Ted Williams, his easy elegance as one of the prime defensive center fielders who ever put on spikes? What ever happened to his gallant battle against injuries and pain, almost from the day he joined the Yankees in 1936? And, need we mention, Joe's fifty-six-game hitting streak of 1941, from May 15 until July 17, an accomplishment that one of the world's great physicists, Nobel laureate Ed Purcell, said was statistically the most unusual and unexpected event in base-ball's history?

Do we care more that Joe had a painful, unfortunate marriage to Marilyn Monroe, the most beautiful girl he'd ever seen, than we do that he had thirteen wonderful seasons (includ-ing ten Yankee pennants) in New York, where he evolved into the legendary Yankee Clipper?

Psychiatrists may be able to emerge with the answers about why Joe acted the way he did. But even to a layman, it isn't too difficult to deduce what formed his personality. He arrived in baseball at a time when the country was still wrestling with its attitude toward eth-nic minorities. Even popular publications such

as *Life* magazine referred to Joe in ugly stereo-types. No, *Life* said, Joe didn't happen to reek of garlic, and he didn't use olive oil on his black hair. The public was also informed that Joe could actually speak English, without an accent, even if his Italian fisherman father spoke not a word of English—and neither did Joe—at their home in Martinez, California. Such ignorant badgering must have contributed to Joe's gen-eral demeanor. Aware of his role as one of the first Italian-American heroes produced by base-ball, Joe stage-managed a profile for himself, including the way he dressed and the way he spoke, or didn't speak, that reflected his sensi-tivity. Generally, he chose to keep his mouth shut, in a nod to the Sicilian mystique. He remained such a private person that one of his fellow Yankees remarked, "Joe led the league in room service."

Joe, whose brothers Dom and Vince also made it to the majors, became the successor to those icons Ruth and Gehrig (the latter was still in the lineup when Joe arrived). Almost from the beginning, he monopolized the atten-tion of the fans and an adoring press. There were immediately high expectations for him in 1936, and he came through with a freshman mark of .323. In 1939, 1941, and 1947, Joe won the MVP Award in his league. But it was the hitting skein in 1941, probably never to be broken, that rocketed him into baseball's pan-theon. During those pre–World War II months, people all across the country woke up each morning and inquired if Joe had "hit one yes-terday." That same summer, Ted Williams bat-ted over .400, but the songwriters penned their lyrics about DiMaggio and not Ted. "I wanted it to go on forever," said Joe, when he was finally stopped one night in Cleveland. The owners wanted it to go on forever too, for the daily challenge caused thousands more to go to the ballpark to root for DiMaggio, even if he played in an enemy uniform.

In 1949, Joe added to his legend when he ignored a painful, slow-healing injury to his heel and returned to the Yankee lineup in a crucial three-game series with Boston. In those games, Joe hit four home runs, leading his team

OPPOSITE
Joe DiMaggio (right) in 1936, his rookie year, posing happily with two kindred spirits, Frank Crosetti (left) and Tony Lazzeri. Just two years later, Joe's play established him as a genuine superstar. His poise created an aura of invincibility. Yankee pitcher Red Ruffing said, "You saw him standing there and you knew you had a damn good chance to win the baseball game."

Joe D. arming himself before playing against the Red Sox on the night of June 28, 1949, marking his first appearance that season. In his first at bat, he singled to center off left-hander Mickey McDermott, and then in the third, he homered into Fenway Park's left-field screen. With the tying run on third in the last of the ninth, Ted Williams sent a towering shot into Fenway's deepest center-field corner, but Joe tracked it down and caught it almost nonchalantly to end the game.

OPPOSITE
Showing little trace of discomfort after sixty-five days of treatment to an injured heel, Joe DiMaggio is seen here singling to center in his first plate appearance against the Red Sox in Boston. He went on to wreck the Red Sox that weekend, hitting four home runs in three games. When a Boston reporter asked him how he did it, DiMag answered, with perhaps a wink, "Just go up and swing and manage to hit the ball. There is, of course, no skill involved."

*He remained such a private person that one of his fellow Yankees remarked,* "JOE LED THE LEAGUE IN ROOM SERVICE."

to a sweep. The victories put the Yankees on the path to another flag.

With a lifetime batting average of .325, 361 home runs (he would have hit more in Yankee Stadium if he hadn't been right-handed), and bundles of RBIs in every year when his body wasn't plagued by injuries, Joe retired after the 1951 season. As he passed from the picture, along came Mantle, to continue the center-field tradition. The Yankees offered Joe $100,000 to stay for one more year, but he felt that he couldn't play up to the demanding standard he'd always set for himself.

A reporter once asked Joe why he continued to play so hard every day. Joe responded that he did it because some fan in the stands may never have seen him before, and he wanted to do his best for that person. Such a personal work ethic probably revealed more about him than any of the unpleasant revelations that surfaced after he died in 1999, at the age of eighty-four.

There are certain moments one would prefer to forget—but can't. I'm thinking about the day more than sixty years ago when I walked into a flea-circus museum off Times Square in New York City and saw GROVER CLEVELAND ALEXANDER slumped in a threadbare chair perched atop a shaky wooden platform. If you asked him, he'd tell you a story, perhaps for a few pennies. Or, if you chose, you could watch other sideshow attractions, such as the half-boy, half-seal, or several mice racing madly around the insides of a little cage.

I don't know if Alexander (who was named after one two-term president, and had another two-term president, Ronald Reagan, play him in a 1952 movie that bore scant resemblance to the truth) ever got paid for his appearance at the flea circus. I do know that I was too embarrassed to speak to him. When I walked out a few moments later, I kept wondering how and why he had ended up this way, his body frail, his face and nose splotched with red booze lines.

What I knew about Alex was that he had won 373 National League games, tying him with Christy Mathewson for the third-highest total of all time. I also knew that he was

"Somebody said if Alex didn't drink he'd probably have won more games," [RUBE] BRESSLER SAID. *"How much better can you get? Maybe drinking helped him. Maybe it let him relax."*

one-half of one of the game's most dramatic confrontations: Alexander versus Tony Lazzeri, 1926 World Series, seventh game, seventh inning, bases loaded, two out, Cardinals ahead, 3–2. That he struck out the young Yankee slugger is what put Alexander into baseball's memory lane. What makes that long-ago strikeout so irresistible to age is that both men suffered from epilepsy, though neither one, so it is claimed, had ever had a seizure on the playing field. The other fact that continues to demand our attention is that Alex had become an alcoholic, who kept belting down Prohibition whiskey to throttle whatever demons besieged him.

One theory about Alex's addiction was that he'd been traumatized by his battlefield experiences during World War I, when he served as a doughboy in a field-artillery unit in France. His epilepsy could also possibly have been triggered by such exposure. Today, we have a name for it: post-traumatic stress disorder.

Returning from France, Alex pitched for the Chicago Cubs in 1919, winning sixteen games, including nine shutouts, and leading the league with a 1.72 ERA. Considering his personal bout in hell, it was a remarkable performance.

Alexander came from central Nebraska, where he was born in the little town of St. Paul in 1887. He was a big, rangy kid, who worked his father's farm and soon graduated to playing ball on neighborhood teams. With Galesburg, in the Illinois-Missouri League, he won fifteen games in 1909 but suffered a serious injury when his head collided with a shortstop's throw. He was unconscious for almost two days. In time he made a decent recovery and wound up with Syracuse in the New York State League, where his sidearm motion baffled enough hitters for him to win twenty-nine games. Within days, the Phillies bought him from Syracuse, thus beginning one of the great careers in pitching history.

The astounding numbers that Alex put together in the ensuing years caused him to be ranked right alongside the nearly invincible Matty and that other farmer's son, Walter Johnson. He had three straight seasons of thirty or more wins, in 1915, 1916, and 1917. His

Grover Cleveland "Old Pete" Alexander, striding confidently onto the playing field in 1911, his rookie year with the Phillies. Pitching in Baker Bowl, a hurler's chamber of horrors, he won twenty-eight games that season, and nineteen or more in the next six campaigns. Giants catcher Chief Meyers said, "Boy he had stuff. Don't think he didn't."

OPPOSITE
A well-documented drinking problem didn't seem to compromise Alexander's performances on the mound. In the opinion of Rube Bressler, who batted against him many times, drinking actually may have benefited him. "Somebody said if Alex didn't drink he'd probably have won more games," Bressler said. "How much better can you get? Maybe drinking helped him. Maybe it let him relax."

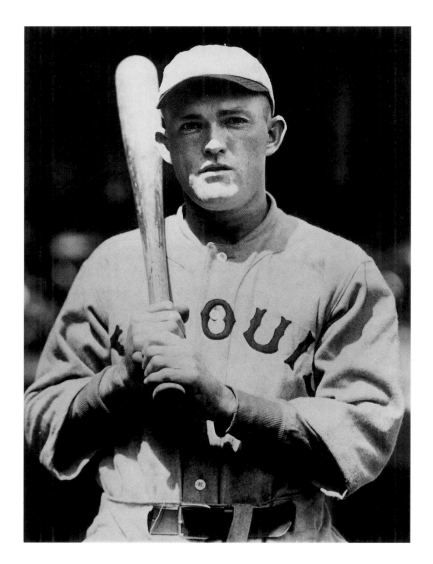

Dave Egan, a longtime Boston sportswriter (and Ted Williams nemesis), wrote in a 1944 *Boston Herald* article that Rogers Hornsby "is the Barrymore of baseball.... No more turbulent figures ever took such twisted routes to their individual halls of fame, and no two gentlemen ever got more action wherever they went."

*"It's the only thing I can talk about,"* [HORNSBY] SAID. *"I wait all winter long for the season to start up again."*

capacity for hard, grueling work, which puts modern-day pitchers to shame, is demonstrated by his average of 384 innings pitched in each of those seasons. In 1915, when he hurled four one-hit games, he also helped the Phillies get into their first World Series. Although the Red Sox beat them, Alex—now hailed as Alexander the Great—pitched and won the first game, 3–1. In his other losing start, he gave up only two runs. In 1916 and again in 1917, Alex pitched and won two games in a single day, a feat that few, outside of Iron Man Joe McGinnity, had ever even attempted.

The Phillies traded Alex to Chicago in 1918, and he had two more twenty-win seasons in his time in the Windy City. The Cardinals chose to overlook the increasing evidence that Alex was a prisoner of his alcohol habit when they dealt for him in 1926. Their faith in their decision was supported by Alex's two triumphs over the Yankees in the 1926 World Series. That was followed by his surprising twenty-one victories in 1927, when he had turned forty. Yet one teammate said of him at the time, "He just wanted to be by himself and drink."

At the end of his life—he lasted until he was sixty-three, which had to surprise many who had observed him—Alex died in a St. Paul rooming house. He was alone with his fading memories of a gray afternoon in 1926 when he turned back one of the most formidable Yankee lineups of all time.

Of all of baseball's immortals, **ROGERS HORNSBY** would probably finish in a flat-footed tie with Ty Cobb as the most boorish and unpleasant of men. Yet there Hornsby is, the greatest right-handed hitter of the twentieth century, with his .424 average in 1924 (along with 227 hits) for the St. Louis Cardinals the best mark of the century. Put that with his seven National League batting crowns, six of them consecutively, and you have the raw statistical story of a monomaniacal man who believed he knew more about hitting than anyone else. He may have been right. On the other hand, when it came to teaching others about the art, he wasn't very good at it, primarily because of a brusque temperament that couldn't abide the failures of others.

To be evenhanded, however, it is not fair to rate Hornsby on his personality. He had a long and lambent career, from 1915, when he joined the St. Louis Cardinals, until 1937, when he finished up with the St. Louis Browns in the American League. He also served as manager of the Cards, Giants, Braves, Cubs, Browns, and Reds, along with coaching for the Cubs and Mets. In the course of this travelogue, he batted over .300 in nineteen of his twenty-three seasons. He usually played at second base, but he also played every other position at one time or another, except pitcher and catcher.

Hornsby had a passion for hitting that he picked up as a youngster in Texas. But unlike that other single-minded hitter, Ted Williams, who would rather have faced a fastball than catch one in the outfield, Hornsby played second base with more than acceptable ability. It was often said that he didn't fare well on pop flies, but few second basemen of his era could guard the base with his doggedness.

Not a learned or curious fellow, Hornsby believed that anyone playing ball in the big leagues should preserve his eyesight by never attending movies or reading books. On the other hand, Hornsby spent a good deal of his spare time peering at horse-racing tip sheets. He didn't drink or smoke, but he was a chronic bettor and defended that right, even if it had cost him more than he ever won. As a compulsive gambler, Hornsby followed the maxim "I hope that I break even; I need the money."

With other players and the press, Hornsby would never have won any popularity contests—not that he cared. Phrase-making columnist Westbrook Pegler wrote that Rogers had "go-to-hell eyes," while Travis Jackson, a teammate of his on the Giants of 1927, said Hornsby "cared little for what anyone says, and still less for what they think."

With all of his imperfections, Hornsby ended up having a supporter in his biographer Charles C. Alexander, who wrote, "As player, manager, and teacher of young people he may have added to the sum total of human

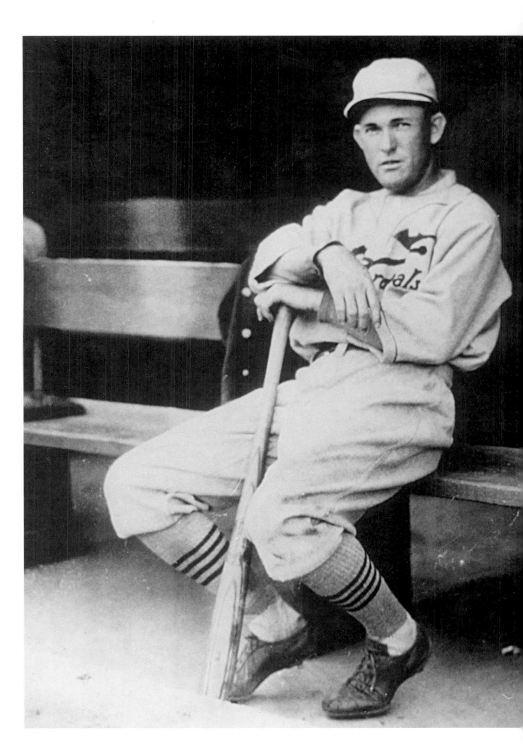

Rogers Hornsby, early in his career, gazing out at the camera with characteristic disdain. Like Ty Cobb, he had a host of admirers, as well as victims of his nasty behavior. As a matter of fact, Cobb had little use for him. He wrote in 1945 that "Hornsby couldn't catch a pop fly, much less go in the outfield after them, could not come in on a slow hit." But even Cobb couldn't find much fault in the Rajah's batting skills.

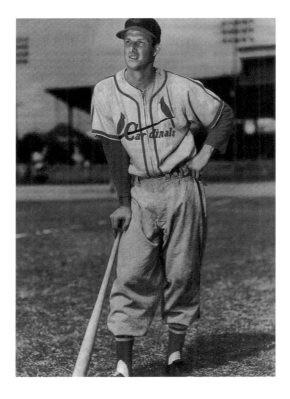

In accepting the Sporting News Player of the Decade Award for 1946–55, Stan Musial said, with a straight face, "I can't hit like Williams, I can't field like DiMaggio, and I certainly can't throw like Feller. I can't figure out why I'm getting this." His modesty was as natural as his ability. He liked to tell the story of what his young son said after The Man hit five home runs in a doubleheader against the Giants. Dickie said, "Gee Dad, they must have been throwing you some fat pitches today."

OPPOSITE
Musial's batting stance was singular and, to most pitchers, menacing. He was a few weeks shy of his twenty-first birthday when he was called up late in the 1941 season. He hit .426 in twelve games, and was a major leaguer to stay. Few hitters have matched the numbers he posted in the summer of 1948: 230 hits, forty-six doubles, thirty-nine homers, 135 RBIs, and a .376 batting average.

*White said Musial was a fellow who was nice to everyone, white or black:* "IT DIDN'T MAKE ANY DIFFERENCE TO HIM WHO YOU WERE."

enjoyment." But Alexander also enumerated Hornsby's flaws, which included a distaste for "colored people," a predisposition that was endemic among many players of his time. It is also possible that Hornsby was a member of the Ku Klux Klan, when that racist organization was at its peak in the United States.

Rogers (the *s* on the end of his name was often omitted in stories about him; it came from his mother's maiden name) was born in 1896. Even at the beginning, baseball was his whole life, and it always remained that way. "It's the only thing I can talk about," he said. "I wait all winter long for the season to start up again." Such a self-appraisal underlined Hornsby's honesty and bluntness, even as it made him out to be one-dimensional.

Ironically, the most dramatic moment of Hornsby's baseball career did not come as a result of his bat. It took place in the 1926 World Series, when, as the Cardinals' manager, Hornsby waved Grover Cleveland Alexander in from the bull pen to face Yankee slugger Tony Lazzeri in a make-or-break situation. It was the seventh inning of the seventh game, two out, bases jammed, Cards in the lead by one run.

Alex had pitched and won a complete game the day before, and it was rumored that he'd spent that night "celebrating." At thirty-nine he was past his prime, with a nasty addiction to the bottle. But Hornsby had the guts—or was it luck?—to call on Alex. After the pitcher came through, the Cards won their first championship flag. "I was never treated more fair by anyone than Rog treated me," said Alex, in a postgame reflection.

Hornsby's reward for his judgment was to be traded off that winter to the Giants for second baseman Frankie Frisch and pitcher Jimmy Ring. In 1927, he batted .361 for John McGraw's team, making the point that it was always the same for him, when it came to hitting. It didn't matter where he was.

In the days when Ebbets Field, that old dump of a ballpark, was still the roost of the Brooklyn Dodgers, **STAN MUSIAL** couldn't wait to get there from St. Louis. When he arrived, the

Enos Slaughter, though a teammate of Stan Musial's, was an exacting critic, and not given to perfunctory compliments. He told author Donald Honig, "I don't think anybody knew what a great hitter he was going to be because of that odd batting stance he had. I know I heard a lot of pitchers say he could be pitched to, but I never saw anybody do it successfully."

Dodgers pitchers were well advised to leave, for Musial's bat would turn Ebbets into a Little League park. He banged doubles, triples, home runs, and singles off the nearby walls, so frustrating the Dodgers diehards that they took to calling him "that man, that man." In time, Musial simply became Stan the Man. Anyway, that's the story they used to tell in Brooklyn.

Musial may have been the most chronically nice guy ever to put on a big-league uniform. "Numbingly amiable" is what one admirer dubbed him. He smiled and laughed his way through his years with the Cardinals, from 1941 through 1963, with only a year out, in 1945, for military service. He ended up with a lifetime average of .331, 475 home runs, and three National League Most Valuable Player Awards. Seven times he won the batting crown, the last when he was nearly thirty-seven, in 1957. The fans in St. Louis loved him so much they wanted to stuff him and keep him in the lineup forever. They settled for a statue of him in front of the St. Louis ballpark, portraying him in his inimitable batting style, which has been described as a man looking furtively around a corner. While his chief left-handed competitor for immortality, Ted Williams, often played in a tempest, Stan went largely unnoticed and uncriticized. All he did was help the Cards win four flags and three World Series. Geniality, in his case, was never a drawback.

Stanley Frank Musial was born in Donora, Pennsylvania, a bleak mill town of some fifteen thousand souls on the banks of the sluggish Monongahela River. Donora is twenty-five miles from Pittsburgh, so most kids grew up rooting for the Pittsburgh Pirates. But after 1941, when Stan made his debut in a Cards uniform, they all turned into Cards fans—and Stan fans. Stan's father, Lukasz, a Polish immigrant, had a job lifting heavy bundles of wire, so physically demanding that he hurt his back and took to drinking too much. But Lukasz also knew that the way to get ahead in America was to get a good education. So he was determined that Stan, who was a talented basketball player at Donora High, should attend a fine university. However, Stan's love of baseball got in the way.

Honus Wagner, his sinewy arms and long hands in evidence, joined the Pirates in 1900. He was just twenty-six at the time but looked twenty years older, and his appearance may have lulled some opponents into a fatal complacency. He was a speedy base runner and a deft fielder, and as a hitter he had few peers. He is still regarded as one of the most popular players ever to put on a Pittsburgh uniform.

OPPOSITE
During his twenty-one-year career, Honus Wagner batted .299 or better in fifteen consecutive seasons, and he was about forty years old before he dropped below that figure. Larry "Nap" Lajoie said, "You know, except for Cobb and Ruth, there's only one other man, Wagner, who is unanimous. People quibble over the pitchers, catchers, first basemen, and so forth, but never about those three."

Lukasz couldn't comprehend such devotion to a silly game. But in time he relented and let his son, then a skinny southpaw pitcher, sign with the Cardinals for $65 a month. Thus, Stan became part of the Rickey Chain Gang—and never left it, being one of the few great players to spend his entire career with only one club.

After Stan got married in 1939, he went to Daytona Beach, in the D Florida State League. There he experienced the seminal moment of his life. He stumbled while trying to catch a fly ball (he was playing in the outfield that day) and suffered a painful injury to his left shoulder. It didn't take long for his manager, little Dickie Kerr, who had won two games for a bunch of White Sox teammates who were conspiring to fix the 1919 World Series, to inform Stan he was no longer a pitcher. "You've got more of a future in this game as a hitter," predicted Kerr.

How right Kerr was. Many years later, when Kerr was going through hard times, Stan gave him $10,000 to buy a house in Houston. The act was typical of Musial. When the story leaked to the press, nobody who knew Stan was the least bit surprised.

Musial's decency was also evidenced by his relationships with teammates and foes alike. He may not have been a professional crusader for civil rights, but, in the testimony of Bill White, a teammate and black man who later became president of the National League, "Stan was helpful to anyone who asked him for advice." White said Musial was a fellow who was nice to everyone, white or black: "It didn't make any difference to him who you were." The quipster Joe Garagiola chimed in with his assessment of Stan: "A saint with money," he said.

By 1958, Stan, the human hitting machine, was on his way to becoming a member of the elite 3,000-hit club. To speed the process, he had banged out 42 hits in twenty-two games in early spring. After he reached his 2,999th hit, Cards manager Fred Hutchinson, sensing the value of having Stan make his 3,000th hit in front of a hometown St. Louis crowd, held Stan out of the lineup for the next game at Chicago's Wrigley Field. This type of manipulation is often frowned upon in purist baseball circles, and it should be. But by the sixth inning, with the Cards trailing, 3–1, Hutchinson called on Stan to pinch-hit. In came Stan from the bull pen, where he'd been basking in the midday May sun. With a count of two and two against southpaw Moe Drabowsky, Stan lashed the next pitch into the left-field corner, far out of the reach of Walt Moryn. Stan made it to second base, another of his typical two-baggers; he'd led his league in doubles eight times. This one gave him his 3,000th hit. At the end of his career, Stan had 3,630 hits, behind only Pete Rose and Ty Cobb.

Even in his time, Ty Cobb, that grouchy immortal, didn't win the vote of that other grouch, John J. McGraw, as the greatest player in the game. Instead, McGraw named **JOHN PETER "HONUS" WAGNER** in that role, which may surprise some. But Wahoo Sam Crawford, who played with Cobb on the Tigers, agreed with McGraw. He said he wasn't putting Cobb down when he named Wagner as the best all-around player he'd ever seen.

From the time Wagner joined Louisville, in the National League, in 1897, until he finished up with Pittsburgh in 1917, he was a dominant player in every department: hitting, fielding, and baserunning. Yet, somehow, he was frequently overshadowed by others such as Cobb. Perhaps one of the reasons for this second-banana status was that he didn't really look as good as he was. He may have been the greatest shortstop in the history of the universe, but he just didn't have the image. If you took a good look at his physique, you had to be stunned that he could move as fast as a rabbit. His personality was unprepossessing and shy. His choice would have been to drink beer with his friends, rather than get broiled by the sun during an afternoon game. He was a bulging, squat man, more than two hundred pounds, with a chest that was more a wrestler's than a shortstop's. He had enormous, hamlike hands, fingers that never seemed to end, and exaggerated bowlegs under which you could have walked your dog. The face was melancholy and undistinguished, with a

"Idaho Phenom Will Pitch Today," announced a small headline in the *Washington Post* on August 2, 1907. Walter Johnson lost his first game, but five days later he beat the Indians, 7–2. The *Post* reported, "His speed was so terrific that several Cleveland players acted as if they did not take particular delight in being at the plate."

*Ty Cobb was saying that "the busher [Johnson] throws faster than anyone I've ever seen."* IN TIME, NOBODY EVER DISAGREED WITH HIM.

long, hooked nose that nearly curved over his mouth. Some kidded that his arms were so long he could have tied his shoelaces without bending over. In short, he was an ungainly and awkward-looking fellow.

Yet his quick, powerful swing from the right side of the plate terrorized pitchers for almost two decades. When ground balls came his way, he swooped down on them like an enraged eagle and then threw to first base with such velocity and certainty that pebbles that might have been under the ball flew across the diamond at the same time.

This homely man won the batting title eight times. From 1899 until 1914, he never hit under .300; his top mark was .381 in 1900. He led in doubles eight times and played in one hundred or more games in each of nineteen consecutive seasons. On five occasions, he led the National League in stolen bases; he had 722 steals when he finally stopped running.

Wagner was born in Carnegie, Pennsylvania, in 1874. The town was originally called Mansfield, but in deference to the steel tycoon Andrew Carnegie, who set up shop in nearby Pittsburgh, the name was changed. Honus was one of nine children of a Bavarian immigrant, who eked out a living in the coal mines. Wagner's name had metamorphosed from John to the Germanic Johannes, to the nickname Hans, then to Honus, a name affixed to him by other ballplayers. When he was still Hans, he was making $3.50 a week in the mines, hardly enough to keep the beer flowing. In due course, he wound up playing in the minors, where, at Steubenville, his salary rocketed to $35 a week. It was there that he was discovered by Ed Barrow, the baseball savant whose nose could sniff out talent a mile away. (He was the same fellow who had sniffed out the transition of Babe Ruth from pitcher to outfielder.)

Barrow signed Wagner for his Paterson, New Jersey, club in the Atlantic League, where Honus played two seasons, batting well over .300 each year. Cashing in quickly on his disciple, Barrow sold Wagner to Louisville. When the Louisville franchise collapsed, Wagner wound up with Pittsburgh, which meant that

Honus could play in front of his delighted family and neighbors. By 1903, Honus had settled in at shortstop, after spending the previous years at first base, at third base, and in the outfield. By 1909, Wagner and Cobb were generally acclaimed as the best players in baseball. As luck would have it, they finally confronted each other in a World Series: Pittsburgh versus Detroit. In pre-Series photo ops (yes, Virginia, they engaged in such folderol then too), the two men made small talk about the size of their respective bats. On the field, Wagner responded to Cobb's ugly threat that he was going to cut Honus to pieces when he slid into second, by tagging Ty so hard on his braggart mouth that three stitches had to be taken to sew up the wound. "Krauthead" (that's what Cobb called him) Wagner said the Series was his greatest thrill because the Pirates ended up winning in seven games. Honus outhit Cobb, .334 to .231, as he got eight hits to Cobb's six. He also stole six bases, including a steal of home, while Cobb stole only twice successfully.

"He really surprised me by playing a clean Series," remarked Honus, his tongue planted squarely in his cheek.

It was **WALTER PERRY JOHNSON**'s misfortune to have pitched for the Washington Senators from 1907 to 1927, a trial by torture, for Washington was ridiculed in those times as "first in war, first in peace, and last in the American League." When the Senators finally won the American League pennant in 1924, Johnson was nearly thirty-seven years old and his once-blazing fastball—probably the hottest in history—was a whisper of what it had been in the early 1900s. However, Johnson now had his chance to win his first World Series game. It would be against the New York Giants, who had won four straight National League flags. A national poll taken at that moment would have made Johnson the overwhelming sentimental favorite to pitch his Washington team to victory.

But there was no such easy scenario. Johnson lost the opening game, 4–3, in twelve harrowing innings, in which he was blasted for

Walter Johnson posing with his brother Leslie before the fifth game of the 1924 World Series. The Giants beat him that day, but Walter was redeemed in the seventh game when he came in as a reliever and ended up the winning pitcher. It was, he would say, the most satisfying victory of his storied twenty-one-year career.

fourteen hits by John McGraw's team. In the fifth game Johnson lost again, as he gave up an uncharacteristic thirteen hits. But Barney (a nickname bestowed on him because he could throw a ball as fast as premier race-car driver Barney Oldfield could drive) was given one last chance—and he came through. During the decisive seventh game, manager Bucky Harris of Washington brought in Johnson in the ninth inning of a tie game. Through four perilous innings, and helped by five strikeouts, Johnson kept his team alive. Then, thanks to a rascally pebble that sent a ground ball hopping over third baseman Freddy Lindstrom's head, the Senators won the game and the Series. And Johnson had his long-sought Series triumph. After eighteen years of slavish devotion to mediocre teams, Johnson was rewarded at last.

The next year, Washington was in the Series again, and Johnson won his first two starts against the Pittsburgh Pirates. But this time he lost the seventh game, under a barrage of Pittsburgh hits. He threw only three strikeouts that long afternoon, but Harris let him pitch all the way, letting his heart overrule his judgment.

In the land of the game's greatest right-handers, Johnson has always rated next to—or above—Christy Mathewson. Only Cy Young won more games than "the Big Train," which was Johnson's other nickname. Johnson won 417 games in all, and for ten straight years, from 1910 to 1919, he won twenty or more games. In one hard-to-believe week in 1908, Johnson shut out the Yankees (then called the Highlanders, and long before their prime) three times. In 1912, he won sixteen straight games, a mark equaled only by Joe Wood, Lefty Grove, and Schoolboy Rowe.

Johnson may have thrown only one pitch—his fastball—but it was enough to top his league in strikeouts twelve times, including eight years in a row. He specialized in nerve-racking 1–0 games, winning 38 of them and losing 26. His total of 110 shutouts is the highest of any pitcher in the record books.

The virtues possessed by Johnson—decency, generosity, and humility—are said not to add up to a killer instinct on the mound. But he threw with such eye-defying speed that he didn't have to be mean. It's probably true that he never purposely threw at a batter. He didn't have to. He added up to a prototypical American hero, the kind that used to be written about in children's books about baseball. He wasn't colorful, profane, or eccentric. But he was beloved by those who followed the game.

This baseball legend was born in Humboldt, Kansas, in 1887. He grew up to be big, strong, and long-armed, and when he threw a baseball he seemed to release it underhand. Amazingly, his right foot never appeared to move. Thus, all the power came from his arm. Under normal circumstances, that should have curtailed his career, but it didn't. When Johnson's family moved west, the young man found work in Idaho digging postholes for a telephone company. But he also pitched for the company team, which soon led to his discovery by a traveling salesman, who must have known a thing or two about pitching. The salesman reported back to the Washington Senators about this phenom he'd just seen, and the Senators sent their injured catcher, Cliff Blankenship, out to Idaho to take a look. Oddly, he never got to see Johnson, but relying on the scuttlebutt, he signed the lad for $100, plus $350 a month. Johnson left for the sophisticated East immediately. He may have been as guileless a fellow as ever came out of Idaho, but within a year Ty Cobb was saying that "the busher throws faster than anyone I've ever seen." In time, nobody ever disagreed with him.

After his long career was over, the mild-mannered Johnson managed the Senators from 1929 to 1932, then piloted Cleveland for two years. He died in Washington in 1946, at the age of fifty-nine, remembered always for his sweetness of character and a fastball that few could ever catch up with.

The only player who ever had catcher **GORDON STANLEY "MICKEY" COCHRANE**'s number was Pepper Martin. In the 1931 World Series, Martin, the quintessential Gashouse Gangster, stole five bases—and everything except Cochrane's chest protector—as he led the St. Louis Cardinals to a thrilling seven-game triumph over the Philadelphia Athletics. In one week, Pepper became a household word, while Mickey was reduced to humiliated onlooker.

Aside from that embarrassment, which could have been blamed partially on his pitchers, Cochrane was as good a receiver as the game has ever seen. Proof of that was his election to the Hall of Fame in 1947.

The image of Mickey Cochrane, dynamic catcher, was best described by baseball historian Robert Smith: "He was a man who would shout defiance into the face of an oncoming Sherman tank, or would have snatched a baseball, if it happened to be in play, out of the mouth of a hungry tiger."

When Mickey was a teenager in Bridgewater, Massachusetts, where he was born in 1903, there wasn't anything he couldn't do in sports. Big-eared, black-haired, muscular, and square-jawed, he played outfield and third base for Boston University and was equally proud of the undefeated record he had as an intercollegiate heavyweight boxer. That he had only one fight made no difference. The important thing was that he had competed, and won.

He was a running back in football, he was a talented field-goal kicker, and, when he had spare time, he ran on the track team and played basketball. Those familiar with Boston U's sports history rate him as the best all-around athlete in the school's history. That he also played saxophone and acted in Shakespearean plays marked him as a very eclectic young man.

Mickey began his professional baseball career with a team in Saranac Lake, in upstate New York. Later he joined Dover in the Eastern Shore League, where he played mostly in the outfield. However, he soon switched to catcher, where his basic combativeness would ultimately stand him in good stead.

By 1924, he was with Portland in the Pacific Coast League, where he batted .333. Before long, Connie Mack bought the Portland franchise and immediately brought Mickey up to the big-league Athletics. Although the A's had a fine receiver in Cy Perkins, it was hard to

Sturdy Mickey Cochrane, pictured n the 1932 season, during which he hit twenty-three homers and drove in 112 runs. Lefty Grove, a hard man to impress, said Cochrane was "the best I ever saw. Good hitter, good runner, good arm, smart. Hardly ever shook him off. . . . Like he was reading my mind. That's the kind of catcher he was."

OVERLEAF
During his four seasons as player-manager for the Tigers, Mickey Cochrane averaged .320 at the plate, and he steered his team to two pennants and a world championship. "Cochrane was great, a great inspirational leader," said second baseman Charlie Gehringer. "Cochrane was in charge out there. That's what you could say about him. He was in charge."

keep Mickey out of the lineup. In fact, Perkins was such a team-spirited fellow that he volunteered to teach Mickey many of the fine points of catching, including blocking the plate, backing up first base, pouncing on bunts, setting up the batters from pitch to pitch, working diplomatically with pitchers, and so on. Muddy Ruel, a catcher during Mickey's time in the majors, had characterized a catcher's equipment as "the tools of ignorance." That was a catchy (no pun intended) way of putting it, but, in truth, the catcher's job was anything but that.

One day, Mickey was sent up to pinch-hit for Perkins, and he hit a game-winning double. From that moment on, he was Mr. Mack's regular catcher. He remained so through 1933, as he became an integral part of the dynasty that Mack created at Shibe Park. From the start, Mack was impressed by how Mickey handled his job. "I often matched my judgment with his own," said Connie, "and he usually called the same pitches I would have called for." Black Mike, as he was known, worked with some of the best pitchers of his era, men such as Lefty Grove, right-hander George Earnshaw, southpaw Rube Walberg, and knuckleballer Ed Rommel. He did it so well that he was instrumental in three straight A's flags, in 1929, 1930, and 1931, with two world titles in 1929 and 1930.

After Pepper Martin ran the A's crazy in the 1931 Series, Mickey added two more good seasons in Philadelphia. But as the Great Depression emptied ballparks, and Hoovervilles dotted urban landscapes, Mack was forced to sell off his stars. Detroit paid $100,000 for Mickey, an enormous wad of cash in those troubled times. In his first year at the Tigers' helm as player-manager, Mickey led the Tigers to a pennant, and he did it again in 1935. He had help from great stars such as Hank Greenberg, Charlie Gehringer, and Goose Gosling and pitchers like Tommy Bridges, Schoolboy Rowe, and General Al Crowder. In seven tumultuous games in 1934, the Tigers lost the World Series to the Cardinals. Mickey got some solace that year from his Most Valuable Player Award. In 1935,

however, the Tigers beat the Cubs in six games—and Mickey scored the winning run in the final game—to give Detroit its first world crown. But Mickey's reign at the top of the baseball world was, sadly, ephemeral. In May 1937, his career came to a sickening halt at Yankee Stadium, when right-hander Bump Hadley threw a pitch that cracked Mickey's temple. For ten days, Mickey hovered between life and death. Suddenly, his career as a player had been terminated at the age of thirty-four. The next year he managed the Tigers again, but his emotional and physical health had deteriorated, and he was never able to regain the spark that had ignited so many teams. When he died in 1962, at the age of fifty-nine, he left behind a reputation as a Hall of Fame catcher with the best defensive skills of his time.

It is part of baseball tradition to refer to all left-handed pitchers as "stylish." That is applicable even when the southpaw being talked about is much less than that. I can recall Herb Pennock of the Yankees, from my youth. And, yes, the skinny, patrician guy was the epitome of left-handed stylishness. But the lefty who truly earned the expression, perhaps more than any other southpaw, was **WARREN EDWARD SPAHN**.

Even at the end of his long career (363 wins, 245 losses, with 63 shutouts, the most by any National League southpaw), Spahn was a pleasure to watch, rhythm in motion. His right leg would kick high in the air, followed by a long stride toward home plate. The impeccably smooth delivery never changed, from one hitter to another, from one year to another. If you saw Warren Spahn in action, you would be unlikely ever to forget him.

At bat, too, he was a remarkably good hitter, up there with the best-hitting pitchers of all time, such as Red Lucas, Wes Ferrell, and Red Ruffing. He hit thirty-five home runs during his twenty-one-season career and won any number of games with his own clutch hitting.

Spahn had a face that was hard to forget, too. With his long, crooked nose planted in the middle of an angular face, he had "an Old

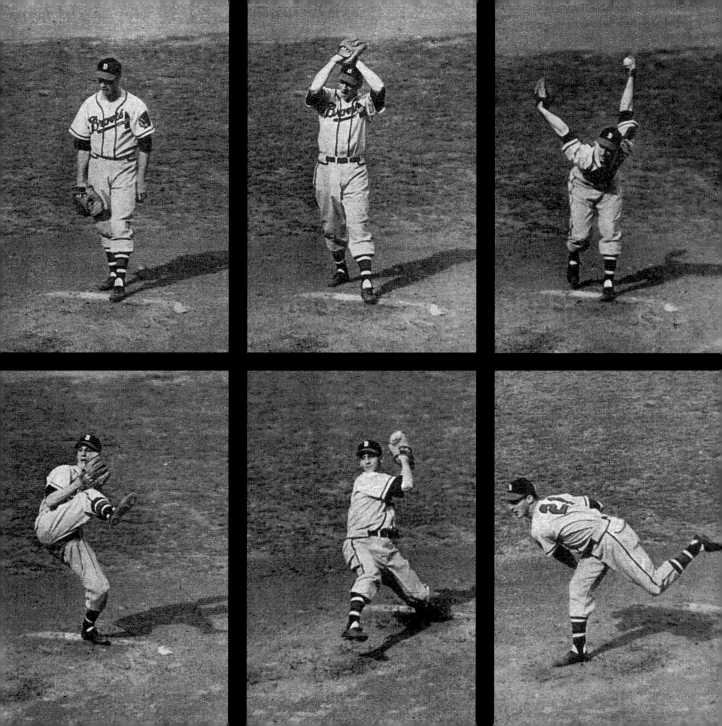

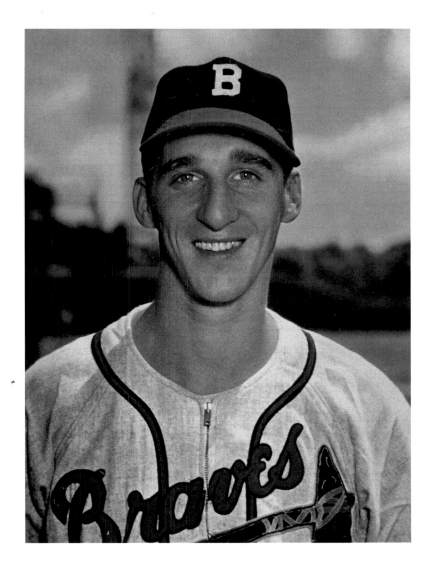

Testament kind of visage," as a *Sports Illustrated* writer put it. But when he talked about pitching, which this cerebral athlete liked to do, there was nothing old or rusty about him. He knew everything there was to know about his craft. "Home plate," he would say, "is seventeen inches wide. All I ever asked for was two inches on each corner. Hitters would have the thirteen inches in between. I made sure never to go there."

In thirteen of Spahn's seasons, he won twenty or more games. He didn't win his first big-league start until he returned from military service in World War II, in 1946. Before he went away, he had pitched for manager Casey Stengel of the Boston Braves in 1942. It was without much success, and with some caustic criticism from Casey. Warren had disregarded orders from Stengel to throw a brushback pitch at the Dodgers' Pee Wee Reese. "I just didn't want to throw at the guy. I pitched in front of him, but I couldn't get one under his chin. Casey was furious at me and cussed me out," recalled Spahn. As a reward for his recalcitrance, Spahn was demoted to the minors, down to Hartford in the Eastern League. Ironically, Stengel wound up managing Spahn more than two decades later, when Warren was about to close out his baseball life. "I knew Casey before and after he was a genius," Spahn said.

Spahn had a grueling war that saw him winning a battlefield commission during the Battle of the Bulge. He nearly lost his life at Remagen Bridge, which became a celebrated, bloody event in the annals of World War II. By the end of hostilities, Spahn had won a Bronze Star and a Purple Heart for his bravery under fire. "They were running out of officers," said Spahn about his commission. He was a wry man, with a knack for putting an edge on a sentence, very much the way he pitched. Always an edge.

Warren was born in Buffalo, New York, in April 1921. His first name was borrowed from Warren G. Harding, then president of the United States. He started to pitch in high school and was soon spotted by the Braves, who signed him for $80 a month. By 1946, Spahn had become a mainstay of the Braves staff. Spahn, Johnny Sain, and Vern Bickford helped the Braves win the

In 1947, his first full season with the Boston Braves, Warren Spahn won twenty-one games and recorded an ERA of 2.33. Sixteen years later, at age forty-two, his record was 23–7 with a 2.60 ERA. Stan Musial said at the close of that season, "I don't think Spahn will ever get into the Hall of Fame. He'll never stop pitching."

OPPOSITE
Warren Spahn's flowing motion mesmerized National League hitters for twenty-one years. Rival manager Chuck Dressen said, "Spahn is what I call a 'go to sleep' pitcher. The manager says Spahn's gonna pitch tomorrow, and then gets a good night's sleep." He pitched in more than 5,200 innings in his career, and he hated to miss a start. He insisted on pitching every fourth day, and he once asked the team's general manager to intercede when his preference wasn't respected.

"*Home plate,*" [SPAHN] WOULD SAY, "*is seventeen inches wide. All I ever asked for was two inches on each corner. Hitters would have the thirteen inches in between. I made sure never to go there.*"

One of the sunniest dispositions in baseball history belongs to Yogi Berra, seen here in 1947, his first full season with the Yankees. Milton Gross wrote in 1950 that Berra had "the looks of the Angel of wrestling, the disposition of an angel of heaven, and the unadorned simplicity of an angel cake." His image notwithstanding, he was one of smartest players ever to take the field; "his intuitive grasp of the mental aspects of the game was exceptional," Leonard Koppett wrote in the *New York Times*.

OPPOSITE

Yogi Berra's swing was not a thing of beauty, but it was lethal, especially in high-stakes contests. Just ask the Dodgers' Don Newcombe. Compounding the difficulty that pitchers faced was Berra's inclination to swing at almost anything inside the strike zone—or out of it. It's reported that he once doubled on a pitchout. Responding to the charge that he was a bad-ball hitter, Yogi said, "A bad pitch isn't a bad pitch anymore when you hit it into the seats."

1948 flag. Together, Spahn and Sain won thirty-nine games that season, with Warren taking fifteen and Johnny winning twenty-four. But in the torrid stretch drive that year, the two men won eight games in a two-week period, as manager Billy Southworth had no reservations about trotting them out every other day. Their durability was soon memorialized in a popular little jingle that went, "Spahn and Sain, and pray for rain."

On many occasions, Spahn remarked that pitching was a lark after what he'd been through in the Bulge. "Pitching is what I did. Hitting is timing. Pitching is upsetting timing. That's it," he said not long before he died in 2003, at the age of eighty-two.

Whether or not LAWRENCE PETER BERRA actually has uttered all of those Yogi-isms credited to him, it's clear that he's still at it. Recently Whitey Ford, his onetime Yankee teammate, told of how he and Yogi looked up at the Yankee Stadium scoreboard not too long ago, just as it flashed the names of some deceased baseball notables. "Boy, I hope I never see my name up there," said Yogi. Yes, that was Yogi Berra, still at the top of his game.

There are perhaps any number of humorless contrarians who try to undermine Yogi's simple—but somehow logical—quotes by informing us that Yogi has probably written more books than he's ever read. Nobody knows that for sure, and I've never seen his library card. But it is certain that for all of his endearing malaprops, Yogi has become a lovable part of America's popular culture.

When those who know Yogi well continue to give testimonials for him, you know he's the genuine article. The astute Bob Costas says that "Yogi is a one-of-a-kind genius," while Tim Russert of *Meet the Press* chips in with the assessment that Yogi is "an American treasure." Bruce Weber of the *New York Times* says Yogi "has a naturally shrewd eccentricity." And what other big-league catcher has ever had a museum named after him? The Yogi Berra Museum and Learning Center, on the campus of Montclair State University of New Jersey, is a little jewel.

Yankee teammates could not resist teasing Yogi Berra, and he seems to have taken it all cheerfully in stride. When he first reported to the Yankees in 1946, he wore his sailor's uniform into the clubhouse. One of the Yankee veterans said he didn't look much like a ballplayer. Another said he didn't look much like a sailor either.

Almost every day you'll see Yogi there, when he isn't off playing golf.

However, Yogi is more than just a squat little fellow whom we like to quote. He was an honest-to-heaven great baseball player, who played in fourteen World Series for the Yankees and hit twelve Series home runs, as he suited up for New York from 1946 through 1963. He even managed the Yankees for one year—1964—and immediately led them into the World Series. For his efforts—after a seven-game loss to the Cardinals in the Series—Yogi was fired. At once he signed on with the New York Mets as a coach. He managed the Mets to a flag in 1973 but was fired in 1975. In 1984, he was back managing the Yankees again, but in 1985 owner George Steinbrenner fired him after only sixteen games. Deeply hurt by the rebuff and the fact that the boss never personally delivered the blow, Yogi refused to set foot in Yankee Stadium for the next fourteen years. He felt that after three decades with the Yankees as player, coach, and manager, he was deserving of better treatment than that. And who could disagree with him? In 1999, Steinbrenner finally apologized to Yogi, and Yogi accepted it. Both men showed maturity—and a sense of commerce—in their rapprochement, and all Yankee fans were delighted that Yogi had come home again.

Although Yogi Berra is a true folk hero of our times, he didn't emerge from a log cabin. He was born in May 1925 in a small, lower-class section of St. Louis called The Hill, a neighborhood crammed with Italian bakeries, grocery stores, butcher shops, and restaurants. His boyhood buddy was Joe Garagiola, who turned out to be a catcher, like Yogi, and a pretty funny guy, like Yogi. The famous yogi nickname evolved out of a visit he took to a movie about India. His pals noticed there was a yogi in the film, and so Lawdie Berra (which is what he'd been called then) became Yogi. He's been known as Yogi ever since, and, somehow, it seems like a perfect fit.

In his teens, Yogi quit school and had a tryout in front of Branch Rickey, who was working for the Cardinals. The odd-looking, shy young Yogi failed to impress Rickey, who politely

*Milton Gross wrote that* **Berra** *had "the looks of the Angel of wrestling, the disposition of an angel of heaven, and the unadorned simplicity of an angel cake."*

advised Yogi to get into another line of work. Rickey may have discovered Jackie Robinson, but he missed the boat on Berra. Meanwhile, a Yankee scout touring the St. Louis area came up with a different opinion of Yogi. He got the New York organization to sign Yogi to a contract in 1942 with Norfolk, Virginia, a Yankee subsidiary, for $90 a month, plus a $500 bonus if he was "retained" until September 1943. Indeed, Yogi was retained for twenty years, and ultimately his salary grew to $5,000 a month, about as compelling an American success story as one can imagine.

In 1944 and 1945, Yogi was in the Navy— not as a poster boy for Navy recruiting but as a sailor on a rocket launcher during the Normandy invasion. When he returned from the war, he quickly proved that he may have looked sort of funny in a baseball uniform, but he seemed to have an unerring eye at the plate. He was a good hitter of bad pitches, and although his first efforts at catching were unpolished, to say the least, he soon developed, under the tutelage of former Yankee catcher Bill Dickey, into a first-rate receiver. He "learned good," as dugout talk had it. And as far as hitting went, he was probably the best clutch hitter in baseball. Satchel Paige, the ancient black sage and pitcher, insisted that Yogi was the "best bad-ball hitter I've ever seen." Yogi won three MVP Awards (1951, 1954, 1955), as well as uncounted needles about his inelegant vocabulary and gnomelike physical appearance. "Aw, nobody hits with their face," he once said in rebuttal. He's been having the last laugh ever since.

The year of 1934, any way you looked at it, was a seminal time for good and bad news in the world. Franklin D. Roosevelt was getting his New Deal under way; dust storms battered the Great Plains; the Dionne quintuplets were born in Canada, making a medical hero out of a small-town doctor; the *Morro Castle* burned off the coast of New Jersey; and Bruno Richard Hauptmann was accused of the fatal kidnapping of Charles A. Lindbergh's baby. In this tumultuous time, **DIZZY DEAN** tried to chase

the blues away, in a world of empty iceboxes and empty wallets, by winning thirty games for the St. Louis Cardinals and leading his team to a World Series victory over Detroit.

If the nation was ever in need of comic relief, Dean provided it. Often declaring that he'd been born in three different states— Arkansas, Mississippi, and Oklahoma—Dizzy Dean was the charismatic country boy who ambled onto the baseball scene just at the moment when Babe Ruth was beginning to suffer from advanced decrepitude. He boasted, kidded, lied, played hooky and practical jokes, and was a veritable "three-ringed circus performer" (in the happy words of Donald Honig). One day he said his name was Jerome Herman Dean, the next he said it was Jay Hanna Dean. It didn't make any difference what he called himself, because he was one helluva pitcher. He shrewdly mangled the English language; "A lot of folks who ain't saying ain't, ain't eating" was his economic philosophy, which seemed to be as good as any in those desperate and uncomfortable times.

When I was about fourteen years old, right after Dizzy had absolutely slaughtered the Tigers in the 1934 Series, I was invited backstage at the old Roxy Theatre in New York City to meet Dizzy (and his brother Daffy). The brothers, who won forty-nine games between them that year, had suddenly become vaudevillians, in the tradition of other celebrated athletes who had been trotted out on the boards. I was struck by how enormous Dizzy looked (he was six-foot-three) in his Cardinals uniform, with those well-fed birds balancing a baseball bat on his shirtfront. "How are ya, son?" he said as he grinned, with one of the friendliest smiles I'd ever seen. I don't remember what I said in return, but I felt that his voice came from a mouth that had to be ten feet above the top of my head. A few minutes later, he was on the Roxy stage, telling all sorts of big and little fibs about how he'd taken the National League apart that year.

The game's greatest, most appealing braggart was born in January 1910—possibly in Lucas, Arkansas. His mother died when he was

very young, and Dizzy and his sharecropper dad roamed around like the nomadic characters in John Steinbeck's *The Grapes of Wrath.* When he was sixteen years old, Dean joined the Army at Fort Sam Houston in Texas, lying about his age in order to get in. All he got out of his military stint was his nickname, which stuck to him for the rest of his life.

Dizzy's fastball soon came to the attention of the Cardinals' scouts, who had watched him pitch for a San Antonio company team. By 1930, he had worked his way up to St. Joseph (Missouri) in the Western Association and Houston in the Texas League. Pitching for these two clubs, he rolled up twenty-five wins; by the end of the season, the Cards had called him up—just in time for him to hurl a three-hitter. In the Cards' spring-training camp of 1931, Dizzy devoted himself to sleeping and boasting how many games he was going to win for the Birds. Such behavior, however, failed to endear him to manager Gabby Street, who shipped him back to Houston. There, the unrepentant Dizzy set the Texas League on its head with twenty-six victories.

By 1932, Dizzy was up with the Cards for good. He won eighteen games in 1932, then twenty in 1933, leading the league each year in strikeouts. But it was that year of 1934 which marked him as the most dazzling pitcher in the game. As an integral part of the grimy, profane, colorful Gashouse Gang, Dizzy seemed to be on the mound every day. He started thirty-three games, completed twenty-four, and also relieved seventeen times. The latter accomplishment, which Dizzy forced on a somewhat reluctant manager Frankie Frisch, was unique among starting pitchers, for most of them preferred to remain away from the bull pen. Dizzy's thirty victories that season, including four wins in relief, were the most by a National Leaguer since Grover Cleveland Alexander's thirty wins in 1917. Even Dizzy himself hadn't figured to win that many, probably the only time he ever underestimated what he could do.

Before the World Series against Detroit, Dizzy predicted that "Me 'n' Paul [his brother Daffy] are gonna win four." As usual, he was

After fracturing the big toe on his left foot in the 1937 All-Star Game, Dizzy Dean won only one game over the second half of the season, and in 1938 was sold to the Chicago Cubs. His fastball was gone by then, but he still had a decent curveball, an effective changeup, and not a trace of self-pity.

OPPOSITE
With his team ahead 9–0 in the late innings of the seventh game of the 1934 World Series, Dizzy Dean began to clown around a bit on the mound. Player-manager Frankie Frisch called time, walked over from his position at second base, and told Dean to behave himself or he'd get a new pitcher. "No, you won't," Dean said. Frisch pondered this for a moment, then returned to second base.

right. In the seventh game, Dizzy wrapped it up with an 11–0 shutout, as his rambunctious Gashousers clawed and scratched their way to the top of the baseball world.

The next two seasons, Dizzy, now the biggest drawing card in the game, as well as its foremost nonstop, cracker-barrel voice of immodesty, won 28 and 24 games respectively, giving him a total of 120 wins in five seasons. There's no telling how high and far Dizzy could have gone. But almost as quickly as Dizzy had risen, he plummeted. In the All-Star Game of 1937, as the starting pitcher for the National League—and with 12 wins already in his pocket—Dizzy was scorched by a ferocious line drive off the bat of Earl Averill. The ball smashed into Dizzy's big toe on his left foot. With the toe broken and giving him great pain, Dizzy, ever the impatient rebel, returned to the mound too soon. In a game against the Braves, he employed a stunted delivery that favored the toe. That afternoon, something popped in his right arm—and that meant the end of the road for him.

The mouth still worked, but the arm was shot. So in 1938 the Cards traded Dizzy to the Cubs, who paid $185,000 and a bunch of players for him. But the days of glory were over for him, as a pitcher. What was left was the talk, and he became one of the most amusing and garrulous of baseball broadcasters, even as educators and teachers were critical of his tortured use of language. Did he really know better than to use "slud" instead of slid? Perhaps. He ended up laughing all the way to the bank.

Growing fatter than he'd ever been in his life, Dizzy lasted until 1974, when he died in Reno, Nevada. There's been nothing like him in baseball since.

On the last day of the 1972 season, **ROBERTO CLEMENTE** knocked out the three thousandth hit of his eighteen-year career with the Pittsburgh Pirates. Weeks later, on New Year's Eve, the dynamic right-fielder was dead at the age of thirty-eight, in an air crash into the ocean a few miles off his native Puerto Rico. He had chosen to fly on a mission of mercy to bring supplies to victims of a devastating earthquake in Nica-

ragua. Try as they might, rescuers were never able to find Clemente's body. Only one of his black socks was recovered, nothing else.

But Roberto's spirit is still alive to those who survived him, including his large family, his fans all over Puerto Rico and the world, and his former teammates. Eleven weeks after his death, Roberto became the first Latin American voted into the Hall of Fame. Of those 424 baseball writers who voted, 93 percent approved his quick induction.

"If there is such a thing as a virtue of pride, Roberto Clemente had it," wrote author Wilfrid Sheed. "Pride for him was not an indulgence, but a moral obligation. When his plane crashed we saw what he had meant all along. It was like the old Clemente crashing into the right-field wall in a losing game: the act of a totally serious man."

It has long been said of Clemente that his anger was the single factor that drove him to baseball heights. From the start of his career with the Pirates in 1955, he was subjected to abuse from foes and even some of his teammates. The abuse was directed at his Puerto Rican heritage, which he was intensely proud of, and there were those who patronized him by calling him "Bobby," instead of Roberto. He was also annoyed when writers referred to him as a hypochondriac. In truth, he played many times when he was hurt and injured. But rarely did he receive credit from a hostile press.

When the Pirates reached the World Series in 1960, after Roberto had batted .314 and led the National League in assists, he felt aggrieved about the voting for Most Valuable Player that year. His teammates Dick Groat, who won the MVP, and Don Hoak, who finished second, had attracted the votes that Roberto didn't get. He wound up eighth, and it took him a long time before his anger at the writers simmered down. "I play the game the way it's supposed to be played," he said. "I give everything I have, according to my ability." That statement pretty well expressed his frustration.

The best rebuttal Roberto could provide was with his bat and arm—and he proceeded to do just that. He rang up a lifetime batting average

OPPOSITE
**Many Pirate fans arrived at the ballpark early to watch Clemente during fielding practice. He had a cannon for a throwing arm, and he would treat the early birds to a spectacular show. In 1958, he snuffed out twenty-two heedless base runners, five more than Willie Mays did. "His throws combined strength, accuracy and speed of release in whatever proportions were necessary to get the job done," wrote Bill James.**

"*If there is such a thing as a virtue of pride, Roberto Clemente had it,*" WROTE AUTHOR WILFRID SHEED. "*Pride for him was not an indulgence, but a moral obligation.*"

of .317, and in the process he won four batting crowns. There was also an increased awareness that he was as good a defensive right-fielder as the game could boast. His arm was as intimidating a weapon as his bat, and that's saying something.

In 1958, he hit three triples in one game versus Cincinnati, and he played in twelve All-Star games and batted over .300 in thirteen seasons. In August 1970, he connected for ten consecutive hits in two games, a record in the National League. From 1961 to 1972, he won twelve Gold Gloves for fielding excellence. "He was poetry in air," wrote his biographer Kal Wagenheim. When he heard people say that he had one of the best arms in baseball, he interjected, "Can you find me anyone with a better arm?"

But it wasn't until he literally took over the 1971 World Series, when he almost single-handedly defeated Baltimore in a seven-game Series, that the nation's fans finally gave him his due. He hit in every game, as he had also done in the 1960 Series. He crashed out twelve hits, including two doubles, a triple, and two homers. He had a Series average of .414 and won the MVP Award by acclamation.

Roberto's assessment of himself, usually spoken with a quirky sense of humor, was often mistaken for boasting. He wasn't boasting; he was telling the truth. Bowie Kuhn, then the baseball commissioner, had always watched Roberto's exploits with amazement. What he said about Roberto could have been an appropriate epitaph: "He was a wonderfully good man, with a touch of royalty."

After the Yankees made their earth-quivering trade to acquire the wonder boy Alex Rodriguez in the winter of 2004, joining an already stellar lineup, they seemed to be without a second baseman. So writer Tyler Kepner of the *New York Times* suggested that the Yankees might try "to rouse Nap Lajoie from the dead."

Now, how many current Yankee fans know who Lajoie was? Not many, I would think. But to many of the cognoscenti, who pay humble respect to the past, **NAPOLEON LAJOIE**

was the best second baseman in the game, playing from the turn of the twentieth century until 1916.

Lajoie was good enough to compete on more than an equal level with shortstop Honus Wagner, his celebrated contemporary. In many respects, he was better than Wagner. He outhit Honus over his lifetime, by .338 to .327. He had the highest single-season American League batting average of all time, with his .423 mark in 1901. His total of 3,242 hits fell short of Wagner's 3,430, but Nap made far fewer errors than Honus. In physical appearance, you couldn't compare the two men. Wagner was awkward and not graceful in the field, while Lajoie was the epitome of style, on and off the field.

Born in Woonsocket, Rhode Island, in 1874, Lajoie was the only man in the history of organized baseball ever to be blessed, or cursed, with the given name of Napoleon. Nap was handsome, intelligent, and tall (six-foot-one). But he never quite seized the public imagination the way that such early icons as Matty, Cobb, and Wagner did. However, when he played for Cleveland from 1903 to 1914, the team was named the "Naps," in his honor.

It was said of Lajoie (some pronounced it "Lazhoway") that he could take a third baseman's head off with one vicious swing of his bat. One day in 1908, minor league southpaw Rube Marquard, soon acquired by the Giants, received some advice from Cleveland third baseman Bill Bradley prior to an exhibition game in French Lick Springs, Indiana. "Be careful of the Frenchman," said Bradley. "The Frenchman is very sharp and he's been hitting terrific line drives this past week. He's almost killed three of our own pitchers in practice, so there's no telling what he'll do in a real game, even if it's just an exhibition game." According to Lawrence Ritter's book *The Glory of Their Times*, Lajoie did connect for two hits against the alerted Marquard that afternoon.

In 1896, Nap was playing with Fall River in the New England League for $100 a month. He batted .429 and hit sixteen homers, which was mighty production in that dead-ball era. The Philadelphia Phillies then obtained him, in a

*"Be careful of the Frenchman,"* said Bradley.
*"The Frenchman is very sharp and he's been hitting terrific line drives this past week. He's almost killed three of our own pitchers in practice."*

deal in which he was a throw-in. He started out playing first base, but within a year he'd been switched to second by manager George Stallings, a move that made second-base history.

Nap made another bit of history when he found the money being waved in his face by the new American League's Philadelphia Athletics more appealing than the maximum salary of $2,400 that he was making with the Phillies. So he jumped to Connie Mack's team in the same town as the Phillies, thus precipitating a lawsuit, *Philadelphia Ball Club v. Lajoie*, which came before the Supreme Court of Pennsylvania in January 1902. The Phillies sought an injunction that would have prevented Lajoie from continuing to play for the Athletics (he'd already put in a sensational year under Mack, batting .422 and hitting fourteen homers). In effect, the case brought against Nap was the first major litigation involving the pernicious reserve clause. His argument was that the Phillies could easily replace him, since he didn't really offer any "unique service," an astonishing display of humility that he couldn't possibly have believed. The court ruled for an injunction, causing a temporary impasse that ended only when Mack agreed to send Nap to Cleveland. That move would get him out of Philadelphia, which some legal beagles said was the only area in which the injunction applied.

In Cleveland, Lajoie became one of the best performers in that city's history, though blood poisoning from a spike wound almost ruined his 1905 season. An interesting footnote (no pun intended) to this incident is that it caused players in future years to wear sanitary socks, with colored stirrups over them.

Managing the Naps didn't work out too well for Lajoie. His team never won a flag, although in 1908 they trailed Detroit by only a half game. He resigned from the thankless job in 1909, while remaining as second baseman. That year he batted .324; the next he hit .384.

Somehow, controversy seemed to pursue Nap in 1910, despite his good nature. He competed closely with Cobb for the batting title. Few familiar with Cobb rooted for him, for he was disliked as much as Nap was liked. With

"Did you ever see . . . Lajoie bat? No? Then you have missed something. I want to tell you that there was one of the greatest hitters—and fielders too, ever in baseball," wrote former White Sox pitcher Ed Walsh in a 1945 article for the *Chicago Daily News*. Walsh was writing about the afternoon he fanned Lajoie with the bases loaded and the 1908 pennant at stake. "Not many pitchers ever did that," he wrote.

OPPOSITE
The 1919 issue of the *Reach Guide* had this to say about Napoleon Lajoie's fielding: "He was the personification of a peculiar grace, in the expression of which he made the hardest plays look easy." As for his batting skills, a lifetime average of .338 is persuasive testimony. From 1901 through 1906, playing for the Phillies and then Cleveland, he averaged .372.

Pie Traynor's throwing arm was powerful and deadly accurate. John McGraw said, "He could come up with a ball and throw a runner out before he had a chance to drop his bat and start running." Combine this talent with a .320 average over seventeen seasons, and you have a Hall of Famer, and one of the two or three finest third basemen in baseball history.

two days to go, Cobb chose to sit out the last two games. It was hardly a sportsmanlike gesture, but it was a move designed to give him the batting title, plus a Chalmers 30 automobile that would go to the winner.

Meanwhile, Nap played his last two games against the Browns and went eight for eight. But the collusion of the Browns' manager, Jack O'Connor, may have opened the floodgates for Nap to acquire his eight hits. Despising Cobb, O'Connor suggested that his third baseman play deep with Nap at bat, thus encouraging Lajoie to bunt deftly to the left side six straight times for what were recorded as base hits. The verdict on two of the hits was questionable: one hit could have been ruled a sacrifice; the other could have been judged an error. In spite of the tainted scenario, Cobb still wound up as batting champ, .385 to .384. As a reward for his dubious strategy, O'Connor was fired.

By 1914, Lajoie had gained three thousand hits, behind only Cap Anson and Wagner. Still playing at forty-one in 1917, Nap hit .380 as player-manager for Toronto in the International League. Twenty years later, in 1937, he was elected to the Hall of Fame. Needless to say, he had few words to exchange with Cobb at the induction ceremony in 1939.

In the words of that revered philosopher Leo Durocher, "Nice guys don't win pennants." This dictum turned out to be true in the case of **HAROLD "PIE" TRAYNOR**, who played from 1920 to 1937 for the Pittsburgh Pirates and is often hailed as the best third baseman of his era. But when it came to managing, which is what Pie did for the Pirates from 1934 to 1939, his decency and popularity simply failed to ignite his charges.

However, Pie did come close on one occasion. On a late September afternoon in 1938, as darkness descended on Wrigley Field, and with thirty-four thousand fans holding their breath, catcher-manager Gabby Hartnett of the Cubs hit a two-out, two-strikes home run to give Chicago a 6–5 victory over the Pirates. As the ball sailed into the left-field bleachers, the Pirates' chances of winning the pennant disappeared. Traynor had had his team in front since early July. Now they were finished for the season.

After the game, often memorialized in the Cubs' lugubrious mythology, Pie walked mournfully (he was known to walk a hundred blocks before and after some games) from Wrigley to the downtown hotel where his team was staying. He was accompanied by a Pittsburgh writer and the club's trainer. "If either of them had said one word, I would have slugged him," said Pie, who was normally one of the most mild-mannered of men.

Traynor was born in Framingham, Massachusetts, in 1899, and carried his odd nickname and typical New England bray all of his life. Where did the nickname Pie come from? Well, some people said Traynor just liked to eat lots of pie. But a more likely explanation was that his father, a printer, noted how blotched with dirt his little son was one day when he came back to the house and, at once, growled that the boy looked like "pied type." The name stuck.

Pie played sandlot ball as a teenager in Somerville, Massachusetts, where he came to the attention of the nearby Red Sox. It would have been expected that the Sox would sign him, but for some reason he was turned down. W. O. McGeehan, writing about the bad judgment of the Red Sox (weren't they the guys who also got rid of Babe Ruth?), said that someone—maybe Ed Barrow—had advised Pie "to get the hell out of Fenway Park. . . . I'm tired of watching your spikes cutting up our field!" Thus, Pie went to the Pirates, who paid the Portsmouth club of the Virginia League $10,000 for him.

By 1921, Pie was in the Pirates lineup, and he never left until his last active year, 1937. He compiled a lifetime batting average of .320. In each of seven seasons, he knocked in more than one hundred runs, helping to win him recognition year in and year out as the premier third baseman in the National League.

In 1925, his .320 average and 114 runs scored, as well as his impeccable fielding, helped the Pirates win their first pennant in sixteen years. "The left side of the Pittsburgh infield," wrote Fred Lieb, a veteran observer of the baseball

In 1971, *Boston Globe* columnist Harold Kaese wrote a piece comparing third basemen. He wrote that Pie Traynor was the Brooks Robinson of his generation. Several days later, a woman from Pittsburgh called and objected to the comparison. "Robinson couldn't carry his glove," she told Kaese. She then identified herself as Traynor's wife. He had many other admirers. In 1929, John McGraw called him "the best team player in baseball today."

JOHN MCGRAW SAID, *"[Traynor] could come up with a ball and throw a runner out before he had a chance to drop his bat and start running."*

Bob Feller, blazing away en route to an opening-day no-hitter in 1940, the year he won twenty-seven games. Cleveland scout Cy Slapnicka, after watching fifteen-year-old Feller pitch in a sandlot game, wired his boss, "Grab him at any price." Several years later, when asked about six-figure signing bonuses, he said, "I think you're supposed to get paid after you do your job."

scene, "was the toast of the nation, and never before in baseball history have fans in any city seen any better defensive ball than Traynor and Glenn Wright (at shortstop) flashed that season." In the World Series against Washington, Traynor, batting .346 over seven games, contributed to the Pirates' exciting come-from-behind victory. Pie's homer against the great Walter Johnson in the opening game was the only run Johnson permitted in that contest.

As the Pirates captured the flag again in 1927, they had the ill luck to come up against the Yankees, in a year when the New Yorkers may have assembled the most talented club of all time. Pie batted only .200 as the Pirates lost four straight to the Yankees. If there was a high point for Pie, it was the single he hit off southpaw Herb Pennock in the eighth inning of the third game. Until that moment, Pennock had been pitching a perfect game. The single, however, accounted for no difference in the final result: the Pirates lost that day and the next. Despite the Pirates' toothless performance in the Series, John McGraw, the New York Giants' manager, who had been around the game almost since its infancy, insisted that Pie was "the greatest team player in all of baseball." Considering that Pittsburgh had such splendid players as Paul and Lloyd Waner, Glenn Wright, Max Carey, and Clyde Barnhart, McGraw's comment was a meaningful tribute.

Pie was equally important to the Pirates at bat and in the field. A man with great range, he could guard the third-base line as aggressively as anyone in his time. Admirers of Baltimore's Brooks Robinson, who performed his third-base acrobatics many years later, have suggested that Brooks was a superior fielder to Pie. They may be right. But Pie's arm, when it wasn't hurt, was certainly the equal of Robinson's. Pie was elected to the Hall of Fame in 1948. In 1972, he died in Pittsburgh, a city that admired and respected him as a fierce competitor, even if he'd been thrown out of only one game in his long career.

Put back the nearly four years that **ROBERT WILLIAM ANDREW FELLER** spent in the U.S. Navy during World War II, and you have a pitcher with well over 300 victories. But even with those years lost to Bob Feller's record, he was a winner of 266 games, including three no-hitters and twelve one-hitters. All of these achievements could have been previewed near the Raccoon River in Van Meter, Iowa, when the earnest young farm boy was only fourteen years old.

One of Feller's no-hitters came on the opening day of the 1940 season against the White Sox, the only time in major-league history that a pitcher has done that. Ultimately that season, Bob won twenty-seven games, his top total in eighteen years of pitching for Cleveland.

Bob Feller was the Great Depression pitcher, just as Herbert Hoover, who also hailed from Iowa (West Branch), was the Great Depression president. Feller's background—his dad built him a ball field on their land—was straight out of a Hollywood scenario. Bob did chores on the farm: milked the cows, fed the hogs, chopped wood, and kept the roads clear in the wintertime when the snow swirled through the countryside. But he never neglected his early ambition, encouraged by his father, William, to become a pitcher. In that lush heartland, boys preferred to grow up throwing baseballs, rather than reading Shakespeare or playing musical instruments. Oddly, when Bob grew up he also developed a sophistication and urbanity that belied his humble background. He flew his own plane, formed his own corporation, attached attendance bonus clauses to his contract, and haggled over money with the avidity of a Harvard-educated business major.

In the early 1930s, he became a teen legend, as he pitched in American Legion ball. Those who witnessed his mind-boggling fastball (later it was timed at 98.6 miles per hour by Army devices) shouted out the news of the boy's magnificence to Cleveland scout Cy Slapnicka, who had come to Iowa to take a look at a right-hander named Claude Passeau. He didn't get to see Claude. But he did get a view of Bob. Within a few days, Slapnicka proclaimed that he'd just seen "the greatest young pitcher in the world." And not long after that, Cleveland signed the lad for one dollar and an autographed ball, plus seventy-five bucks a month. A nonsensical legend? No, the unvarnished truth.

By July 1936, Bob hurled a few innings in an exhibition game in Cleveland against the St. Louis Cardinals. After fanning eight men in three innings, there were no naysayers around. Everyone waited for Bob's first start in a regular game, in mid-August versus the lowly St. Louis Browns. At the age of seventeen, Bob fanned fifteen of the Brownies, who, despite their overall miseries, had several good hitters in their lineup. The next morning, Bob was America's corn-fed headliner, probably the most famous kid in the land outside of the dimpled Shirley Temple.

In September 1936, he whiffed seventeen Philadelphia A's, tying Dizzy Dean's record—and also establishing that he was a country boy who was vying with another country boy to win the hearts and minds of the fans.

If Bob had a problem during his career, it was his control. In 1938, he passed 208 batters, a record at the time. At the same time, he fanned 240, to earn his first strikeout crown. It had become clear by then that if batters couldn't see through the smoke Bob threw at them, they could at least keep their bats on their shoulders. Even when he fanned eighteen Tigers on the last day of the 1938 season, Bob lost because he doled out seven walks. However, in a duel mano a mano with Hank Greenberg, who had fifty-eight homers and was trying to unseat Babe Ruth, Bob struck out Greenberg twice. When the winds of war enveloped America in December 1941, Bob joined up with the Navy, a day after Pearl Harbor. He was one of the first big leaguers to answer the call. He had tough combat duty on the battleship *Alabama* and ended up with five campaign ribbons and eight battle stars.

Picking up his career in 1945, Bob introduced another pitch to his repertoire: a slider. It helped him ring up a 20–11 mark in 1947. The next year, as Cleveland captured the pennant, Bob had 19 wins, but by that time Bob Lemon and Gene Bearden had preceded him in the rotation. The Indians won that World Series over the Boston Braves, even as Bob suffered

For several seasons, Bob Feller (far right) was part of a peerless four-man pitching rotation. In 1951, the year this picture was taken, Bob Lemon, Mike Garcia, and Early Wynn (left to right) won a total of fifty-seven games, and Feller added twenty-two, the best in the American League that season. "He had more stuff than anybody," Ted Williams said.

*Cleveland scout Cy Slapnicka, after watching fifteen-year-old Feller pitch in a sandlot game, wired his boss,* "GRAB HIM AT ANY PRICE."

two losses. In the first game, Bob lost 1–0, a wrenching defeat after a disputed play at second base late in the game cost the Indians the only run scored.

In 1962, Feller was elected to the Hall of Fame. All those days on the farm in his youth had paid off for him.

Every bit as combative as Jackie Robinson, who preceded him to the majors, **FRANK ROBINSON** became the first black manager in baseball history. It was an event that would have made Jackie proud. But Frank was much more than an enduring symbol of racial progress in the sport, for he was also the only player ever to win a Most Valuable Player Award in each league. He did it with Cincinnati in 1961, then with Baltimore in 1966. And thereby hangs a tale of misjudgment that has probably never been equaled.

After Frank won the 1961 prize, but saw his team go down to defeat in the World Series against the Yankees, he spent the following four years still in a Cincy uniform. Two of these seasons were subpar for him, with averages below .300. That led Reds owner Bill DeWitt to suspect that Frank was washed up at the age of thirty. Thus, he engineered a trade in the off-season of 1965 that may well go down as the most crushingly one-sided baseball transaction in the record books. The Reds sent Frank to the Orioles, getting pitcher Milt Pappas and a couple of no-names in return. When Frank then led the Orioles to a pennant in 1966, followed by a World Series win over the Los Angeles Dodgers in four straight, the pundits had a field day with Mr. DeWitt. James Reston, normally a political columnist for the *New York Times*, jumped out of his division to proclaim that DeWitt "had caused Baltimore to make the best deal since the Louisiana Purchase. . . . This superb Negro athlete may do more for sanity on the race question in Maryland than all of the fair-minded politicians in the state."

Oddly, Frank's big numbers over the years— 586 career homers (fifth on the all-time list) and the feat of hitting homers in the greatest number of ballparks (thirty-three), as well as

"If he finishes the season with .270 and fifteen home runs, I'll be happy," said Cincinnati Reds manager Birdie Tebbetts as he watched rookie Frank Robinson play during the 1956 spring-training schedule. He had fifteen homers by the end of June. He finished with thirty-eight, nearly half of which were hit against the Dodgers and Braves, the league's top teams. He also hit twenty points better than his manager's goal, and was a unanimous choice for the Rookie of the Year Award.

OPPOSITE
Due to his combative, plate-crowding style, Frank Robinson was a frequent, and unintimidated, victim of brushbacks and pitched balls aimed at his head and body. Phillies manager Gene Mauch reportedly fined any of his pitchers who knocked Robinson down, believing that he was twice as dangerous when aggravated.

PALMER: *"Frank was a true super-star who started the Orioles on the road to greatness."*

his penchant for getting hit by pitchers (third on the list)—had still not won him the acclaim it should have. He was, in a sense, baseball's "invisible man"—which was the title of a book by Ralph Ellison about black men in America. This is not said to disparage Robinson, but rather to emphasize how he has played in the shadow of other African-American stars such as Mays, Aaron, and Barry Bonds.

Born in Beaumont, Texas, in 1935, one of ten children, Frank moved with his family to Oakland, California, at an early age. His all-around talent soon came to the attention of big-league scouts. By 1956, he was signed by Cincinnati, after General Manager Gabe Paul discovered that "he's the type of player you dream about."

But in 1961, Frank made an imprudent decision one night in Cincinnati that could have cost him dearly. Walking into an all-night restaurant, he flashed a gun during an altercation, and he was arrested and indicted. He pleaded guilty to a charge of carrying a concealed weapon and was fined $250 plus court costs. Later he tried to explain that he was carrying the gun because he had large sums of money in his pockets. On this occasion, he added, the walk from his garage to his apartment was along a badly lit road. "It was for my peace of mind that I had the gun," Frank said.

Whatever thoughts Frank offered on the subject failed to have much impact on rival bench jockeys, who seized on the incident to assail him with rude insults and barbs. "I wanted to forget about it, and play ball," said Frank, "but I kept getting it from all sides, in every town. It wasn't very pleasant."

However, a steady flow of game-winning base hits and aggressive play in right field ultimately helped Frank drown out the discordant notes. In that way, he proved both to himself and to those who had portrayed him as a malcontent that he had what it takes to survive in the rough-and-tumble of his profession.

When DeWitt made the mistake of jettisoning Frank, Robinson had already posted 1,009 runs batted in during his ten years in Cincinnati. Coming to Baltimore, where he teamed up with

the superb third baseman Brooks Robinson, Frank's stubborn pride paid off. By winning the Triple Crown in his first year in the American League, he put all those misguided rumors about his character and temperament to rest. In 1966, he was everybody's MVP. "He should have been the MVP of *both* leagues," said one writer. He hit forty-nine homers, a personal all-time high, and knocked in 122 runs. In the World Series against Los Angeles, he started and finished the scoring with home runs.

As the years went by, it wasn't a secret that Frank yearned for a chance to become the pioneer black manager in the majors. He took basic training for such a job by managing in the Caribbean winter leagues, even as he kept his trim, muscular body (six-foot-one, 194 pounds) in excellent shape. When he finally got the call to manage, it was with the Cleveland Indians in 1975. On his first day as player-manager of the Indians, Frank blasted a first-inning home run to help turn back the Yankees. Unfortunately, the Indians were not stocked with seven other players of Frank's quality, so after two years he wrote another first into the book by becoming the first black manager to be fired. "I did the best I could. Race was not a factor," Frank said.

In 1981, the San Francisco Giants hired Frank as manager, and he led the club to a third-place finish. For his work, Frank won designation from United Press International as the National League's Manager of the Year. Later he got to manage his old team, the Orioles, for a couple of years, and he was glad to be back in familiar territory. A lifetime of achievements in baseball could only please Robinson. But what he cherished more than anything else were assessments about him made by Brooks Robinson and Orioles hurler Jim Palmer. Brooks said that "Frank could do everything that Mays and Aaron could do," while Palmer stated that "Frank was a true super-star who started the Orioles on the road to greatness." In 1982, Frank Robinson was named to the Hall of Fame.

In many respects, **NOLAN RYAN** may be the most remarkable right-handed pitcher in history.

Nolan Ryan in 1968, his rookie year with the New York Mets. No one, least of all the Mets' management, would have predicted twenty-seven years of brilliance for the young man. Pat Jarvis, who pitched briefly for Atlanta and Montreal, was Ryan's first strikeout victim. "Everybody knew of him, but he was so wild no one wanted to dig in on this guy," he said. "I'm sure I was standing way in the back of the box and giving him the whole plate."

He started out in baseball life in 1968 as a chronically wild young fellow on the staff of the New York Mets, where he was clearly overshadowed by the bright ex-Marine Tom Seaver. Then, in a trade that rates up there with the worst of them, he was shipped in 1971 to the California Angels, after the Mets began to look upon Nolan as something of a lost cause. In four years with the Mets, Nolan had rung up only twenty-nine wins, against thirty-eight losses. He managed to win ten games one year, but manager Gil Hodges didn't believe that was the kind of production worthy of further patience. Nolan tried to account for his reputation as a loser on the Mets. "They take kids out of high school," he said, "and he's ready for instruction, but there's nobody to instruct him. I didn't learn the fundamentals."

With California, Nolan immediately became a winner—nineteen games in 1972, and twenty-one in 1973—as he suddenly went about establishing himself as a rival to those legendary fastballers Walter Johnson and Rube Waddell. In 1973, he rang up 383 strikeouts, which surpassed Sandy Koufax's mark. He did that in spite of his penchant for walking batters; he had league-leading totals in that dubious department, even as he led the National League in strikeouts.

Even worthier of mention was Nolan's ability, as he grew old in baseball terms, to withstand innumerable injuries that would most assuredly have sidelined a lesser man. From time to time, he pitched with injuries to his neck, his groin, his hamstring, his legs, his shoulders, his elbows. The only part of his sturdy body (six-foot-two, 212 pounds) that didn't wilt at any time was his heart. That proud organ would eventually carry him through 1993—yes, 1993, some twenty-seven years of pitching. Even in his final year, Nolan, winding up his career with Texas at the age of forty-six, struck out forty-six batters in sixty-six innings. The man who had led his league in strikeouts in eleven seasons, and in his prime had completed as many as twenty-six games (in 1973 and 1974), was still capable of whiffing batters with the best of them.

Nolan's lifetime total of 324 victories, against a rather high total of 292 defeats, should also be kept in perspective, for he was generally working for California, Houston, and Texas teams that were rarely in serious contention.

How did this happen to a man who was all but ignored in New York? The pitching coach with the Angels, Tom Morgan, supposedly performed minor miracles with Nolan's delivery (naturally called Ryan's Express). But Nolan felt his renaissance was due more to the fact that "I began pitching every four days—that's what did it for me."

Born in Refugio, Texas, in 1947, Nolan has to be the Lone Star State's most significant contribution to pitching—and that doesn't exclude the formidable Roger Clemens. Nolan's numbers are astounding, including seven no-hitters and twelve one-hitters. One of the stat rats figured out that in his 5,714 lifetime strikeouts, Nolan had victimized 1,176 different players. On the negative side was his profligacy in doling out bases on balls, a habit that caused him to throw more pitches in each game. However, that never seemed to daunt him.

At the age of forty-four, in 1991, Nolan hurled his seventh, and last, no-hitter. This one came at the expense of Toronto, a team that boasted a number of good hitters. He was working on four days of rest, and before the contest he had told his manager that "everything hurts." To make matters worse, he had just torn a callus on his index finger. So what did Nolan do? He faced only twenty-nine batters, striking out sixteen. Needless to say, he was the oldest pitcher ever to throw a seventh no-hitter, a record that is sure to be as imperishable as DiMaggio's fifty-six-game string. As Geoffrey Ward and Ken Burns point out in their book *Baseball*, the last batter to face Nolan on that charmed day was Roberto Alomar, whose dad, Sandy, had been California's second baseman eighteen years before, when Nolan had carved his first no-hitter.

The old Texas quail hunter, now confined to making TV commercials and advising future generations of flamethrowers, used to toss more than two hundred pitches in an outing. That was much more than the six-inning pitchers of the current generation are accustomed to throwing. But Nolan never counted his pitches, or his injuries. That's what got him elected to the Hall of Fame in 1999.

GEORGE SISLER was acknowledged as a defensive genius among first basemen. He may have even surpassed the despicable rogue Hal Chase with his artistry around the bag. But, like those great batsmen Babe Ruth and Stan Musial, Sisler started out as a pitcher before others decided he was too good a hitter to be used only every four or five days. What's more, in 1915, his first year with the St. Louis Browns, Sisler pitched in fifteen games, and finished with a 4–4 mark. His proudest victory was a shocking 2–1 win over Walter Johnson, who had been his boyhood idol. George became so emotionally unstrung after the game that he was tempted to apologize to Johnson for his act of heresy.

A year later, Sisler was no longer a left-handed pitcher. Instead, he had become the Browns' regular first baseman and, as it turned out, a magical fielder and a splendid all-around player. Within a few seasons, he was the chief challenger to Cobb as the game's best hitter. Of course, there was little doubt that he was a person of better character and disposition. In 1920, when he was twenty-seven (he was born in Manchester, Ohio, in 1893), Sisler put together a year ranking with the best that any other first baseman—or ballplayer of any kind—has ever produced. Yet today, if you ask a battery of baseball historians about that year, they would have difficulty spelling out the precise details. Because Sisler was never a self-promoter or a grabber of headlines, his achievements have been largely overlooked, and that goes for the remarkable year of 1920. Here's what George did: he batted .407 and collected 257 hits, the record for the century (broken by Ichiro Suzuki in 2004). Eighty-six of those hits were for extra bases, including 18 triples, 49 doubles, and 19 home runs. He drove in 122 runs and scored 137 times, as well as stealing

Third baseman Jimmy Austin, a longtime St. Louis Browns teammate of George Sisler's, weighed in on the Sisler versus Hal Chase competition for Larry Ritter, the author of *The Glory of Their Times*, one of baseball's indispensable books. "Of the two, I guess I'd have to say that Chase was the better fielder," Austin said. "In a way I hate to say that, but you have to give the devil his due. Sis was a better all-around ball player."

*Within a few seasons, he was the chief challenger to Cobb as the game's best hitter.*

42 bases. Truly a complete ballplayer! Those monumental figures were supplemented by his prowess in the field, as well as his participation in all of his team's 154 games.

To prove that 1920 was hardly an aberration, Sisler batted .420 in 1922, the second-highest average in American League history (Lajoie hit .426 in 1901). He knocked out 246 hits and rolled up a forty-one-game hitting streak, which lasted until Joe DiMaggio passed it in 1941.

Considering that Sisler's life was never marred by controversy, it was odd that his career began on a note of rancor. While pitching for Akron High, in Ohio, as a teenager, George signed a contract with the local team in the Ohio-Pennsylvania League. He received no money from Akron, but the club maintained that he was its property, even while he was attending the University of Michigan as a mechanical engineering student. Akron transferred the contract to its parent club, Columbus. In turn, Columbus sold the contract to the Pittsburgh Pirates. But there was a subtext to all of this maneuvering: Branch Rickey, a scout for the St. Louis Browns, was also Sisler's coach at Michigan and believed that Sisler was the best college player he'd ever seen. He was determined to void the contract that George had signed when he was a minor, without parental consent. When the issue was put before the National Commission, a baseball bureau that preceded the appointment of a baseball commissioner, the contract was declared null and void. Thereupon, George signed with the Browns, where, mirabile dictu, Mr. Rickey had become the manager. Sisler received a $5,000 bonus and $400 a month, more than peanuts in those parsimonious times.

It was a tribute to Rickey's shrewdness that he saw such great potential in this slim (170-pound) young man. He may also have been much taken by Sisler's civility, in contrast to what Ty Cobb had once said about the game: "It's as gentlemanly as a kick in the crotch." The bond between Rickey and his disciple would last for the rest of their lives, with Rickey always being referred to as "Coach" by Sisler.

George Sisler loved hitting in Sportsman's Park. In 1920, he hit .473 there, with fifteen homers and eighty-seven RBIs. On the road, he managed only four homers and thirty-five RBIs, but he still recorded a .340 average. He played with a contending team just once during his seventeen-year career, and he never displayed his gifts on the World Series stage.

Sisler played for the Browns for thirteen years. Only in 1922 did the team come close to winning; it finished behind the Yankees by a single game. "We desperately wanted to win," said a disappointed Sisler. In 1927, Sisler was sold to Washington for $25,000. But before that, in 1923, he suffered a serious medical setback. Due to an acute eye infection, he became the victim of double vision. As a result, he had to sit out the whole season. When he returned to St. Louis in 1924, he was made player-manager, a popular decision in that hot baseball town. However, he was never quite the dominant hitter he had once been. He managed, with some difficulty, to adapt to his poor eyesight and actually hit .345 in 1925 and .327 in 1927. But those were disappointing averages to the perfectionist Sisler. Some said he was "swinging on memory," which was still sufficient to help him end up with a .340 lifetime average. After he left the game in 1931, Sisler became the head of a true baseball family. Two of his three sons, Dick and Dave, became big leaguers. Dick hit a clutch home run for the Phillies in 1950 that beat out Brooklyn for the pennant.

When Sisler, a Hall of Famer, died in 1973 at the age of eighty, a question lingered about him: what heights might he have reached had he not been bedeviled by his eye disability? We will never know. Nevertheless, he remained Rickey's finest gift to baseball.

Lou Gehrig was to Babe Ruth what **TRISTRAM SPEAKER** was to Ty Cobb. Both Lou and Tris played in relative anonymity because they were overshadowed by larger-than-life characters. Speaker's career ran from 1907 to 1928, and Cobb's career ran almost concurrently with that of Tris. Speaker achieved much, as one of the most agile center fielders in the game's history, but he always had to be compared with Cobb as a hitter. In that department, Cobb rang up so many batting titles, plus a lifetime average of .367, that Tris's facility in the field was easily overlooked.

Yet Speaker was no slouch at the plate. He had a career average of .344 and hit over .300 in eighteen seasons, mainly with the Boston

In 1912, Tris Speaker, playing for the Red Sox in his fourth full year in the majors, was at bat in the last game of the World Series when a foul pop fly he hit in the last of the tenth inning dropped beyond the reach of the Giants' catcher Chief Meyers, whom pitcher Christy Mathewson had called to grab it. Speaker yelled out to Matty, "Well you just called for the wrong man. It's gonna cost you this ball game." On the next pitch, Speaker singled to center, driving in the tying run. Shortly after that, the winning run crossed on a sacrifice fly.

OPPOSITE
As he was during his playing career, Tris Speaker was compared with Ty Cobb during their coinciding years as managers, and here Speaker proved to be the more successful. Doc Cramer, a twenty-year major leaguer, felt that Speaker was the better teacher. "He'd take you out there and show you how to do it," Cramer said. "Cobb wouldn't do that. He'd talk to you, tell you all about it, but he wouldn't take you out there."

Babe showed his appreciation:
*"I'd be pitching and hear the crack of the bat and say to myself, 'There goes the ball game!' But* Tris *would race back to the fences, and at the last moment make a diving catch. Not once, but a thousand times."*

Red Sox and the Cleveland Indians. In another department, managing, he was more successful than the angry Cobb. In 1920, he piloted the Indians to a pennant, then a World Series victory over Brooklyn. Cobb failed to accomplish anything like that as a manager.

From 1910 to 1915, Speaker, who was popularly known as the "Grey Eagle," was the middleman in one of the most impregnable outfields ever assembled. Duffy Lewis was on the left and Harry Hooper was on the right for the Red Sox. In center, Speaker made a specialty of throwing out base runners trying to advance. He was so good that in each of two seasons, he threw out thirty-five runners, an American League record.

This wonderful trio helped immeasurably in bringing pennants to Boston in 1912 and 1915. In each World Series, the Red Sox won. In the 1912 Series against the Giants, as the Red Sox emerged in an eight-game battle, Speaker topped his team with a .300 average. In addition, he turned in the only unassisted double play by an outfielder ever recorded in a World Series game.

Speaker made it a habit to play close behind second base, perhaps closer than any other outfielder ever had. This enabled him to get many hitters out on ordinary line drives over the base. There's not much doubt that many of these balls would have dropped in for singles had Tris not been on hand to snuff them out. But Tris could also go back on a ball. When a long fly was hit behind him, he was invariably there to snag those drives too. He seemed to take off even before the batter had completed his swing. He would then capture the ball on the dead run, invariably catching the ball over his shoulder, almost as if the ball had been casually thrown to him. It wasn't speed afoot that did the job for Tris; it was anticipation. When latter-day outfielders such as Willie Mays and Joe DiMaggio went back on balls à la Speaker—as Willie did in the World Series of 1954—it was most unusual. With Speaker it was commonplace.

DiMaggio never saw Speaker play. But he fully understood how Tris's style of play could

be invaluable to his team. "He certainly could catch many Texas Leaguers that ordinarily might fall in for base-hits," said DiMaggio. "In fact in one season Tris made two unassisted double plays at second because of his ability to catch those bloopers just over the infield. From all that I've heard about him Speaker was a genius and certainly one of the great outfielders that ever lived."

Speaker was born in Hubbard City, Texas, in April 1888. He was one of seven children. When he was ten years old, his father died, leaving his mother, Jennie, in charge of a family without many resources. Jennie's distaste for baseball, which Tris loved, was accentuated when her son fell off a horse and broke his arm. She felt that this would surely put an end to his ball playing. Instead, Tris adapted to his situation by learning to bat and throw from the left side. At the age of seventeen, he signed to play with a team in the North Texas League. By 1907, he was playing for Houston in the Texas League, where he made some starts as a pitcher. But his hitting ability stamped him as a natural, causing his contract to be sold to the Red Sox. In Boston, he batted .309 as a rookie in 1909, thus beginning ten consecutive seasons for him as a .300 hitter.

Soon he gained renown for his fielding talent. He revolutionized outfield play, to the extent that he was almost regarded as a fifth infielder. After the Red Sox won the flag in 1912, Speaker got the MVP Award, aided by numbers—a .383 average on 222 hits—that were as impressive as those his friendly enemy, Cobb, had posted. The two men actually got along reasonably well, which took surprising diplomacy on Tris's part. Perhaps there was some common ground between the two based on the rumors that once placed Speaker in the ranks of the Ku Klux Klan.

Even as Tris batted .363 and .338 the next two seasons, the Red Sox failed to repeat their league championship. But in 1915, with a young fellow named Babe Ruth pitching, the Red Sox again won the American League pennant. Babe showed his appreciation for Tris's presence in center field with this appraisal of his

teammate: "Spoke was really something special. I'd be pitching and hear the crack of the bat and say to myself, 'There goes the ball game!' But Tris would race back to the fences, and at the last moment make a diving catch. Not once, but a thousand times."

However, the Red Sox management, by this time paying Tris $18,000 a year, was not as appreciative as Ruth. It tried to cut Speaker down to $9,000, after the Federal League folded. Tris had been making eyes at the rebel loop, and the Red Sox resented it. This led to a nasty brouhaha, which ended with Tris's being sold to Cleveland for $50,000. In his new home, Tris picked up where he had left off. In his first year with the Indians, he won the batting title with a .386 mark, breaking Cobb's run of nine straight crowns. By 1919, Tris replaced Lee Fohl as Cleveland's manager, perhaps contributing to a decline in his batting. He finished at .296, the only time he was below .300 from 1909 to 1927. But the next year, he brought his club home in first place, with some push from his own .388 batting average. The year was marred by the death of the Indians' shortstop Ray Chapman, who was hit in the head by a sidearm throw from the Yankees' Carl Mays, the only instance in major-league history of a player being killed during a game.

In his twilight time, Speaker was accused—along with Cobb—of trying to fix a game that had been played some years before. Both men were ultimately exonerated by Commissioner Kenesaw Mountain Landis, though the incident was hardly a happy way to finish out a career. Many prominent people defended Tris and Cobb, including the witty "poet lariat" Will Rogers, who said, "If Cobb and Speaker had been selling out all those years, I'd like to see them play when they weren't selling."

Despite the ugliness, Tris was still named to the Hall of Fame in 1937. When he died in Texas in 1958, his 3,514 hits were second only to Cobb's.

After **DENTON TRUE "CY" YOUNG** pitched a perfect game against the Philadelphia Athletics in 1904, at the age of thirty-seven, he discussed the subject in his usual modest fashion. "I guess," he said, "that I had pretty good speed and stuff." Chances are that was as accurate as Young's middle name, for he permitted only six balls to be hit out of the infield that day.

In a career that began with Cleveland in 1890 and ended with Boston in 1911, when he was forty-four years old, Cy Young won more games—511—than any pitcher in history. That he also lost 316 games, also more than any other pitcher, was testimony to the fact that he was more durable than anyone else in the books, with the possible exception of Nolan Ryan.

Cy insisted that he never suffered from a sore arm in his life. We'll have to take his word for that. But when you win thirty or more games five times, and win twenty or more fifteen times, that's darned good evidence that nothing has ever bothered you, outside of mosquitoes on a scalding afternoon. In fact, Cy lived a life of consistency in every respect. He was born in Ohio in 1867, and he died in Ohio in 1955. He literally never left home, outside of those mound appearances he made in various big-league cities. As Robert Smith wrote, "He lasted so long in the majors that it seemed they'd have to shoot him on Judgment Day, with his baseball shoes still on."

That Young pitched in the so-called deadball era, starting out when pitchers were just fifty feet from batters, when there was an emphasis on struggling for one run at a time, and when home runs were as rare as kind words from umpires, still doesn't diminish this man.

When Young first came off a farm in eastern Ohio, he wasn't yet known as Cy. The nickname may have been derived from the fact that he threw the ball like a cyclone or that rural lads were often referred to as Cy, a shortening of the disparaging Cyrus. Take your pick. His pitching life began with Canton in the Tri-State League. He looked so good that the Cleveland Spiders plunked down $300 for him. Showing up for his first big-time start against Cap Anson's Chicago White Sox, he had on a dirty uniform and looked like a country bumpkin. But he won, giving up only three hits. Anson had been dismissive before the game, but after it he offered

"Shucks, they've taken too much away from the pitchers with the lively ball they're using now," said seventy-six-year-old Cy Young in 1943 to a reporter from the *Washington Evening Star*. The ball was certainly livelier in 1943 than it was when Young pitched, but it's safe to say that the right-hander would have dominated any era. "I never had a sore arm until the day I quit," he said. "I guess it was about time. I was forty-five years old then."

AS ROBERT SMITH WROTE, *"[Young] lasted so long in the majors that it seemed they'd have to shoot him on Judgment Day, with his baseball shoes still on."*

In 1947, at an Old-Timers Day observance at Yankee Stadium, Cy Young (far left) suited up with Ty Cobb (far right) and Duffy Lewis, Tris Speaker, and Harry Hooper (left to right), who were teammates on the Red Sox from 1910 through 1915, forming a brilliant outfield. Bill James described Young as a right-handed Warren Spahn, among the best for almost three generations of competitors.

$1,000 for Young. However, the Spiders quickly turned him down. Cy won nine games that year. Then, in 1891, he won twenty-seven times, followed by thirty-six victories in 1892. Young stayed with Cleveland until 1899, when the franchise was moved to St. Louis, a town that in summer was too hot for Cy's taste. So he couldn't have been more receptive to an offer to jump to the Boston Red Sox in the newly constructed American League. The Red Sox were willing to pay him $600 more than he earned in St. Louis.

In the first modern World Series, in 1903, Cy pitched in four games against the heavily favored Pittsburgh Pirates. He won two of those games and lost one, though the Red Sox won. He appeared in thirty-four innings, giving up thirty-one hits and striking out seventeen. These statistics were typical for Young. Sometimes he appeared easy to hit, but in the crunch he could get batters out. In Cy's last season with the Red Sox, in 1908 (he ended up with the National League Boston Braves), he won twenty-one games. Grateful fans gave him a special day at the Boston ballpark on Huntington Avenue, and more than twenty thousand showed up. They presented Cy with a check for $6,000. It was the first such acknowledgment of a ballplayer in that era.

When he retired in 1912, Cy returned to Ohio farm country, but he always retained an interest in the game. He loved to reminisce about the old days, but he never made too much about his achievements. "I just had good control, and a good fastball," he'd say. He was voted into the Hall of Fame in 1937. A year after his death, baseball inaugurated a yearly pitcher's award in his name, a much-cherished emblem of pitching excellence.

Though caught in a vortex of suspicion and media exposure, **BARRY LAMAR BONDS** has been measured for immortality even as he plays. At the start of the 2004 season, this enigmatic athlete hit seven home runs in seven games, in a display of batting that astonished many followers of the sport. Since he turned thirty-seven three years ago, Bonds has made all other home-run sluggers look like under-

achievers. In those three years he hit 164 homers, including his mind-boggling single-season mark of 73. He also reached base 523 times, as he continued to entice walks, intentional or otherwise.

Early in 2004, he passed his godfather, Willie Mays, when he hit his 661st homer. Does anyone doubt that he will ultimately pass Babe Ruth's 714, and then go on, when he is in his early forties, to obliterate Hank Aaron's total of 755? The only thing that can stall his progress toward that goal is pitchers who are fearful of serving up good pitches for him to hit. Like Ted Williams, who had eyes that could pierce a London fog, Bonds has always refused to swing at pitches that are a speck out of the strike zone.

If Bonds had the easy personality of, say, an Alex Rodriguez, his assault on the home-run crown would be hailed by fans from coast to coast. But he isn't Alex, and he isn't the outgoing Babe Ruth. He's Barry Bonds, and he has indicated to the world that he likes it that way. It has frequently been pointed out that many of baseball's most capable hitters have also been afflicted with character and behavioral defects. Williams may have mellowed in his last years, but he was often rude and unpleasant. Need we remind anyone of the paranoid Ty Cobb, or of Joe DiMaggio, who preferred dining alone in his hotel room?

But Barry Bonds does not think he is running for anything. If he prefers spending his off-hours with his children, that hardly makes him a bad guy.

Bonds has been the left-field fixture with San Francisco since 1993, after spending 1986 to 1992 with Pittsburgh. His current manager, Felipe Alou, told *New York Times* reporter Lee Jenkins that the game's greatest hitters are never easy to approach. "I always presumed," remarked Alou, "that it was because they were concentrating. It's not always easy to understand them. They are at such a high altitude." The political columnist George Will, who has a passion for baseball, says that Bonds's refusal to cater to anyone is "refreshing." This is a celebrity, continues Will, "who doesn't care a fig about pandering."

Bonds was literally born into baseball, in Riverside, California, in 1964. His father was Bobby Bonds, a pretty fair country hitter himself, who played with a number of teams. The most home runs that Bobby ever hit was thirty-nine, which tells you how far his son has surpassed him. When Bobby died in 2003, Barry was visibly upset, becoming more remote than usual. Those around him respected his grief and his affection for a man who had meant so much to him.

Many of today's players pay scant attention to baseball's history. But Barry has an awareness of his own place in the game's pantheon. If one could read his mind, it would probably reveal the way he feels about his exalted position in the record books. However, it's the distractions away from the playing field that annoy him. Certainly the steroids scandal is an issue that he has refused to discuss. It's a subject that he has treated with as much disdain as he does unfamiliar autograph seekers. In a period in which his achievements should give him great pleasure, he has said that the last time baseball was fun for him was when he attended Arizona State for three years.

While many focus on Barry's precision hitting, it is often overlooked that he is one of the best all-around players that the game has produced. He is still a fine outfielder, an intelligent base runner, and a man apt to take command of any game he is in. He has now won the National League Most Valuable Player Award seven times, four more than anyone else has ever done it. As Barry keeps pumping his home runs into San Francisco's McCovey Cove, and as fans paddle around in kayaks to retrieve each of those blasts, the locals will continue to cheer him to the echo. It is sad that in other venues he is usually regarded with coldness, even when, beneath the surface, there is admiration for him.

"Barry never feels pressure," insists Felipe Alou. If the veteran Dominican is correct, that makes Bonds even more remarkable than he already appears to be.

Barry Bonds always gestures in this fashion after hitting a homer, pointing to heaven (and, since 2003, sending a message to his father). This picture was taken on October 7, 2001, the day he hit his seventy-third home run of the season. His son Nikolai is the first to greet him.

OPPOSITE
Unfortunately, a cloud of controversy has dimmed the lustre of Barry Bonds' homerun achievements, especially over the past several seasons. Some have even suggested that an asterisk be added to his final total; as bad an idea now as it was when proposed for Roger Maris in 1961.

*Bonds's refusal to cater to anyone is "refreshing." This is a celebrity, continues* WILL, *"who doesn't care a fig about pandering."*

# 2. *The* PERSONALITIES

There are hundreds of Bill Veeck stories, each one better than the last. One such had to do with a party he threw for his St. Louis Browns players in 1952, after they'd lost eight games in a row. He hired a piano player and provided a generous spread of food and drink. At about one in the morning, when a few players started to leave, he opened some champagne and began to squirt it at everyone. Max Lanier remembers that the team went out the next day nice and loose—and lost their ninth in a row.

PREVIOUS
Judge Landis, seen here in a comradely pose with Ty Cobb, was appointed the commissioner of baseball in 1920 primarily to impose damage control resulting from the 1919 Black Sox disgrace. Even though the eight accused players were acquitted, he made it clear that baseball still found them guilty: "No player who throws a ball game, or sits in a conference with a bunch of crooked players and gamblers, will ever play professional baseball." The "sits in a conference" line was probably in reference to Joe Jackson, who evidently knew about the fix but didn't participate.

*Until the day he died, Veeck remained the champion of "the little guy."*

WILLIAM "BILL" VEECK was an unlikely enemy of gloom, for he had spent almost half his life in pain. When he was in the Marines in World War II, one of his legs was injured in an accident. The leg was operated on so many times that only a stump was left. But what was most important about the irrepressible Veeck (pronounced to rhyme with "wreck") was that he was an innovator, a man of ideas and originality. Always ahead of his time, and a friend of the fans, Veeck had to be the game's most brilliant maverick. He fought against the status quo and was a rebel of many causes, a foe of pretense and pomposity. Did anybody ever see him with a tie, or without a smile on his face?

Unfortunately, more people probably remember him as the guy who sent up the midget Eddie Gaedel to bat in a 1951 game (with strict instructions not to swing at any pitch) than for his efforts to speed up the process of getting black players into big-league uniforms.

Several years before Jackie Robinson broke the color line with Brooklyn, Veeck tried to purchase the Philadelphia Phillies, a team going nowhere. But other owners sniffed out Bill's "plot," and they contrived to put the club into other hands. However, Veeck was relentless and resilient. In 1947, he signed Larry Doby, then playing for Newark in the Negro National League, for his Cleveland team, making the outfielder the first African-American in the junior circuit. Branch Rickey hadn't paid a dime to Robinson's Negro Leagues team, but Veeck paid the Newark owner $10,000 for Doby.

The coming of Doby to Cleveland was hardly greeted with acclaim by many Cleveland supporters. More than fifteen thousand letters landed on Veeck's desk, many reflecting hatred and unflinching redneck negativism about Doby. "Had my father listened to this stuff, where would we be?" asked Mike Veeck, Bill's son, who is now an executive with Detroit. Years later, when outfielder Curt Flood contested baseball's reserve clause, Veeck was there, testifying in Flood's behalf.

Until the day he died, at seventy-two, in 1986, Veeck remained the champion of "the little guy." His plaque, whether some of the mossbacks like it or not, now hangs in the Hall of Fame.

Without rewriting history, it's fair to say that Chicago White Sox owner **CHARLES ALBERT COMISKEY**, who was much revered in his time, *didn't* actually cause the Black Sox Scandal of 1919. But his actions did play a negative role in that shabby episode. There's no getting around the fact that the Old Roman vastly underpaid his players. Stars such as Shoeless Joe Jackson and Eddie Cicotte were making much less than players on other teams. He even gave orders for players to cut down on laundry bills and meal money. After Cicotte won twenty-eight games in 1917, Comiskey offered him a paltry salary of $4,500. "A war is going on. Baseball has to pull in its belt," explained Commy.

Despite this evidence of Comiskey's parsimony, David Pietrusza, author of *Rothstein*, a book about the gambler who presumably fixed the 1919 World Series, insists the players were such bad guys that the fix would have happened even if Comiskey had paid better wages.

Oddly, in his early years in baseball, when a National Brotherhood of Professional Baseball Players was formed to fight the owners, Comiskey was adamantly on the side of the players. "I couldn't do anything else and still play square with the boys," he said.

Comiskey was born in Chicago in 1859 and spent a lifetime in baseball as one of its true pioneers. He played, he managed, and then he became the owner of the White Sox when they entered the new American League in the early 1900s. Comiskey worked with Byron Bancroft "Ban" Johnson to found the league, but with the passage of years the two men had a falling-out and got to hate each other. The Black Sox Scandal exacerbated the rift.

The son of Honest John Comiskey, a city alderman in Chicago, Commy started playing ball in 1878 with Dubuque, Iowa, for $50 a month. Four years later, he was making $90 a month with the St. Louis Browns of the American Association. By the time he was twenty-four years old, in 1882, he was player-

On August 2, 1921, the day eight Chicago White Sox players were acquitted of charges that they had conspired with gamblers to lose the 1919 World Series, team owner Charles Comiskey made the following statement to the press: "Cicotte confessed to me that he and seven other players conspired to throw the World Series of 1919. Until this confession can be explained away, not one of these men can play on the White Sox." And not one of them ever did.

*After Cicotte won twenty-eight games in 1917, Comiskey offered him a paltry salary of $4,500. "A war is going on. Baseball has to pull in its belt."*

Garry Schumacher, a publicist for the New York Giants during the 1940s and 1950s, had this to offer as a guide for talking business with Branch Rickey: "Don't drink the night before, keep your mouth shut, and your hands in your pockets." This picture captures perfectly the beguiling shrewdness of Rickey. A writer for a Brooklyn newspaper once wrote, "He is a man of many faucets, all turned on."

TOP
"He painted a ball game" was the way one admirer described Red Barber's skills. He is justly famous for his tenure with the Brooklyn Dodgers, but he also worked for the Yankees for twelve years, beginning in 1954. When he circulated through the Yankee clubhouse prior to his first broadcast, a few players told him that they often tried to get home from their games in time to hear Red broadcasting from Ebbets Field. Red always said that this was the ultimate tribute.

manager of the team—and enormously successful in that role: the Browns won four straight flags and two world titles. Comiskey's salary was $8,000, high for the time, but it did underline how valuable he was in his job.

During this time, Commy was one of the prime innovators in first-base play. He encouraged first basemen to play deep and away from the bag. In order that the first baseman and the other infielders could make more plays on batters, Commy had them shift position for different batters, and he also encouraged them to back up throws to thwart runs. Commy also devised new ways to defend against bunts, which were then commonplace.

When he took over the reins of the White Sox, Comiskey became known for his thirst for winning and making money. By 1910, with the help of his own input of $500,000, he built a new stadium in Chicago, inevitably named Comiskey Park. By 1917, due to the acquisition of players such as Joe Jackson, Eddie Collins, and Happy Felsch, he brought a pennant to Chicago, followed by a World Series triumph. When the team won again in 1919, many overexuberant locals urged Commy to run for mayor of Chicago. The scandal changed all that. But Commy was still boss of the White Sox when he died in 1931.

With his Southern-bred charm, crackling intelligence, and self-effacing manner, **WALTER LANIER "RED" BARBER** was a broadcasting gem. His precise, unemotional reporting, buttressed by his delightful metaphors and literary references, set a high standard for others in his profession. From the days when he was a "green pea announcer" in Cincinnati in the 1930s through his years as the voice of the Brooklyn Dodgers, followed by his time with the New York Yankees, Red's "Barberisms" became an institution. Those who tuned in to him will never forget that Ebbets Field was a "rhubarb patch," that when a team collected lots of hits it "was tearing up the pea patch," and that a team with a good lead was "sittin' in the catbird seat." When "the ducks are on the pond," that meant there were Dodgers on the bases. One afternoon, when a Dodgers shortstop botched two ground balls out of three tries, Red's mellow voice told us that "like the Ancient Mariner, he stoppeth one of three."

Red always felt that "the radio announcer is the supreme, the complete artist. . . . You paint the picture and that is satisfying to the human ego." He also felt that the prime mission of the announcer was to relate exactly what was happening, without any shading of the truth. Judge Kenesaw Mountain Landis, the commissioner of baseball, once instructed him to report "everything you see." One day in 1966, during a disastrous Yankee season, he told his television viewers that "the smallest crowd in the history of Yankee Stadium" had come to see that game with the White Sox. When he went on the radio side, he announced the exact number as 413. The truth may set some people free. In this instance, it cost Red his job.

The greatest contribution that Red made to his profession and to baseball was in the way he described Jackie Robinson's entry into the major leagues. Without any doubt, he helped immeasurably in easing the general acceptance of that embattled black pioneer. Red, who had been raised in a South where black men had been tarred and feathered, became the sender of a message. Robinson never was identified by Red as a "Negro" or "black" or "colored." He was always just "Robinson" or an "infielder" on the Dodgers. Red once told Bob Edwards of National Public Radio that "Robinson had done more for him than he had ever done for Robinson."

Red was born in 1908 in Columbus, Mississippi. His father was a railroad engineer. His mother, a schoolteacher, taught Greek and Roman mythology to her children. When Red was ten years old, the family moved to Sanford, Florida. His sixty-two-year broadcasting career began in Florida in 1930, and it included his doing the play-by-play of the first big-league game ever televised—in August 1939 at Ebbets Field—and the first night game in the majors. He worked the afternoon when Johnny Vander Meer pitched his first of two consecutive no-hitters in 1938, but Red persistently defied the taboo in baseball broadcasting that announcers

shouldn't tell their listeners that a no-hit game was in the works; he always told his listeners about it, and he even did it when pitcher Bill Bevens of the Yankees had a no-hitter going in the ninth inning of the 1947 World Series.

The Ol' Redhead died in 1992, in Tallahassee, Florida. He had been very ill in the last year or so of his life. But he kept doing a wonderful morning show for National Public Radio, because he believed that you "should do a little plowin' every day, 'cause if you stop, you're a goner."

How fitting it was that WESLEY BRANCH RICKEY died with his boots on—which means he was talking when the end came for him in 1965. He was in the middle of a lengthy acceptance speech at the Missouri Hall of Fame when he collapsed.

That ended a career that was devoted to baseball almost from the moment he was born in Lucasville, Ohio, in 1881. Funny thing about Branch Rickey: To some he was a reincarnation of Abraham Lincoln, a voluble, brilliant man, full of biblical references and vision, who paved the way for his beloved game to bring fairness and acceptance to a beleaguered black population. To others, who disliked his flatulent sermonizing, smelly cigars, and penny-pinching, he was nothing but a pompous opportunist, who altered the culture of baseball merely for commercial reasons. However, for us, the jury is not out on assessing Mr. Rickey. Whether we like him or not, he was the man who changed the game and, in so doing, helped to put America on the right track.

Many of those men who played for Rickey (he was often referred to as the Non-Alcoholic Rickey and the Mahatma) charged that he was cheap and stingy. Enos Slaughter, always underpaid by Rickey when he was with the Cardinals, once said that Rickey "would go into the vault to make change for a nickel." The extraordinary but exploitative farm system was a creation of Rickey's genius. It was designed to attack the supply side of the game as well as engage in recruiting, developing, and teaching young men who wanted to be pros. Many angrily referred to it as "Rickey's Chain Gang." At its peak, the system had more than one thousand players under its umbrella, on fifty different minor-league teams. Rickey always insisted that his invention gave opportunity to Depression-era youngsters. But many felt it was a form of slavery—"baseball factories" that put a lid on player freedom and wages.

As a youth, Rickey attended Ohio Wesleyan University. It was there, he said, that his mission to integrate baseball took shape. He had been a halfback on the football team and a catcher with the baseball players. Staying on to be the coach of the baseball team, Rickey had a youngster named Charley Thomas on his squad. When Ohio Wesleyan went to South Bend, Indiana, to play Notre Dame, Thomas, a black man, was not permitted into a local hotel room. Thereupon, Rickey had Charley share his own room with him. That night, Rickey found Charley crying and rubbing his hands. "It's my skin. If I could just make it go away I'd be like everybody else," he wailed. The incident was never forgotten by Rickey. Forty years later, he finally could do something to right the wrong for Thomas and so many others.

Rickey was not as great a player as he was a thinker and diviner. He caught for the St. Louis Browns and Yankees in 1906 and 1907, hitting a total of three home runs. In one game against Washington, thirteen runners stole bases on him—a conspicuously negative mark that still stands. Later he managed the Cardinals and Browns, without any meaningful success. It was only when he moved into the front office of the Cardinals, from 1925 to 1942, that his touch emerged. He had flag winners in six of those seasons. His 1926 club, with such players as Sunny Jim Bottomley, Chick Hafey, Rogers Hornsby, Bill Hallahan, and Grover Cleveland Alexander, beat the Ruth-Gehrig Yankees in a seven-game World Series. Of all of his players, his favorite was Dizzy Dean, whom he always referred to as "Jerome."

In 1942, he moved over to Brooklyn, where he became president and general manager. In that city of rabid fans and polyglot popula-

tion, Rickey fulfilled his private dream of desegregation. The payoff was a dramatic decade of baseball and Dodgers pennant winners in 1947 and 1949. Even after he left to join the front office of Pittsburgh in 1950, the team he had helped construct in Brooklyn kept winning.

Columnist Heywood Broun, a troubadour of the 1920s, once suggested that **JUDGE KENESAW MOUNTAIN LANDIS**, of the granitic, scolding persona, should have gone on the stage. In fact, baseball became Landis's stage following the Black Sox improprieties of 1919. Just how would baseball survive after an urchin weepingly approached the White Sox outfielder Shoeless Joe Jackson outside a Chicago courthouse and implored him, "Say it ain't so, Joe"? Out of that tearful—and possibly apocryphal—moment came the emergence of Judge Landis, the soi-disant savior of the game's integrity.

Not only did Judge Landis wield his power as baseball commissioner with harshness and firmness from 1921 to 1944, but he did it in such a way that he has often been credited with keeping the game alive. If everything seemed to be out of control in the dizzy decade of the 1920s, from the poker-playing cronyism in the Harding White House to crime-inducing Prohibition, Landis was the stabilizing force in baseball, the man with his finger in the dike. However, along with Landis came the implausible Babe Ruth—and which man was the true rescuer is arguable.

Where did this avenging angel come from? Landis was born in 1866 in Millville, Ohio, and spent most of his youth in Logansport, Indiana. He acquired his history-book name from a Civil War battle in northern Georgia in which his father, a Union surgeon, lost his leg. Kennesaw Mountain, with two *n*'s, was where the battle took place, but Dr. Landis was not guilty of a misspelling, for both spellings have long been acceptable to the purists. His son grew up a little fellow, and not much of an athlete. He hustled around like many Hoosier kids, from one odd job to another. He didn't finish high school, yet he wound up studying law. Isn't that what Abe Lincoln did by candlelight? As he became

*To some [Rickey] was a reincarnation of Abraham Lincoln. To others, who disliked his smelly cigars, and penny-pinching, he was nothing but a pompous opportunist.*

**[LANDIS] MADE IT CLEAR:** *"No player who throws a ball game, or sits in a conference with a bunch of crooked players and gamblers, will ever play professional baseball."*

known for his stubbornness and unchallenged patriotism, Landis came to the attention of President Teddy Roosevelt, who was a hero to Kenesaw. By 1905, Roosevelt had named Landis a federal judge in northern Illinois. At once, Landis won a reputation as a trustbuster, which was also the specialty of his mentor Teddy.

When a freight-rebate case involving John D. Rockefeller's Standard Oil Company came before him, the "hangin' judge" threw the book at the old robber baron, fining his company more than $29 million. He also compelled John D. to testify in court, surely an act of lèse-majesté. The fact that the Supreme Court eventually overturned Landis's decision did little to persuade the judge that he was wrong. He remained tough on almost anyone who was too rich, or too radical, and ruled accordingly. Often he applied a form of tough justice that was appalling. One time he sentenced a sick, seventy-five-year-old man to fifteen years in prison for robbing a bank.

In 1920, when baseball found itself in a pickle over the World Series peccadilloes, the owners agreed that what was needed was some kind of hard-hitting czar who would take charge and clean up the barn. A number of military men, including the World War I hero General John J. Pershing, were considered for the post. But in the end, Landis, who told the beleaguered owners that baseball had to be preserved for the sake of the country's kids, won the nod. The owners got what they wanted, for the white-haired jurist, with the fierce look of an eagle, showed no patience, even with the legal system from which he had emerged. When a Chicago court acquitted all of the Black Sox players, Landis still ruled that none of these men could darken baseball's diamonds again; they were through for life. Buck Weaver, one of the Black Sox, pleaded several times to Landis for reinstatement, alleging that he had had nothing to do with the infamous caper. But Landis turned him down flat each time.

When Branch Rickey's farm system came under fire from many owners and players alike, Landis took up their case. He disliked Rickey and his system, which he called "un-American."

With one swipe of his pen in the 1930s, Landis "freed" a number of players who had been "covered up" by Rickey. On still another front, Landis, before he died in 1944, was uncharacteristically missing in action: that was the heated issue of blacks in baseball. Landis's biographer David Pietrusza asserted that Landis provided scant leadership, "yet to ascribe to him actions that he never took whitewashes an entire generation of baseball leadership."

The baseball owners went to the archconservative Judge Landis to repair the game's gaping wounds in 1920. Forty years later, the players went to a liberal labor economist, **MARVIN J. MILLER**, to achieve some equity in the distributions of the game's dividends.

Miller not only took the players out of their relative peonage but also presided over the dissolution of the reserve clause, an infamous weapon that the owners had used since the game's invention. In so doing, Miller's players union became all-powerful in the baseball universe, so powerful that it turned some six hundred players into wealthy men with annual incomes they had never dreamed of achieving. Studs Terkel (who could interview a lamppost) said of Miller, "He was the most effective union organizer since John L. Lewis."

Before Miller took the helm of the Players Association, ballplayers had only one option: if they didn't like what an owner served up to them in terms of wages, they could quit. They had as much bargaining leverage as three-year-olds. "The owners had themselves a plantation," said Red Barber. But Miller changed all that in the next two turbulent decades.

A soft-spoken man with a well-groomed mustache, Miller (born in 1917 in New York) was an unlikely candidate to change the money mores of baseball. His only previous connection to the sport had been his partisan passion for the Brooklyn Dodgers. His garment-worker father had rooted for the Giants. A lifelong deformity in the younger Miller's right arm didn't deter him from leading a vigorous life, both in union activities and on the tennis courts. But it must have come as a surprise to him when the Players Association, through pitchers Robin Roberts and Jim Bunning (the latter became a conservative Republican senator from Kentucky some years later), approached him about taking the organization's post of executive director. The group had heard of Miller's work with the National Labor Relations Board during World War II and as a labor adviser to various unions such as those of the machinists, autoworkers, and steelworkers; he'd been adviser to the steelworkers' president for sixteen years.

However, before Miller signed on with the players for $50,000 a year, there was a slight hitch. Roberts asked Miller if he could work with former Vice President Richard M. Nixon, who would be his special counsel. In his usual quiet manner, Miller was most emphatic. "No way," he said. So Miller came aboard without Nixon. Roberts won 286 games in his career mainly as a Phillie, but this turned out to be his biggest win of all.

Miller insisted that the players ratify his appointment, so he campaigned ceaselessly among the athletes during spring training of 1966, finally winning approval by a 489–136 vote. In the process, he was subjected to hard questioning by the players, normally a conservative group, or at least apolitical. There were also some efforts to disrupt his meetings. But somehow Miller's commitment, energy, and intelligence won over the players. (In 1973, manager Leo Durocher of Houston tried to disrupt one of Miller's meetings by hitting fungoes into the outfield while Miller was talking.)

When Miller took over, a big leaguer's minimum salary was $7,000. It had taken twenty years to get to that level. But within a year, Miller bargained the minimum to $10,000. In addition, the owners agreed to participate more equitably in the players' pension fund. It was only the beginning for Miller, for in the next fifteen years there would be many improvements for players. During this period, there were several acrimonious strikes, which found the players suffering some hits from public opinion. But in the end, Miller was usually vindicated. With the advent of free agency, won under Miller's aegis, the players would be paid more than fifty times what the average fan earned. However, conservative columnist George Will could applaud Miller's persistence as an advocate, even as some fans rued the fact that once-exploited players had morphed into millionaires.

LELAND STANFORD "LARRY" MACPHAIL was never a baseball player. But he compared favorably with some of the game's most bibulous performers. He enlisted in World War I at the age of twenty-seven, and it is likely that he was under the influence when, with a group of his doughboy pals, he supposedly attempted to kidnap Germany's kaiser shortly before the conflict ended. He could have been court-martialed, but he escaped such punishment. When he was a lieutenant colonel in World War II, he did not attempt to kidnap Adolf Hitler, but the notion must have occurred to him.

The restless MacPhail, the son of a Michigan banker, and a resident of Ohio after World War I, tried his hand at any number of unrelated things: construction, an auto dealership, refereeing college football games. But it wasn't until he ran across Branch Rickey, as temperate as Larry was intemperate, that he entered a baseball world that had never seen his like before. For audacity, energy, and imagination, nobody in the pastime would ever compare with him.

Rickey agreed to let Larry run his minor-league Columbus farm team, which was having Depression blues, as most ball clubs were at the time. In a short while, Columbus was drawing big crowds, because MacPhail, a swaggering redhead with a voice like a bullhorn, had brought night baseball to the town. He was also in constant defiance of the Prohibition law, which caused him to part company with Rickey. On the other hand, Rickey appreciated his qualities to such an extent that he recommended Larry to the Cincinnati Reds, who were badly in need of resuscitation. MacPhail got the Cincinnati job in 1934, and at once he introduced night baseball, against the opposition of the Luddites. The team also traveled by commercial airline, a historic first. Another of his accomplishments was the hiring of Red Barber

STUDS TERKEL SAID OF *Miller,*

*"He was the most effective union organizer since John L. Lewis."*

"*There's a thin line between genius and insanity,*" *Leo Durocher once said about Larry.* "*In MacPhail's case it's pretty thin.*"

to announce the Reds' games on radio. For that alone, his memory should be revered.

But restlessness, and McPhail's own self-destructive habits, caused him to depart Cincinnati in 1936, some say voluntarily. "There's a thin line between genius and insanity," Leo Durocher once said about Larry. "In MacPhail's case it's pretty thin."

By 1938, Larry reemerged with the nearly bankrupt Brooklyn Dodgers, and he quickly became, as he always did, a catalyst for change. He did all that he could to improve the physical appearance of a decaying Ebbets Field. He had a fresh coat of paint put on the place, and the toilets were cleaned up and fumigated. A new press box was installed, and booze often flowed there. On the playing field, he brought in a platoon of hustling, hungry players, including Pete Reiser, Pee Wee Reese, Dolf Camilli, Dixie Walker, and Whitlow Wyatt. For the radio broadcasts, he commissioned Red Barber, from Cincinnati, who quickly won his way into Brooklyn hearts, as he should have. As manager, MacPhail installed Leo Durocher, the profane former pool-hall hustler from West Springfield, Massachusetts. His P. T. Barnum instinct told him he would attract fans by installing the embittered Babe Ruth on the first-base coaching line. He was right. Even as a noncombatant, Babe was a drawing card.

The Dodgers had become MacPhail's and Durocher's team, and by 1941 they won the National League flag, Brooklyn's first since who could remember!

When the triumphant Dodgers returned home from Boston after wrapping up the pennant, MacPhail wired ahead that he'd be waiting for the conquering heroes at the 125th Street station. Unaware of MacPhail's plan, Durocher ordered the train not to stop there, since he feared that many players might get off before their adoring fans could see them. This evolved into another stormy MacPhailian flap. As MacPhail waited, the train sped by him. When the Dodgers arrived at Grand Central Station, MacPhail hustled there to inform Durocher that he was fired—perhaps for the fiftieth time. The next day, Larry rehired

Baseball's stormy petrel Larry MacPhail (left) is seen here in 1947 with Bucky Harris, the Yankees' field manager at the time. Larry quit at the end of the season, much to the relief of the players, who'd grown weary of his tantrums and threats. After the seventh game of the 1947 World Series, Larry, with tears streaming down his cheeks, shouted to everyone in the victors' clubhouse, "I'm through, I'm through! My heart won't stand it!"

TOP
Marvin Miller was eighty-five years old when this close-up picture was taken in his home early in 2003. He had a lot to be proud of. One of the many players he rescued from baseball's feudal system was Curt Flood, a talented Cardinal outfielder who refused a trade to the Phillies in 1970. "Marvin Miller was probably the greatest thing that ever happened to baseball as far as the players are concerned," said Flood.

Bill James's reputation as a thoughtful and creative student of baseball landed him a job in November 2002 with the Boston Red Sox as their senior baseball operations adviser. Such a concept might have amused him twenty years earlier, when his icono- clastic analyses of the game were first published. In the introduction to the first edition of *The Bill James Historical Abstract*, published in 1986, he wrote, "I write an annual book about baseball called *The Baseball Abstract*. . . . It's sort of like *Street and Smith's Baseball Annual*, only it's for adults."

*"Statistics create identity,"* JAMES SAYS. *"In the baseball world everybody knows where you stand."*

Leo, in time to face the Yankees in the World Series.

In the fourth game, it looked as if the Dodgers were about to tie the series at two games all, but bad things happened again. With one out and two strikes on Tommy Henrich in the ninth inning, Dodgers pitcher Hugh Casey threw a breaking ball that got Henrich to strike out—but the third strike got past catcher Mickey Owen. After that, the distressed Casey couldn't get anyone out, and the Yankees ended up win- ning, 7–4. The following day, the Dodgers lost the Series.

MacPhail's reaction was to get roaring drunk, and he threatened to fire everyone on the club. He spent one more year—1942— at the Dodgers' helm. Again, there was a bitter ending. The Dodgers won 104 games, a record for them, but they lost the pennant to St. Louis on the last day of the season. Soon after, MacPhail enlisted in the Army as a fifty-two- year-old lieutenant colonel. He always wanted to be where the action was.

After the war, MacPhail couldn't remain away from his obsession. He became co-owner of the Yankees for three years. Determined to modernize the club, he brought the Yankees night baseball in May 1946, built a Stadium Club where well-heeled folks could pay inordi- nate prices for hamburgers, and staged fashion shows and track meets to pull in the largest yearly stadium attendance of all time: 2,265,512 fans. It should have been Larry's greatest triumph. But although he was a visionary on almost all baseball matters, he was a hard- crusted reactionary on the racial issue. From the start, he had opposed Rickey's move to bring Jackie Robinson to Ebbets Field.

After the Dodgers' stirring seven-game World Series loss to the Yankees in 1947, MacPhail shocked the baseball world by sud- denly quitting. No doubt, alcohol had played a part in this drama. MacPhail had done some remarkable things for the game in his tempes- tuous years as an executive. But much of it had gone down the drain in the way he chose to make his exit.

Baseball's first Bill James was a right-handed pitcher for the Miracle Boston Braves who dominated the 1914 World Series against the Philadelphia Athletics. The second **BILL JAMES**—no relation to the pitcher—never threw a ball in anger. He came along in the 1980s with his sabermetrics—or New Statistics—to create a revolution in the use of mathematical formulas to judge the effectiveness of hitters, pitchers, and teams. Some observers have rejected James's use of stats and his occasional acerbic estimations of individual players and teams. But there is little doubt that James has rippled the waters in the stats bureaucracy. At the least, his analyses have gained wide acceptance and been regarded as useful.

Bill James has his roots in Kansas, where he was born in 1948. He majored in English and economics at the University of Kansas, served in the Army, and then became a high-school teacher. There was little in his background to suggest that one day he would employ his love of baseball and his fascination with numbers to challenge many of the certainties that previous generations of baseball fans had accepted as final truth. In doubting many of these fixed notions, James was prepared to rebut much conventional wisdom. For example, he suggested that batting averages could be misleading in evaluating players. Instead, he offered getting on base and runs created as more valid barometers. He has also promised that in the future, there will be many additional means of assessing players and teams. "Statistics create identity," James says. "In the baseball world everybody knows where you stand."

At first when James published his yearly analyses, he won relatively few buyers. But as time passed, his zealous fans and celebrators bought his abstracts and made him a best-selling author. As an indication of how much James's theories have been welcomed, one doesn't have to search any further than the Boston Red Sox front office. He is now on the Red Sox payroll as a consultant. Did James help them whip the Yankees in 2004?

James's stats-based predictions have occasionally gone astray. Like any worthy stats freak, he has been wrong at times. He was, for example, as author Jules Tygiel has pointed out, quite critical of the Phillies before they surprised him by winning the World Series in 1980. However, he has become the premier stats savant at a time when computers produce carloads of arcane information that was previously ignored by the purists.

The ne plus ultra of baseball writers, Roger Angell, regards James's use of stats as "dazzling." Jim Bouton, the former pitcher and author of the once-controversial *Ball Four*, feels that James's analyses "take a different perspective on stats, and that's very worthwhile. When the old-time stats people seem to reject the James approach out of hand, then you know that James must be doing something right!" Baseball historian Donald Honig agrees that "James has had a formidable influence in recent times, yet I still don't feel that you can program the progress of a ball game. . . . I also don't think that it's worthwhile for managers to be inhibited by any rules set down by James or anybody else."

Would Bill James's creative use of statistics be a better way to assess and measure the nation's social health, rather than the loose punditry of so-called financial experts and ambiguous economists? Just asking!

# 3. *The* MANAGERS

Owing to his free-spirit reputation and mediocre managerial performances with National League teams, not much was expected of Casey Stengel as he began his tenure with the Yankees in 1949. He went on to lead an injury-riddled team to a thrilling pennant win and a World's Championship, then won four more World Series in succession. By 1960, Casey had won ten pennants and seven world titles, but after losing the 1960 World Series to the Pirates, he was fired. "It's a shabby way to treat the man," Arthur Daley wrote in his *New York Times* column, adding, "so long, Case. You gave us twelve unforgettable years."

PREVIOUS
Connie Mack supposedly positioned his fielders with the wave of a scorecard, but it's just as likely that the scorecard was used for keeping cool. Mr. Mack wore street clothes, including high, starched collars, in the hottest summer months. After nearly six decades playing and managing in the big leagues, he retired at the end of the 1950 season. "I'm not quitting because I'm too old," he told the press, "but because I think people want me to."

When the Yankees won their first World Series in 1923, the New York Giants' outfielder **CHARLES DILLON "CASEY" STENGEL** "ran a home run home" in the first game. Despite such base-running heroics, Casey wound up on the losing side. Twenty-five years later, Casey Stengel got himself on the winning side. He was hired as the Yankees' manager, to the utter astonishment of most of the baseball world. Such a mass reaction had to do with Stengel's previous managerial record.

In dismal stints as pilot of the Brooklyn Dodgers and Boston Braves in the 1930s and 1940s, Casey had been a chronic loser. In 1943, when he was managing the Braves, Casey was run over by a cab, resulting in a badly smashed leg. Commenting wryly on the accident, columnist Dave Egan nominated the driver as "the man who has done the most for Boston baseball."

Things changed radically for Casey once he came to the Yankees, though few had ever envisioned him as the rightful heir to Miller Huggins and Joe McCarthy. Taking over an injury-riddled Yankees in 1949 and staying around until 1960, Casey shepherded the team to ten flags and seven World Series victories. From clown and double-talker (many of the writers who covered Stengel's extraordinary filibusters called it "Stengelese"), Casey became equally known for his astute knowledge and for a precise memory of almost everything about the game—except the names of the men who played for him. Needless to say, he had better players to direct in New York than he had at other ports, men such as Joe DiMaggio, Mickey Mantle, Yogi Berra, Whitey Ford, Phil Rizzuto, and on and on. Casey took special delight in the development of Mantle.

If the Yankees hadn't come in second behind Cleveland in 1954, Casey would have presided over ten straight American League winners. During this remarkable period, he specialized in platooning his players, in never having a fixed pitching rotation, and in "keeping the five guys who hate you away from the five guys who are undecided." When the Yankees chose to bring an end to the Stengel reign in 1960, after

*The Mets didn't do much under Casey except lose.*
## *"Can't anybody here play this game?"*
*Casey wondered out loud about his inept troops.*

New York lost the World Series to Pittsburgh, the front office explained that he was getting too old for the job. "I'll never make the mistake of being seventy again," Casey responded.

However, the New York Mets, starting out in life at Shea Stadium, hired old Casey as their manager in 1962, and he hung around until 1965. The Mets didn't do much under Casey except lose, but in the process he added to his extensive myth. "Can't anybody here play this game?" Casey wondered out loud about his inept troops. (The quote was probably helped along a little by the inventive Jimmy Breslin.)

Casey was born in 1890 in Kansas City; thus his famous nickname, a contraction of his hometown initials. Two years before he was born, Ernest Lawrence Thayer wrote his famous "Casey at the Bat" poem, so it wasn't Stengel who was the inspiration, as so many think today. Casey grew up as a bowlegged halfback and a left-handed third baseman, although he did turn to the mound on occasion. After Casey enrolled at Kansas City Western Dental College, he realized he didn't like blood that much, so he quit to play baseball. From 1910 to 1912, he kicked around with minor-league teams in Kankakee, Maysville, and Aurora, at last arriving with the major-league Brooklyn Dodgers in 1912. His first time up with the Dodgers, he was told to bunt. He swung away and singled, probably a tip-off on how he would conduct the rest of his career. Until 1918, he played in the phone-booth intimacy of Ebbets Field, becoming a favorite of the fans. His antics were legion. On one occasion, he arranged for a grapefruit to be dropped out of a biplane onto the head of the Dodgers' estimable manager, Wilbert Robinson.

Later he played for Pittsburgh, the Phillies, the Giants, and the Braves, moving around like a traveling salesman. But for all of his transience, he was always more than a journeyman. However, it was as manager of the Yankees that he won his spurs as an improviser and crafty handler of players and the press. "I knew him before he was a genius," remarked pitcher Warren Spahn, who had played for Casey on the Braves. Maybe he wasn't a genius, but his

achievements did get him elected to the Hall of Fame in 1966.

"When you think so many men have done such amazing things and not made it," he said at the induction ceremony, "it's an amazing honor and you shouldn't blow about it." Before Casey died in 1975, he summed up his career. "There comes a time in every man's life and I've had plenty of them," he signed off. As usual, he was good to the last word.

**CONNIE MACK** is to baseball what George Washington is to American patriotism. He was around for sixty years and went through glorious times as well as ignominious times, which pretty much sums up almost all baseball experiences. In the early days of the twentieth century—1910 to 1914—his Philadelphia Athletics were the cream of the game, with only his 1912 club finishing out of first place. The Athletics were the first of the American League's super-teams, featuring mainly great pitching and the so-called $100,000 Infield, consisting of Stuffy McInnis at first base, Eddie Collins at second base, Jack Barry at shortstop, and Home Run Baker at third base. Two of those stars were products of Connie's intelligent scouting operation: Collins came off the Columbia campus, and Barry was from Holy Cross.

When Connie broke up that winning combination, as he did after the Miracle Boston Braves upended the A's in four straight games in the 1914 World Series, his team plunged to stygian depths. It wasn't until 1929 that Connie rose to the top again, with a wondrous assortment of athletes headed by Lefty Grove, who had a 31–4 record in 1931. The team was so jammed with stars that it was difficult to rate one ahead of the other: catcher Mickey Cochrane, outfielder Al Simmons, murderous-hitting Jimmie Foxx, the patrician right-hander George Earnshaw, and second baseman Max Bishop, all at the height of their productivity. When this platoon of players lost the 1931 World Series, after winning the Series in 1929 and 1930, Mr. Mack went at it again. He broke up the club, selling off many of his stars. Although he went on managing the A's until

1950, when he was eighty-eight years old, he never brought home another winner. Through all of those later years, his team finished in the first division only once in seventeen seasons—and he rolled up a lifetime total of 4,025 defeats. Most assuredly, that figure will never be surpassed. Another manager would have been fired, but since Connie was also the owner of the A's, he was not about to fire himself.

Connie was born in East Brookfield, Massachusetts, in 1862, three years before Abe Lincoln was assassinated. His real name—Cornelius Alexander McGillicudy—was as long as a handball court, and when he grew to manhood, his ascetic, wiry frame seemed longer than that. His father, Michael, served with the Union Army, in the 51st Massachusetts Infantry. As a youth, Connie performed many odd jobs, including picking vegetables and working in a cotton mill. But he also engaged in four-o'cat, an early version of baseball for kids. Soon he got his first job in baseball, as a catcher with Meriden, in the Connecticut League, for $90 a month. Considering that Connie graduated into baseball's moral conscience, it's odd that he saw nothing wrong about utilizing some tactics that were, to say the least, questionable. He liked to needle and distract batters from behind the plate, and he was not above interfering with a batter's swing, just enough to cause him to miss the pitch.

As Connie moved up the minor-league ladder, he didn't claim to be much of a batter. But wearing no protection as a catcher, he proved to be an innovator. He encouraged his pitchers to throw overhand and showed great patience in handling them. His first managing post was with Pittsburgh in the last years of the nineteenth century, and although he was not a winner, he projected civility and kindness, traits that were quite rare in the rough-and-tumble game.

By 1901, Connie was managing the first American League team, the Philadelphia Athletics. His team won the flag in 1902 and won again in 1905, though they lost to the New York Giants in the World Series. Losing to Christy Mathewson three times in six days was too much for Connie's guile to overcome. Now known as the Tall Tactician, Connie conducted crafty raids of talent from the National League, discovered players tucked away on college campuses, and managed to put up with the likes of the irrepressible oddball southpaw Rube Waddell, who Connie thought was the best lefty he'd ever seen. He also proved to be a smart, watch-the-bottom-line businessman, which accounted for his breaking up two dynasties once these clubs couldn't make money for him.

Connie never wore a uniform in the dugout. Under his straw brimmer, a hat then popular in America, he wore a high, starched collar, and he was said to have constantly flashed directions to his outfielders with his trademark scorecard. An expert handler of pitchers, he often couldn't remember their names. He disliked foul language, but he never fired a player for using it. "He looked like a stately, well-plucked gobbler," wrote Bob Considine, but no turkey ever had to manage so many culls and mediocrities as Connie did. Somehow, he never lost his temper or his reputation, which accounted for sportswriter Grantland Rice's saying that "nobody else could ever match his contribution to the game as player, manager and owner."

He was a friend of saloonkeepers, crooked policemen, pool-hall hustlers, racetrack bookies, low-life gamblers (the infamous Arnold Rothstein was an intimate), and showgirl celebrities. But the contentious JOHN JOSEPH MCGRAW was much more than that: he was also one of the most enterprising managers who ever sat in a dugout. In thirty years as manager of the New York Giants, after he'd come to the National League from the Baltimore Orioles in 1902, he won ten pennants, plus three world titles.

McGraw did it with an imagination unrivaled by others in his line of work. Throw in bellicosity, skill, aggressiveness, and an implacable hostility toward all those who occupied enemy uniforms, and you have a profile of John McGraw. His almost demonic desire to win was perhaps exceeded only by Ty Cobb's. Psychologists might say that he arrived at this point because he suffered a dreadful youth in the

## *"[Connie Mack] looked like a stately, well-plucked gobbler," wrote Bob Considine.*

little upstate New York town of Truxton, some sixty miles from, you guessed it, Cooperstown.

He was born in 1873, the third of eight children, in a dirt-poor family. In the winter of 1884, when John was twelve, his mother, Ellen, and four of her children succumbed to what was called "black Diphtheria." Depressed and embittered, John's father turned on John, berating and physically beating him. He scoffed at John's time-wasting interest in baseball. When his father's behavior became too much for him to bear, John moved out, to be taken in by an elderly widow who lived nearby.

Before long, John, like many young Irishmen living in poverty in those days, saw baseball as a way out. Even at five-foot-five and not much more than 110 pounds, John was a formidable competitor. At the beginning, he was a pitcher, and then he shifted to third base, as he played at various stops in the Western New York League. Thus began the career of the man who would come to be called "the Little Napoleon." Ultimately, as the manager of the tough-edged Orioles in Baltimore (truly the first town in America to be gripped by baseball madness), and then as guiding genius of the Giants, McGraw took on the image of "a supergeneral plotting victory and avoiding defeat." This was, wrote Leonard Koppett of the *New York Times*, "part and parcel of McGraw's public image."

Many tales have been told about McGraw's temperament. Perhaps most typical was the afternoon he ordered a player to bunt a man to second base. Instead, the player swung away and hit a game-winning home run. Was McGraw happy? Certainly not. He fined the player for disobeying him!

McGraw introduced the hit-and-run to baseball, refined the art of bunting, and signed players just to pinch-hit. One of his early innovations was the relief pitcher, and he also employed signals the way admirals did on the high seas. If that wasn't enough, he often insisted on calling the pitches thrown by his moundsmen. In short, there was little he didn't seek to control on the ball field. Under his aegis, some of the most skilled players of all

time developed. Mel Ott, Bill Terry, Frankie Frisch, Ross Youngs, Casey Stengel, Carl Hubbell, the incomparable Christy Mathewson—they all benefited from his tutelage. In Matty's case, the two men actually shared an apartment in New York, a most unusual circumstance, especially considering how different their temperaments were.

In 1918, 1919, and 1920, the Giants finished second each year. Then the years of dominance and glory came to McGraw and his Giants. The Giants won flags in 1921 and 1922, each time beating their neighbors, the Yankees, in the World Series. In 1922, McGraw was credited with masterminding a four-game sweep of the Yankees. "We set that big fellow (Babe Ruth) on his rear end with slow stuff," McGraw openly gloated.

The Giants won pennants again in 1923 and 1924, giving McGraw four National League pennants in a row, still a league record. But never again did this combative man battle to the top.

By 1934, he was dead of cancer, at the age of sixty. Fittingly, he was buried in Baltimore.

JOSEPH VINCENT MCCARTHY never played a single inning of major-league baseball. In spite of this deprivation, he became one of the best managers of his time, sufficiently successful to get himself elected to the Hall of Fame in 1957. It was Marse Joe's brilliant record as the twelfth manager of the Yankees—from 1931 to 1946—that gave him the credentials for admittance to the Hall. Those eight pennants and seven world titles spoke louder than any words the normally reticent McCarthy had ever emitted in his own behalf.

Before he came to the Yankees, McCarthy managed the Chicago Cubs and did rather admirably, getting into a losing World Series with the Athletics in 1929. Even in his last active baseball years, as manager of the Boston Red Sox, he came within a single game of upending his old Yankee team in one of the most memorable American League pennant scrambles in history, in 1949. But it was his lengthy stay with the Yankees that established

# McGraw took on the image of "A SUPER-GENERAL plotting victory and avoiding defeat."

When John McGraw announced his retirement as the Giants' field manager on June 3, 1932, dozens of current and former colleagues and foes expressed their regrets. Joe McCarthy, the Yankees' manager, said, "McGraw must have been pretty sick, for he is not the kind to give up baseball without a reason." Bill Terry, McGraw's successor, told the press that he would ease up on the strict discipline that characterized McGraw's regime. "I am going to let them relax a bit and see what they can do to get us out of last place," he said.

BELOW

Joe McCarthy, posing here with the Cubs' manager Gabby Hartnett before the opener of the 1932 World Series, fielded four consecutive World Championship teams from 1936 through 1939. One of the stalwart Yankee players during that run was Tommy "Old Reliable" Henrich, who said McCarthy was one of the greatest men he ever knew. "I don't know where in the heck he learned all his psychology about ballplayers," Henrich said. "He could handle almost anybody. And if he couldn't handle them, he'd trade them, I'll tell you that."

## *"You're Yankees—act like Yankees!"*

his reputation. The first words he uttered in coming to the Bronx were "You're Yankees—act like Yankees!" For most of his reign at the stadium, his team did exactly that.

New York fans were puzzled at first by the choice of McCarthy as manager, after he had resigned as Cubs pilot in the final week of the 1930 season. But they soon realized that the lantern-jawed Philadelphian (who had attended Niagara University in Buffalo, New York, for two years) was strictly an all-business guy. That he later developed a nagging problem with booze, an addiction that he managed to hide pretty well from the baseball public, never interfered with his competence. He appeared in command at all times, and he seemed to have total recall of everything that occurred on the field and in the clubhouse. McCarthy was a coldly efficient operator, unlike his flamboyant, aging icon Babe Ruth, and some in the press sought to disparage him by proclaiming he was a "push-button manager." But as he invariably seemed to press the right buttons, the criticisms never had much substance.

McCarthy hated to lose, and he refused to coddle his players. He believed that teaching pitchers to field their position was equally important as teaching them to make pitches. He invoked rigid dress codes with his Yankees—jackets and ties in the dining room, gentlemen—and he was a stickler for physical conditioning long before modern-day players made a fetish out of it. If he made rooting for the Yankees about as exhilarating as rooting for U.S. Steel, as sore losers often grumbled, he managed to remain around Yankee Stadium longer than anyone dreamed he would.

When Joe first arrived in New York, his main problem came from the overt hostility of Babe Ruth. As Babe's power faded and his stomach expanded, he yearned to end his career as the Yankees' manager. But behind his back, his detractors hissed that if he couldn't handle himself, he could never be expected to handle a ball club full of disparate personalities. Regarding McCarthy as a second-rate pretender, Babe made no effort at conciliation, while McCarthy wisely decided his best course was simply to

ignore the big man. In following this course of diplomacy, McCarthy also went out of his way to develop amicable relationships with other players. He became close to Lou Gehrig, for example, which was quite an achievement, considering Lou's previous attachment to the deceased manager Miller Huggins.

When McCarthy steered the Yankees into the 1932 World Series, he then extracted a measure of revenge against the Chicago Cubs. The Yankees took the Cubs in four straight games, making it twelve victories in a row in the Series. The games themselves were all but forgotten, because Babe again swiped the headlines with his magisterial "called-shot home run" in the third game at Wrigley Field. It also amounted to Babe's valedictory, for his overall production fell appreciably in 1933 and 1934, and the Yankees failed to win each year.

But with the coming of the highly regarded Joe DiMaggio in 1936, McCarthy again became a winner. From 1936 through 1939, the club took four world titles. This team, including men such as DiMaggio, Gehrig, catcher Bill Dickey, shortstop Frankie Crosetti, third baseman Red Rolfe, second baseman Tony Lazzeri, and bulldog winning pitchers Red Ruffing and Lefty Gomez, couldn't help but make McCarthy look like a genius. Joe himself admitted that it was surely one of the greatest teams ever assembled. He just let them play, which was his mantra. Before McCarthy died, at the age of ninety, he lived to see a plaque honoring him placed in Monument Park at Yankee Stadium. There he was, alongside all of the other Yankee immortals—and today, few would deny him his niche in such a group.

They called him Captain Hook because, as manager of the vaunted Cincinnati Reds' Big Red Machine from 1970 to 1978, **GEORGE LEE "SPARKY" ANDERSON** had no compunctions about removing pitchers. Strange thing about this policy—it worked brilliantly, enough to make Sparky Anderson the only manager ever to win a World Series in both the National and American Leagues. Among managers, Sparky Anderson—like Walter Alston, who bossed the

Dodgers for years without anyone paying too much attention to him—was the rarest of birds. His players actually liked him, and, as the official publication of the Hall of Fame points out, "he was treasured by fans and players alike."

In twenty-six years of managing, first with Cincinnati and then with the Detroit Tigers, Sparky was at the helm for 2,194 victories. That puts him behind only John McGraw and Connie Mack for most wins as a manager. Sparky would be happy to inform you, in his most congenial way, that the true secret of his success was his dependence on the hired help. He enrolled good coaches, then delegated responsibility to them, for he was convinced that managing should not be an act of unchallenged autocracy. In the modern game, a manager needs help, Sparky believed.

Anderson came from a humble background, although he was not the kind to complain about it. He was born in Bridgewater, South Dakota (population less than seven hundred), in 1934, at the height of the Great Depression. His father worked in the post office and also painted barns and silos. Nine members of the Anderson brood lived in a two-story house, but Sparky thought that was the way all people lived. When Sparky was nine years old, the family moved to Los Angeles, into the neighborhood that later became known as the Watts ghetto. But this new venue gave Sparky his chance to learn about baseball.

One day, when he was walking past the field where the University of Southern California baseball team practiced, a ball came whizzing over the fence. Like any red-blooded youngster, Sparky retrieved the ball and went inside the enclosure to return it. USC's coach, Rod Dedeaux, took a liking to the boy almost at once and made him the team's batboy. If this story sounds like the one about George Gipp retrieving a football at Notre Dame and kicking it back, thus enabling Knute Rockne to discover him, so be it. The Gipp story was apocryphal; the Sparky story is true.

In time, Sparky, a hustling little infielder (but not yet featuring the snow white hair that became familiar to a future generation of fans),

played American Legion ball, then joined the Los Angeles Dodgers' farm system. Dedeaux wanted Sparky to attend USC, but Sparky didn't have any such aspirations. Even then, his grammar wasn't of the highest grade.

In six seasons in the minors, Sparky proved to be a competent fielder, but no great shakes as a hitter. But he advanced to the majors when the Dodgers traded him to the Phillies. In his one big-league year, Sparky batted a lordly .218 with the Phillies, who would, as they say, have finished last with or without him. Back in the minors for another four campaigns, Sparky never batted higher than .257. This convinced him that he should try to become a manager. He wound up doing just that, with Toronto in the minors.

By this time, he'd come to the attention of Bob Howsam, who had worked in the Cardinals' front office. It was Howsam who got Anderson a coaching job in the majors with San Diego. When Howsam then moved on to Cincinnati, he chose Sparky to manage the Reds, provoking an outcry from those who didn't know much about him. But Anderson soon showed them. With his talent for dealing kindly with players, with his enthusiasm and alertness, with an ability to deal with the media (which Sparky always believed was an important element of the job), and with a belief (borrowed from Franklin D. Roosevelt, perhaps) that fear was only a recipe for failure, Sparky broke out of the starting gate with a pennant in 1970. The World Series that year went to Baltimore. However, in 1975, Sparky's Big Red Machine, helped along by Pete Rose, Joe Morgan, Tony Perez, Johnny Bench, and others, won a celebrated World Series victory over the Boston Red Sox in seven games. The games were stirring, and a nation that had begun to be turned off by baseball watched on TV as Sparky led his boys to triumph. Many believe it was that group of games that restored the sport into the good graces of the public. The next year, the Reds mauled the Yankees in four straight games in the World Series.

In his nine years in Cincinnati, Sparky's teams won an average of ninety-six games a year. Despite such results, Sparky was shockingly fired after a disagreement over coaching personnel. True to his character, Sparky refused to bellyache, and by 1979 he had signed to manage the Detroit Tigers. It took him a few years to apply the Anderson treatment, but his Tigers of 1984 went all the way, after starting the year with thirty-five wins in their first forty games—the best-ever start by any team in history. They took the World Series against San Diego in five games, thus making Sparky the first to do it in both leagues.

By 1989, however, the Tigers weren't a very good team. They started poorly and wound up losing 103 games, the most Sparky had ever lost. For a man who had always been committed to winning, it was a disaster. The events had a terrible impact on his emotions, producing what he thought was a nervous breakdown. After deciding to take an extended vacation, Sparky concluded he'd been a "winaholic" who was injuring his family and himself. Such introspection was probably rare for a baseball man, and even for a big-league manager. He has been a happier man ever since.

*"[Sparky] was treasured by fans and players alike."*

George "Sparky" Anderson had every right to look content while filling out a lineup card. During most of the 1970s, his Cincinnati Reds team, the Big Red Machine, was one of the best teams in baseball. After the Reds won the turbulent 1975 World Series, Anderson told the press, "The true test of a great club is what they do over a 162-game season. . . . In a short series only luck prevails." An Associated Press reporter wrote, "For a change, lady luck had a kiss, rather than a slap in the face for the Reds."

# 4. *The* GREATEST GAMES

Dodgers announcer VIN SCULLY *proclaimed that "most assuredly
this was the greatest game ever pitched in the history of baseball."*

In the Yankees' clubhouse after his perfect game, Don Larsen signed a baseball for the
Dodgers' owner, Walter O'Malley, who a year later would be cursed by Brooklyn fans
for moving their beloved team to California. Casey Stengel told John Lardner, one of
the dozens of writers swarming around Larsen and his teammates, that "when this
fella has control, he is quite useful."

## October 8, 1956: Yankees 2, Dodgers 0

Right-hander Donald James Larsen, six-foot-four, 235 pounds, was hardly the best-conditioned man in New York the day he hurled the first (and, so far, only) perfect game in World Series history. He had been out on the town the night before, as was his custom in those days. But the next afternoon, in the fifth game of the Series, he threw ninety-seven pitches, including seventy-one strikes and twenty-six balls, yielding no hits, no walks, no hit batsmen, no errors, no runs. In short, Larsen gave up absolutely nothing to a Brooklyn Dodgers lineup that included Duke Snider, Jackie Robinson, Roy Campanella, Pee Wee Reese, and Gil Hodges. With two out in the ninth, more than 64,000 fans roared as Larsen finished his masterpiece by throwing a called third strike past pinch hitter Dale Mitchell. Game time: two hours, six minutes. Dodgers announcer Vin Scully proclaimed that "most assuredly this was the greatest game ever pitched in the history of baseball."

## October 12, 1929: Athletics 10, Cubs 8

If Connie Mack's teams of the 1940s and 1950s were "a gentle comedy" (in the words of John Updike), his Philadelphia club of 1929 was something quite apart from that. Going into the seventh inning of the fourth game of the World Series, the Cubs held a dominating 8–0 lead and appeared ready to tie the Series at two games all. Then came the deluge, started by an Al Simmons home run, followed by an avalanche of base hits. In the nightmare ten-run inning, Simmons singled when he came up again and Jimmie Foxx singled twice. The play that sealed the doom of the Cubs was a fly ball misplayed by center fielder Hack Wilson. When he lost Mule Haas's line drive in the sun, three runners came across and Haas was given credit for an inside-the-park home run. It was the greatest rally in World Series history, and a Series record for runs scored in a single inning. For good measure, it was the most hits—ten—ever achieved in a single inning. Although he was the goat of the game (and the Series), Wilson managed to make a joke about it. That night, in a Philadelphia restaurant, Hack asked the headwaiter to dim the lights so he wouldn't misjudge his soup.

Al Simmons hit a home run in the last of the seventh inning against the Cubs in the fourth game of the 1929 World Series. It did not thrill his teammates, since it was the Athletics' first run of the afternoon, making the score 8–1. Jimmie Dykes remembers saying at the time, "Well, we won't be shut out anyway." Later, when the lead was narrowed to 8–7, Dykes leaped to his feet and pounded the person next to him and sent him crashing into the bat rack. The fallen man turned out to be Connie Mack, who said, "That's all right, Jimmy. . . . Isn't this wonderful?"

PAGE 131
The Yankee Stadium scoreboard registers Don Larsen's masterpiece. This picture was taken a few seconds after pinch hitter Dale Mitchell was called out on strikes to end the game. As the top of the ninth inning began, *New York Times* columnist Arthur Daley wrote, "Out from the stands swept a low murmur of excitement, almost like surf rumbling against a distant shore." Under the circumstances, such expressiveness is completely understandable.

Hack Wilson (left), seen here with Rogers Hornsby and Kiki Cuyler, hit .471 in the 1929 World Series, but he will always be remembered for misplaying Mule Haas's fly ball, which allowed three runs and got the Athletics back into the game. Lefty Grove, who won the game in relief, offered some solace when he said, "It was tough out there, what with the sun coming just over the edge of the stands."

### October 21, 1975: Red Sox 7, Reds 6

By the sixth game of the 1975 World Series at Boston's Fenway Park, Cincinnati's Big Red Machine led the Red Sox, three games to two. As the game rolled along, the Reds took the lead by the seventh inning, after the Sox had been ahead, 3–0, behind their colorful right-hander, Luis Tiant. But the drama was yet to unfold. As the late-night minutes ticked away, a national TV audience became entranced at what was evolving into one of the most thrilling games in history. The Reds tacked on a run in the eighth, making the score 6–3, as they moved closer to their first world title in thirty-five years. But with two out and two on in the bottom of the eighth inning, pinch hitter Bernie Carbo smashed a home run to tie the score at 6–6. It was Carbo's second pinch-hit homer in the Series. As the game moved into extra innings, sensational plays were the order of the night. Dwight Evans leaped into the right-field seats to deprive the Reds' Joe Morgan of a homer in the eleventh inning. In the bottom of the twelfth, New England's own, catcher Carlton Fisk, hit Pat Darcy's second pitch high into the darkness above the left-field foul line. As Fisk started toward first base, his arms high in the air, he seemed to be willing the ball to go fair. It did, setting off church bells throughout Massachusetts. The blow won the game for the Red Sox—who lost the Series the next day. There are many who credit this game—and this World Series—for bringing about a resurgence of public interest in baseball.

### September 9, 1965: Dodgers 1, Cubs 0

In 1965, Sandy Koufax was the greatest pitcher in the universe. By the end of the year, he would post twenty-six victories and 382 strikeouts, his all-time high. Bob Hendley, his mound foe on this day, was also a lefty. The most games he'd ever won had been eleven in 1962. But neither man ever pitched a better game than this one—a perfect game for Sandy, a one-hitter for Hendley. In completing his classic, Sandy struck out seven of the last nine batters he faced, five of them swinging. The one run that the Los Angeles Dodgers scored came on a

Carlton Fisk, willing his drive down the left-field line to stay fair. It did, of course, and decided one of the most exciting World Series games ever played. Ray Fitzgerald wrote in the *Boston Globe,* "Call it off. Call the seventh game off. Let the World Series stand this way, three games for the Cincinnati Reds, and three for the Red Sox."

*There are many who credit this [Red Sox vs. Reds] game—and this World Series—for bringing about a resurgence of public interest in baseball.*

*A perfect game ...* "As total as it's ever been," [Sandy] said.

walk, a sacrifice, a stolen base, and a bad throw. Later Sandy agreed that he'd never pitched a better game in his life. "As total as it's ever been," he said. The record books reveal that only one runner was left on base, while only two runners (for both teams) even reached base, also a record. "It was the greatest loss in history," said Kenny Holtzman, a teammate of Hendley's. It also happened to be the fourth no-hitter of Sandy's career, a record at the time. Oddly, five days later Hendley beat Sandy, 2–1, in a rematch at Wrigley Field.

**September 23, 1908: Giants 1, Cubs 1**
In 1908, the New York Giants and the Chicago Cubs, bitter rivals, were at the end of a torrid pennant race. On the morning of this infamous game, the Giants were six percentage points ahead of the Cubs. John McGraw pitted Christy Mathewson against the Cubs' southpaw Jack Pfiester in this showdown game at the Polo Grounds. After eight and a half innings, the teams were deadlocked at 1–1. In the last of the ninth, after two outs, Moose McCormick singled and went to third when nineteen-year-old Fred Merkle, a backup first baseman from Wisconsin, also singled. Al Bridwell followed with a short single to center field, and, for all intents and purposes, McCormick trotted home with the winning run. As the joyous crowd surged onto the diamond, the Giants seemed well on their way to the flag. But suddenly, the tiny figure of the Cubs' second baseman, Johnny Evers, could be seen waving frantically toward plate umpire Hank O'Day. Evers was insisting to O'Day that Merkle, instead of touching second base, had headed for the dugout, in the false belief that the game was over. In Evers's strict reading of the rules, Merkle was forced at second, because he had not touched up there after Bridwell's hit. In O'Day's book, he was out too. The fact that Evers may have employed the wrong ball when he touched second was beside the point. In this case, the brainy Evers had outthought the brainy McGraw. The game could not possibly continue amid the confusion. Eventually, National League President Harry Pulliam ruled

"Censurable stupidity" was how the *New York Times* described Fred Merkle's failure to touch second base. John McGraw and several teammates loyally defended Merkle. Fred Snodgrass reminded a reporter that the Giants lost five games after the uproar, and then dropped the playoff game. "Hard to blame Merkle for that," he said.

OPPOSITE
Sandy Koufax, surrounded by his admiring teammates, has just completed his perfect game against the Chicago Cubs. Koufax realized in the seventh inning that the achievement was almost in his grasp. "I really wanted that no-hitter," he said. "I didn't think so much about the perfect game, but I really wanted that no-hitter." Ernie Banks, who struck out three times, said, "He was trying to throw the ball by us—and he did."

*"Censurable stupidity" was how the* NEW YORK TIMES *described Fred Merkle's failure to touch second base.*

Giants manager John McGraw posing with Cubs manager Frank Chance, "the Peerless Leader." For the rest of his life, McGraw insisted vehemently that his team was "robbed out of the 1908 pennant by a technicality. . . . We won that game fairly and squarely, for the winning run had crossed the plate, even before Bridwell had reached first on his hit."

that the contest had to be replayed. When it was, the Giants lost. Until the day he died, McGraw felt that the Giants had been robbed of the pennant. As a result of this brouhaha, poor Merkle became the archetypal "bonehead." To his credit, McGraw, usually an unforgiving man, never blamed Merkle. To restore Merkle's confidence, McGraw raised his salary $500 the next year.

## September 30, 1951: Dodgers 9, Phillies 8

Few players have ever been able to dominate a game the way Jackie Robinson could. The most striking example of this happened on the last day of the 1951 season, as the two contenders—the Giants and Dodgers—were deadlocked for the National League lead. The New York Giants, playing in Boston, had already won their game, and the Brooklyn Dodgers trailed the Phillies, 6–5, in Philadelphia. In order to stay alive, the Dodgers had to win, or the Giants would have the pennant. By the end of the eighth inning, the Dodgers had come back to tie the score at 8–8. While the Giants' players were glued to their radios back in Boston—rooting hard, of course, for the Phillies to eliminate the Dodgers from the race—the game proceeded into the twelfth inning. After the Phillies loaded the bases, with one out, Don Newcombe struck out Del Ennis for the second out. But then Eddie Waitkus, once the victim of a hotel shooting, banged a hard, savage liner far to the right of second base. There wasn't a soul in Shibe Park who didn't think Brooklyn's season was over. But out of nowhere, Robinson made a desperate, diving catch. As he did so, he came down hard on his shoulder. After a few moments, he got up, writhing in pain, and groggily walked back to the dugout. A lesser man might have been removed from the lineup. But Jackie stayed around long enough—the fourteenth inning, with two out—to bring the Dodgers back into a tie with the Giants by hitting a home run into the upper deck in left field. That night, Jackie could have been elected Brooklyn's borough president.

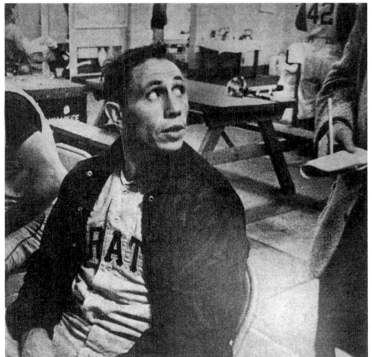

Harvey Haddix, in the Pirates' clubhouse after his "perfect loss," trying to explain to a reporter how he felt about the historic contest. When Haddix came to bat in the ninth inning, the Braves' catcher Del Crandall said, "Hey, you're pitching a pretty good game." Pittsburgh's catcher Smoky Burgess reminded a reporter that Haddix didn't get behind in the count on a single batter until the twelfth inning.

TOP
Jackie Robinson has just snared Eddie Waitkus's line drive in the twelfth, a catch that saved the game for the Dodgers—and left Robinson dazed for several minutes. Red Smith wrote, "Of all the pictures he left upon memory, the one that will always flash back first shows him stretched in full length in the insubstantial twilight, the unconquerable doing the impossible."

### May 26, 1959: Braves 1, Pirates 0

On a damp night in Milwaukee County Stadium, a little southpaw pitcher, Harvey Haddix, faced a brutal right-handed lineup—Hank Aaron, Joe Adcock, Andy Pafko, and Del Crandall among them—with seven men batting over .300 at the time. For twelve innings, not a single man reached base against him. No pitcher had ever arrived at such a point. Haddix, five-foot-nine, weighing 150 pounds, had only once, in 1953, been a winner of twenty games (for St. Louis). Yet here he was, bewildering the Braves with an assortment of pitches. All during his performance, he was aware of what was happening, even though, during the course of his rubbing out one Braves batter after another, his teammates insisted on obeying the time-honored dugout pledge of *omerta*—you don't remind a pitcher he's working on a no-hitter, or, in this case, a perfect game. However, in the thirteenth inning, with the aid of only a single hit, it all came crazily down for the plucky Haddix. On a routine grounder to Don Hoak at third base, Felix Mantilla reached first base when Don made a poor throw. No longer was there a perfect game, though Haddix still had his no-hitter. Mantilla went to second on a sacrifice, and Aaron was walked intentionally. That left it up to Adcock, who hit a shot that cleared the fence in left-center—the only damage any batter had committed all day against the weary Haddix. That Adcock passed Aaron on the base paths meant nothing, for the winning—and only—run had already scored. After the game, the farm boy from South Vienna, Ohio, was philosophical about his near miss for perfection. "My aim was to win," Haddix said. "It was just another loss, but it hurt a little more."

### October 27, 1991: Twins 1, Braves 0

Nobody ever accused Jack Morris, a six-foot-three, two-hundred-pound workhorse of a right-hander, of backing down from a fight. He was as durable as anybody in the modern game. In fourteen years with Detroit, before he joined the Minnesota Twins as a free agent in advance of the 1991 season, he had invariably finished what he started. During that period, he had also won more games than any other pitcher. Now he found himself in the seventh game of the 1991 World Series, facing the Atlanta Braves in a scoreless deadlock after nine innings. Morris's manager, Tom Kelly, wanted to summon a relief pitcher to take over in the top of the tenth inning. But that's not the way Morris saw it. He told Kelly he wanted to go back for the tenth and thwart the Braves. Kelly had Morris's vote, so he asked pitching coach Dick Such what he thought. Such didn't hesitate: leave Jack in there, he advised. Once, many years before, in another World Series, manager Johnny Keane of the Cardinals had left Bob Gibson in a crucial game, because he "believed in Gibson's heart." Kelly now had voted for Morris's heart. So Jack erased three straight Atlanta batters in the top of the tenth, leaving it up to the Twins in their half of the inning. With one out, the Twins loaded the bases, and Gene Larkin was nominated to pinch-hit. The former Columbia University student obliged Morris and Kelly by delivering a game-winning single to left-center, sending the fifty-five thousand screaming, handkerchief-waving fans home happy. It marked only the second seventh game in Series history to go into extra innings, and only the second seventh game in which only one run was scored. Three of the games in this grim Series went into extra innings, seeming to justify Baseball Commissioner Fay Vincent's assessment that this had to be "one of the greatest Series ever."

### October 12, 1986: Red Sox 7, Angels 6

With a lead of three games to one over the Red Sox, the California Angels appeared to be a sure shot to win the 1986 American League Championship Series, and thus advance to the World Series. The Angels' manager and resident genius, Gene Mauch, long had a reputation as a superb strategist, and now he had his club inches away from a title. Going into the ninth inning of Game Five, his team needed to take only one of three games to claim victory. With a 5–2 California lead in the ninth inning, sixty-four thousand fans at Anaheim Stadium were ready to explode with joy. But Don Baylor hit a two-run homer with one out, pulling the

OPPOSITE

"I was mentally prepared for this game since I was a kid," Jack Morris said of his seventh-game victory in the 1991 World Series. "You fantasize about that moment … ninth inning…. Some people want it in that situation, and some don't. I always wanted to be that guy." At the end of the ninth inning, Twins manager Tom Kelly told Morris that he couldn't ask any more of him. Morris said he told Kelly that "I wasn't going anywhere."

Red Sox within one run. Pitcher Mike Witt retired the next Red Sox batter, making it two outs. That brought up lefty swinger Rich Gedman. At this juncture, Mauch, always an assiduous player of percentages, brought in the left-handed pitcher Gary Lucas to face Gedman. Lucas immediately proceeded to hit Gedman with a pitch. That brought up Dave Henderson, who earlier had misplayed a long fly into a home run. Still managing in the orthodox way, Mauch called on right-hander Donnie Moore. Moore got a two-two count on Henderson, who then swung and sent a long home run over the left-field fence, putting the Red Sox ahead 6–5. A tragic footnote to Moore's role is that he committed suicide in 1989, by putting a bullet into his head. Moore's friends said that he had been troubled by having "blown it" with Henderson. "I'll think about that until the day I die," Moore said incessantly. Still, the Angels rallied to tie the score in the ninth. A sacrifice fly would have won it, but two batters failed to come through for Mauch. In the eleventh inning, the Red Sox went ahead on a sacrifice fly by Henderson. The distressed Angels failed to retaliate in the last half of the inning. Although momentum is probably an overused term in baseball, the Angels lost the next two games, 10–4 and 8–1. It was often said that Mauch was always three steps ahead of other managers; it didn't help in this instance. On the other hand, the Red Sox were confounded repeatedly in their own World Series pursuit until 2004. In this case, their luck didn't run out, as it had on so many other occasions, before they made it into the World Series.

**October 15, 1986: Mets 7, Astros 6**
"In 35 years of covering baseball I have never seen a game like it," wrote Jerry Izenberg of the *Newark Star-Ledger* about the contest that decided the 1986 National League pennant. One must always allow for the usual hyperbole when it comes to sports events, but then we must not disallow it when we recall how fascinated millions were when they watched this game for almost five hours on that mid-October night. The games that preceded it were almost as

MAURY ALLEN WROTE, *"the beauty of baseball was glorified by an infinite clock.... I wanted it to go on forever."*

riveting—but Game Six, the longest postseason game in history, may have been unmatched for thrills and unbearable stress. This game began with the Mets, managed by Davey Johnson, falling three runs behind in the first inning. For the next eight innings, the Mets of Gary Carter, Mookie Wilson, Keith Hernandez, Darryl Strawberry, and Lenny Dykstra could do absolutely nothing with junkman southpaw Bob Knepper. Then, in the ninth inning, Dykstra pinch-hit— and shook down the thunder with a leadoff triple. That was followed by a single, a ground out, and a double, producing two runs and a shower—for Knepper. Reliever Dave Smith gave Astros manager Hal Lanier a case of shudders by walking the next two men to load the bases. But all the Mets could get out of it was the tying run on a fly ball out. Another pinch hitter, Danny Heep, took the count to 3–2, then struck out, as forty-five thousand Texans roared. When the Astros could do nothing in their half of the ninth, the game went into extra innings. Roger McDowell came in to give the Mets five almost-perfect innings of relief, even as three Astros relievers matched him. In the top of the fourteenth, the Mets went ahead on a Wally Backman single. But in the bottom of the inning, after two men went out, Billy Hatcher kept Houston alive with a home run to left field, on a ball that was fair only by inches. In the sixteenth, the Mets got hits out of Strawberry and Ray Knight, combined with a walk and a single by Dykstra, to go ahead, 7–4. With the curtain coming down on them, the Astros rallied again. A walk, plus three singles, brought them within one run of the Mets, and they still had two on, with two out. Kevin Bass worked the count to 3–2, then went down swinging against Jesse Orosco, who instantly leaped high into the air. Within seconds, Orosco was almost maimed by delirious teammates. Mike Scott, the Astros pitcher who won two games in this series and was named its MVP, summed up his feelings. "It was harder to watch than to pitch," he said, glumly. For the Mets, who went on to capture the World Series against Boston, it was, as Dykstra said, "just like a dream game." For the Astros, it was a prolonged nightmare.

Jesse Orosco has just struck out Kevin Bass of the Houston Astros in the last of the sixteenth inning, ending the sixth game of the 1986 National League pennant playoff series. Maury Allen of the *New York Post* wrote, "As the innings passed into history, and the beauty of baseball was glorified by an infinite clock.... I wanted it to go on forever."

OPPOSITE
Dave Henderson (left) and Rich Gedman, returning to the Red Sox dugout after Henderson's two-run, ninth-inning homer gave Boston a one-run lead over the California Angels in Game Five of the 1986 American League Championship Series. Thomas Boswell wrote a piece in 1990 about the late Donnie Moore, the Angels' pitcher who threw the home-run ball. "The reason we don't forgive you is because there's nothing to forgive in the first place," he wrote. "You tried your best and failed. In games, there's a law that says somebody has to lose."

Johnny Vander Meer, pitching to the Dodgers' Buddy Hassett in the fifth inning of his
second no-hit game in a row. The feat coincided with the first night game played at
Ebbets Field. The novelty of night baseball in Brooklyn was the main attraction, but
Vandy literally stole the show. Lou Smith, writing in the *Cincinnati Enquirer,* described
the contest as "Larry MacPhail's inaugural mazda opera."

## June 15, 1938: Reds 6, Dodgers 0

In the summer of 1938, Johnny Vander Meer, the twenty-three-year-old southpaw of the Cincinnati Reds, became a household name. He was a handsome, curly-haired young man out of a church league in Midland Park, New Jersey. Until the night in June when he faced the Brooklyn Dodgers at Ebbets Field in the first night game in the Dodgers' history, few people in that borough of baseball lovers had ever heard of him. In the less than two and a half hours that it took for Vander Meer to stifle the Dodgers for his never-equaled second no-hitter in a row, most of those lovers of Dem Bums had taken their hats off to him—and so did the rest of the bedazzled baseball world. On June 11, Vander Meer had sufficiently tricked enough Boston Bees batters at Cincinnati's Crosley Field, before ten thousand fans, to register his first no-hitter—and the first by a Reds pitcher in nineteen years. When he arrived in Brooklyn a few days later, he had become a headline fellow, preparing to take on a Brooklyn team that was the second in the majors to play under the moon. Some thirty-eight thousand of the Brooklyn faithful stormed the gates to see this new phenom. What they got for their zealousness was one of the weirdest no-hit games ever pitched. Nonetheless, it was a no-hitter, and Vandy's second in a row. He walked eight and fanned seven. But, oh, that ninth inning! With these Brooklyn fans actually rooting for the "foreigner" (for they were fully aware of how close he was to back-to-back no-hitters), Vander Meer got the first batter on a bouncer to the mound. Then all the parts seemed to fall off, as Vandy walked three batters in succession. Was he going to buckle at this stage? His manager, Bill McKechnie, ambled to the mound and purred words of reassurance into his ears. It must have worked, for Vandy then got Ernie Koy to hit into a force-out at home, followed by Leo Durocher's lazy fly to center field. In his next start, Vandy actually added three and two-thirds more innings of no-hit ball to his streak. But Boston's Debs Garms banged a single, and the magic came to an end. Thereafter, Vander Meer was always referred to as "Double No-Hit." Others preferred to call him the Dutch Master.

# 5. *The* GREATEST MOMENTS

Bobby Thomson in 1947, his first full season with the Giants. He hit twenty-nine homers and drove in eighty-five runs that year, and he was apparently establishing a solid major-league career. His running speed and Glasgow birthplace earned him the nickname "the Flying Scot." He played center field prior to the arrival of Willie Mays in 1951, then moved to third base, and was posted there as the epochal playoff against the Dodgers began.

## October 3, 1951: The Shot Heard 'Round the World

It couldn't have happened to two nicer guys. Looking back over fifty-four years, that's a fair way of putting it. Bobby Thomson's ninth-inning, three-run home run against the Brooklyn Dodgers gave the New York Giants the National League pennant, and it gave the language that happy phrase: the Shot Heard 'Round the World. The blow also ended what may have been the most dramatic pennant race in history. If you wanted to cast two men in this compelling scenario, you couldn't have chosen any better than Thomson, who hit the home run that broke the hearts of Brooklyn fans, and Ralph Branca, who threw the pitch that caused columnist Red Smith to declare that "the art of fiction is dead. Reality has strangled invention." Thomson, a Glasgow-born Scot, then not yet twenty-eight years old, had always been a quiet, rather unassuming fellow, as well as a gentleman. To this day, he still doesn't quite comprehend what the fuss was all about. Branca, then twenty-five years old, was born in Mt. Vernon, New York. He was a bright, assertive fellow and, like Thomson, a gentleman. More important than the pitch that made him perversely famous, Branca should also be known as a player who had helped ease the way for his teammate Jackie Robinson's acceptance into the game. As for the home run, "People remember me because of it," Thomson said years later. "I don't think anyone would have paid much attention to me if it hadn't happened." Branca always reacted to his own role with a mixture of acceptance and annoyance. "I don't smoke, drink, or run around," he said, plaintively. "Why me?" But regardless of how unfair it seems, Branca knows that he is inexorably linked with Thomson, in the most golden moment of the golden age of baseball.

## October 15, 1988: Kirk Gibson's Hamstring Trot

Manager Tommy Lasorda of the Los Angeles Dodgers always believed he could talk the birds out of the magnolias. Many agreed with him. Maybe he proved it in the first game of the

Kirk Gibson, celebrating his breathtaking ninth-inning home run that won the opening game of the 1988 World Series for the Los Angeles Dodgers. In his *Los Angeles Times* column, Jim Murray wrote, "I mean this is Rambo IV, right? That was Sylvester Stallone that came out of the dugout in the ninth inning of game one of the 1988 World Series. That wasn't a real player? . . . This is John Wayne saving the fort stuff. Errol Flynn taking the Burma Road."

PREVIOUS
A rare view of Willie Mays's back-to-the-diamond catch of Vic Wertz's 470-foot drive in the eighth inning of the opening game of the 1954 World Series. As he trotted back to the dugout at the end of the inning, Mays said to left fielder Monte Irvin, "I had that one all the way. Had it all the way." Irvin said later, "It was his solemn duty to catch a ball that wasn't in the stands."

The Shot Heard 'Round the World has just cleared the left-field wall at the Polo Grounds, and Bobby Thomson is airborne, while the spectators, most still frozen in disbelief, begin to react. First-base coach Freddie Fitzsimmons has flung his hat skyward. Jackie Robinson can't bear to watch. "All I could think was that we beat the Dodgers," Thomson said. "I never for a moment thought anything but that." When he returned home later that evening, Thomson began to grasp the scope of the event when his brother asked, "Do you realize what you've done?"

[Thomson's] running speed and Glasgow birthplace earned him the nickname *"the Flying Scot."*

1988 World Series, between the heavily favored Oakland Athletics and his own club. With two out in the ninth inning, one man on, and Oakland ahead, 4–3, the Dodgers appeared to be licked. Lasorda made a call to the clubhouse to see if his injured slugger, Kirk Gibson, could go up and take a last, desperate swing in behalf of the Dodgers. Why desperate? Well, Gibson, the six-foot-three, 215-pound, thirty-one-year-old outfielder hadn't even suited up that day, because he was nursing a torn left hamstring and a sprained ligament in his right knee. When he took a few practice swings in the clubhouse, it hurt. But Ben Hines, the Dodgers' batting coach, confided to Lasorda that Gibson might have one good swing in him. Based on that bit of intelligence, Lasorda asked Kirk to pinch-hit, and when Gibson came hobbling onto the field, the manager yelled encouragement at him. As fifty-five thousand fans at Dodger Stadium looked on, many asked themselves what the devil this guy was doing up there. A's reliever Dennis Eckersley, a future Hall of Famer, might have asked himself the same thing. Eckersley threw one pitch, then two, then three, four, and five—and Kirk's bat didn't budge off his shoulder. With the count 3–2, Dennis threw his best pitch, a slider. Kirk swung, mustering all of his strength, and the ball went sailing over the right-field wall. As Gibson made his gimpy, exultant home-run trot around the bases to give the Dodgers a 5–4 victory, the A's players looked on in disbelief. After a football career as a flanker at Michigan State and eight solid years with Detroit, Gibson had come to the Dodgers as a free agent in 1988. He batted .290 that year and hit twenty-five home runs. But until this moment of truth, he always seemed to be a whisper away from true stardom. Manager Sparky Anderson of Detroit had once dubbed him "the next Mickey Mantle." On that October Saturday in 1988, his home run galvanized his teammates, who went on to win the Series in five games.

## September 29, 1954: The Catch

When Willie Mays turned his back on home plate and ran as hard as he could toward the center-field bleachers in the Polo Grounds, it looked as if he didn't have a chance to catch Vic Wertz's long fly ball. Writer Arnold Hano, who was sitting in the bleachers that gray September afternoon, thought the ball would beat Willie and his glove to the wall. "It was forty feet higher than Mays' head, and winging along like a locomotive," Hano wrote in his book *A Day in the Bleachers*, "but he had run so fast and truly that he made this impossible catch look—to me in the bleachers—quite ordinary."

This happened in the first game of the 1954 World Series between the New York Giants, Mays's team, and the Cleveland Indians, who had set an American League record of 111 triumphs that year. Willie's catch helped to win that game. And the Giants won the next three in a row, in a stunning reversal of form that was almost as wondrous as the catch itself.

Hano has always insisted that Mays made other great catches, in a career of great catches. But he acknowledges that it was the circumstances surrounding the highway robbery that accounts for its reputation. Here was the setting: the score was tied at two-all, Cleveland batting in the top of the eighth inning, with two men on base and one out. By outracing Wertz's drive—"the hardest ball I ever hit," Wertz said later—Mays saved one run, and possibly two, from scoring. What is often overlooked in this scenario—and is part and parcel of the catch itself—is the throw by Willie that followed the catch. As Hano describes it: "Willie caught the ball, and then whirled and threw, like some olden statue of a Greek javelin hurler, his head twisted away to the left, as his right arm swept out and around. And, as he turned, or as he threw—the two motions were welded into one—off came the cap, and then Mays himself continued to spin around, after the gigantic effort of returning the ball whence it came, and he went down flat on his belly and out of sight. What an astonishing throw, to make all throws before it seem like the flings of teen-age girls." Larry Doby managed to advance to third after the throw, but Al Rosen, who had been on first, had to remain there. In the tenth inning, pinch hitter Dusty Rhodes hit a puny, 270-foot fly to

This picture reveals dramatically the amount of ground Willie Mays covered in his pursuit of Vic Wertz's bid for a game-breaking extra-base hit. The right-field foul pole, only 257 feet from home plate, is not seen, but it was reached in the last of the tenth inning when Dusty Rhodes lofted a game-winning homer near it. Wertz and Rhodes could testify expertly on the extent to which the old Polo Grounds "gaveth and taketh away."

AS HANO DESCRIBES IT: *"Willie caught the ball, and then whirled and threw,* LIKE SOME OLDEN STATUE OF A GREEK JAVELIN HURLER … *off came the cap … after the gigantic effort of returning the ball … he went down flat on his belly and out of sight."*

A moment before Babe Ruth clubbed this home run into the center-field bleachers at Wrigley Field, the Bambino gestured toward Cubs pitcher Charlie Root, indicating something—maybe his determination to hit a homer on the next pitch, or his understanding that it takes only one pitch to hit a homer. Or perhaps it was merely a gesture of Ruthian hubris. Gordon Cobbledick of the *Cleveland Plain Dealer* was there, and he wrote, "The story has no basis in truth, but it hasn't impeded its circulation. It has become part of the Babe Ruth saga."

right field that just went in for a home run, giving the Giants the victory. But all that anyone could remember was that Willie Mays got a quicker start than anybody else alive—and caught a fly ball.

### October 1, 1932: Did Babe Call His Shot?

As the third game of the 1932 World Series began—with the Yankees having won the first two games—Babe Ruth was being maligned by the Chicago fans and the Cubs bench at a level that was almost unprecedented. The abuse mostly had to do with Ruth's purported "nigger" origins and the size of his thirty-seven-year-old belly. It was caused, in part, because the Yankees had been needling the Cubs over their parsimonious behavior in dividing up their World Series shares. An ex-Yankee, Mark Koenig, now a Cub, had, according to the Yankees, been treated in miserly fashion. When Babe came to bat in the fifth inning against right-hander Charlie Root, obscenities directed at him reached a new pitch, and fans tossed lemons at him. As one strike whistled past him, Babe grinned and held up one finger. Root then threw two balls and another strike, and Babe signaled with two fingers. As Root prepared to unleash his next pitch, Ruth signaled toward the distant center-field wall, his index finger jabbing the air. Some have since decreed that there should be no misinterpreting what Babe had in mind: he was advising the boisterous crowd of more than forty thousand that Root's next delivery was going to wind up outside the ballpark. When that next pitch headed for Babe low and away, it never reached catcher Gabby Hartnett's mitt. Babe swung, and the ball wound up in the center-field bleachers. It was claimed to be the longest home run ever hit in Wrigley Field.

Babe's beau geste continues to be the subject of controversy to this day. Was he signaling that he needed only one more pitch to hit it out of the park, or was he signaling that the next pitch would wind up in the center-field bleachers? It is the opinion of Robert Creamer, Ruth's biographer, that, yes, Babe was challenging

Root and the Cubs, and, yes, he was indicating he was going to hit a home run. But Creamer doesn't think that Ruth was promising to hit it into the center-field bleachers. Whatever the truth happens to be, the story has been embellished and embroidered over the years, as one might expect. In his autobiography, Babe himself garnishes the tale nicely by insisting that he contemplated doing it the night before the game, in his hotel room, after he and his wife had been spat on by Cubs fans in front of the hotel. The most ironic aspect of this episode is that it drew attention away from the one-man show that Lou Gehrig put on during the Series. He hit .529, with nine hits in seventeen at bats, knocked in eight runs, scored nine times, and had three home runs and a double. In fact, Lou followed Babe's swat with a home run on Root's first pitch to him. But who noticed! The called shot remains the single most dramatic incident in Ruth's legend, any way history chooses to look at it.

### September 28, 1938: A Homer in the Gloamin'

As National League pennant races go, it was a beaut. The Cubs and Pirates were vying with each other in 1938 right down to the final days. Gabby Hartnett, the Cubs' excellent catcher—and ultimately a Hall of Famer—had taken over as manager in late July, when Jolly Cholly Grimm was said to have lost his touch. The Cubs then seem to have rallied around Hartnett, thus proving that inspiration from the top sometimes can play a role. The Pirates, with their own Hall of Famer, Pie Traynor, as manager, had started to slip in the home stretch. So when the teams met in late September at Wrigley Field, the pennant was on the line. In the first game of the three-game series, the score was tied at 5–5 going into the bottom of the ninth inning, with Mace Brown pitching for Pittsburgh. He retired the first two Cubs, with Hartnett coming to bat. At this stage of his long playing career, Gabby did not catch every day. In the 1938 season, he would appear in only eighty-eight games. But he was always a potent threat with the bat. If Brown could retire

Hartnett, there was no doubt that the game would be called immediately because of darkness. Brown figured that Gabby could not hit what he couldn't see, so he got the first two pitches over the heart of the plate, and then did the same thing with the third pitch. But Gabby saw enough of the third pitch to hit it out of the ballpark. "I had the kind of feeling you get when the blood rushes out of your head and you get dizzy," said the elated Gabby to reporters. "I knew the minute I hit it, it was gone." Warren Brown, a veteran Chicago writer, said that "there have been many home runs slugged out of Wrigley Field but none before or since created the stir within the place that followed Hartnett's wallop—not even Babe Ruth's so-called Series shot against Charlie Root. Wild-eyed fans broke out of the stands and onto the field. . . . Hartnett had to fight his way through the mobs to find third base and touch it." With Gabby's blast, the Pirates were done. They lost the next day and were finished. However, in the World Series, which the Cubs lost to the Yankees in four straight, Gabby managed only one measly single.

### October 10, 1926: Old Pete Fans Tony
The confrontation between Grover Cleveland Alexander and Tony Lazzeri in the seventh inning of the seventh game of the 1926 World Series has been likened to Aaron Burr dueling with Alexander Hamilton at Weehawken Heights or Jack Dempsey facing Gene Tunney twice, in Philadelphia and Chicago. Overlooking the hyperbole, it is true that that moment still adds up to one of the most stirring episodes in Series history, inextricably linking these two ballplayers forever. Ironically, the two protagonists—Alex, the nearly forty-year-old veteran of many wars, including World War I in the trenches, and Lazzeri, the twenty-two-year-old slugging rookie—both suffered from epilepsy. Here's how the moment occurred: The St. Louis Cardinals led, 3–2, as the Yankees came to bat in the bottom of the seventh. It was a dark, dreary day, which caused Yankee Stadium to be little more than half full. The Yankee team of Ruth and Gehrig loaded the bases,

bringing up Lazzeri, with two out, to face Jesse Haines, who was wearying of his task. Manager Rogers Hornsby of the Cards could have gone to a younger pitcher in his bull pen. But he made the call to Alexander—the man they also called Old Pete. Only the day before, Pete had gone nine innings to beat the Yankees. But Hornsby chose to go with the legend, maybe because Alex had gotten Lazzeri out four straight times in that previous game.

His cap perched comically on his head, Alex shuffled in from the bull pen—taking his time, some later insisted, to ruffle Lazzeri, who had batted in more runs that year than any other Yankee except Ruth. As Hornsby handed Alex the ball, he looked into his eyes, for rumors had it that Alex had had a postgame victory shot or two. Satisfied with what he saw, Hornsby retreated to the Cards' dugout and let Alex take over, which is exactly what he did. Three pitches later, Alex had triumphed. The first roundhouse swing by Tony was a miss. The second produced one of the loudest fouls in Series history, the ball screeching for the left-field stands, then curving foul at the last mini-second. The third pitch sliced the outside corner of the plate, causing Tony to swing again and miss by the proverbial country mile. Overnight, Alex became a national hero (he stayed in to shut down the Yankees the last two innings as well), and Hornsby was proclaimed a genius for plucking the relatively ancient farm boy from Nebraska out of the bull pen. Bob O'Farrell, the Cards' catcher that afternoon, never for a moment believed Alex would fail. "The greatest clutch pitcher I've ever seen," he said. "Lazzeri would have to have been Houdini to get his bat on that last pitch." Alex would win 373 games before he was through. But life after baseball was hard. He died alone, in 1950, in a cheap hotel room in Nebraska, a victim of his fears and alcohol.

### October 18, 1977: Three for Reggie
Reginald Martinez Jackson was a piece of work, an egotist, a showstopper, a fellow who, one pundit said, wanted to die in his own arms. He was boastful, narcissistic, voluble, and, by his

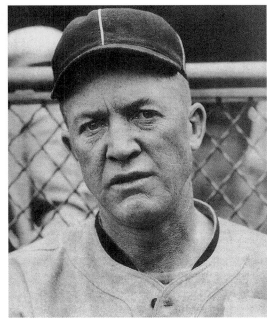

CLOCKWISE FROM ABOVE

Gabby Hartnett was engulfed by teammates and fans alike as he circled the bases in the wake of his ninth-inning, game-winning home run against the Pittsburgh Pirates. "A lot of people have told me they didn't know the ball was in the bleachers," he said. "Well I did. Maybe I was the only one in the park who did. I knew it the minute I hit it."

"We're in a tough spot and there's no place to put this guy," said Cardinals manager Rogers Hornsby as he handed the ball to Grover Cleveland Alexander in the seventh inning of the last game of the 1926 World Series. "This guy" was the Yankees' "Poosh 'Em Up" Tony Lazzeri, who had driven in 114 runs that season. "I'll take care of that," Alexander said. Three pitches later, Lazzeri had struck out, and St. Louis went on to claim the world title.

Badly fooled by a curveball down and away, Tony Lazzeri has just struck out with the bases loaded in the seventh game of the 1926 World Series. The preceding pitch from the Cardinals' Grover Cleveland Alexander, a fastball, was hammered into the left-field stands, foul by no more than a foot. "No more of that for you, my lad," Alexander thought. "A foot or two made all the difference between being a hero and a bum," he said later, recalling the loud foul.

*"I love competition. It stimulates me, it excites me," [Reggie] said.*

own admission, "the straw that stirs the drink." One of his teammates said of him that "he'd give you the shirt off his back, but he'd be sure to call a press conference to announce it." Those are the negatives. The positives are that he was charming, intelligent, tremendously talented, dependable in the clutch (his boss liked to call him "Mr. October," because he was brilliant in postseason play), and someone who seemed to know what to do with his life and his money. He is also the player who is alone in baseball history for bashing three home runs in a single World Series game—all on first pitches, and against three different pitchers. This performance, against the Los Angeles Dodgers and pitchers named Burt Hooton, Elias Sosa, and Charlie Hough (two of whom were knuckleball hurlers, thus making the achievement more perilous), was so stunning that many in the crowd of fifty-seven thousand that night were not aware that the feat was committed on three consecutive pitches. With the three home runs rung up in a row, Reggie totaled five for the Series—a World Series mark—and the output helped the Yankees win their first world title in fifteen years. When Reggie trotted around the bases on his third wallop, first baseman Steve Garvey of the Dodgers couldn't help but appreciate the unique moment. He clapped into his glove and smiled at Jackson. In the Yankee clubhouse after the game, manager Tommy Lasorda paid a visit to Reggie. "The greatest performance I've ever seen," he told the excited Reggie. No doubt Reggie agreed with him. When Jackson first came to the Yankees in November 1976 from Oakland, where he had been instrumental in that team's success, the newly minted millionaire became, in the words of author Donald Honig, "a new, incorporated hero." In another time, before Jackie Robinson paved the way for black men in baseball, Reggie would have been disparaged as "uppity." But Reggie represented—and well—another generation of black men. He refused to be inhibited or thwarted. He gloried in his role and in his multiple skills. "I love competition. It stimulates me, it excites me," he said. He had even predicted that there would be a candy bar

OPPOSITE
Reggie Jackson acknowledges the standing ovation given by Yankee fans after his third consecutive home run in the sixth game of the 1977 World Series. The homers provided the difference in a victory over the Los Angeles Dodgers that captured another World Championship for the New Yorkers. "Nothing can top this," he said in the clubhouse. "Who is gonna hit three home runs and clinch the World Series? I mean, I'm not."

named after him—and there was. The Reggie Bar, almost as sweet as Reggie's swing, wasn't bad eating, either. Reggie is still around, as Mr. Steinbrenner's consultant. He collects cars the way he used to collect homers—and strikeouts.

## October 13, 1960: Maz Ends a Glorious Slugfest

There's only one way to fittingly describe the World Series of 1960 between the Yankees and the Pirates: preposterous. The raw figures of those games would indicate that the Yankees were the superior team. As a club, the Yankees hit .338, the highest in history for a seven-game competition. The three Yankee victories were accomplished by the laughable scores of 16–3, 10–0, and 12–0. Ten of the Yankees' ninety-one hits were home runs, with Mickey Mantle chipping in with three, Roger Maris with two, and Bill Skowron with two. The Pirates totaled only four home runs among their sixty hits. They had a team average of .256, almost 100 points lower than the Yankees' mark. Yet, at the conclusion of this wackiest of all Series, the Pirates, led by the meagerly celebrated Danny Murtaugh, emerged victorious over the New York team, which was ministered to by that most celebrated of all monologists, Casey Stengel. As a reward for this strangest of all defeats, septuagenarian Casey was at once shown the door. How did this all come about? The Pirates got fine performances from Roberto Clemente; pitchers Vernon Law and Harvey Haddix, each of whom contributed two wins; and Bill Virdon, with some timely outfielding. To put the icing on the cake, they reaped a serendipitous clout from the bat of Bill Mazeroski, a winner of eight Gold Gloves at second base, but normally not regarded as much of a home-run hitter.

Maz, born in West Virginia in 1936, teamed up with shortstop Dick Groat to give the Pirates a tenacious double-play tandem. What led up to Maz's game-winning poke was a topsy-turvy game that included a ground ball landing in shortstop Tony Kubek's Adam's apple in the eighth inning, thus helping a late Pirates rally. The game was tied at 9–9 in the top of the ninth, after the Pirates had scored five in the

# *Maz* sent the crowd of thirty-seven thousand into spasms of delight.

Bill Mazeroski hitting the ninth-inning home run that ended the 1960 World Series in a victory for the Pirates over the New York Yankees. "I'd like to hit a home run and win it all," Mazeroski thought as he trotted to the dugout after the Yankees tied the score in the top of the ninth. "A moment after I hit that ball a shiver ran down my back. We always felt we could pull it out . . . but I didn't think I'd be the guy to do it."

OPPOSITE
"I was awful lonely standing out there at first base," Pete Rose said, after breaking Ty Cobb's lifetime hit record, then waiting until the tumult from his fans subsided. "I can't describe what was going through my mind; what was going through my stomach. . . . I was all right until I looked up in the air. I looked up in the air and saw Ty Cobb and my dad. That took care of me."

bottom of the eighth to give them a brief lead. Stengel then summoned right-hander Ralph Terry to face Mazeroski in the last of the ninth. On the second pitch, Maz became a Yankee-slayer. He swung his right-handed bat, sending the ball winging over the left-field wall at Forbes Field, while Yogi Berra, playing in the outfield that afternoon, watched despairingly as the ball disappeared from sight. It was evocative of Andy Pafko of the Dodgers gazing forlornly at Bobby Thomson's home run in 1951. Maz's blow ended the game at 10–9, giving the Pirates their first world title in thirty-five years. It also marked the first time a World Series had ended in a "walk-off" home run. As he leaped around the bases, Maz sent the crowd of thirty-seven thousand into spasms of delight. "I can't even talk," he said. "I'm too tired." Each year since 1960, a group of Pittsburgh admirers has gathered at the site of the historic homer, to honor their shy hero. But Maz has never accepted an invitation to join them.

## September 11, 1985: Pete Passes the Georgia Peach

In January 2004, Pete Rose uttered his long-overdue confession that he had, indeed, bet on baseball games during his playing days. According to most polls on the subject, a majority of fans, much taken by the blue-collar toughness of Rose, support his admission to the Hall of Fame, in spite of his peccadilloes. However, there are also plenty of observers who continue to look askance at Rose dipping his spikes into the Hall, even if he did, on the night of September 11, 1985, break Ty Cobb's all-time hit mark of 4,191. Ultimately, Rose's total went to 4,256 before he decided it was time for him to leave baseball. Nobody has any doubt that Rose's compilation of hits is as unassailable as Joe DiMaggio's fifty-six-game hitting streak. On that night in 1985, before a packed house in Cincinnati, forty-four-year-old Rose faced Eric Show of San Diego. Hunched over the plate, his left-handed bat cocked in menacing style, Rose went to a 2–2 count on Show, then connected on the next pitch for a clean hit to left-center. It was base hit number 4,192, the one that would

FIVE STRIKEOUTS *in a row* AGAINST FIVE HALL OF FAMERS.
*When Hubbell finished the third inning by striking out pitcher
Lefty Gomez, the notoriously weak-hitting hurler of the Yankees,*
HE HAD GONE FROM THE SUBLIME *to the ridiculous.*

Carl Hubbell (left) and Lefty Gomez, the starting pitchers in the 1934 All-Star Game,
played at the Polo Grounds on July 10. After Hubbell struck out five American League
sluggers, Gomez came to bat in the second inning and said to catcher Gabby Hartnett,
"You are now looking at a man whose batting average is .104. What the Hell am I
doing up here?" Lefty then struck out.

pass Ty Cobb. The Reds fans went wild, fireworks shot into the heavens, and a blimp hovering over the ballpark flashed "Pete Rose, 4,192." In the midst of this admiring scenario, Rose was tearful. "Clear in the sky I saw my dad, Harry Francis Rose, and Ty Cobb," Rose said, choking up.

Rose had long been obsessed with Cobb. One of his sons was named Ty. Rose once even said that he thought Cobb's reputation as a bad guy had been exaggerated. Rose played with the Reds and Phillies for twenty-four years, helping to drive the Phillies to their first world title, in 1980. For intensity and total devotion on the field, Rose was probably unsurpassed. Yet, by violating the game's most sacrosanct rule—no betting on games—he had sadly breached his compact with the fans. "Is Charlie Hustle still hustling us?" asked TV commentator Chris Matthews, after Rose finally 'fessed up to his compulsive gambling activities. The ubiquitous, baseball-wise Larry King said he'd have still cast a ballot for Rose to join the Hall. But, he added, "he should not be allowed back into the game. Let his plaque read that he bet on baseball." George Vecsey, columnist of the *New York Times*, points to Rose's 3,562 games, and all of those hits, as the reason for letting Rose in the Hall. "A lifetime of probation and lingering scorn is worth the price of admission," Vecsey wrote.

## July 10, 1934: The Story of a Screwball

Carl Hubbell, who was fondly called "the Meal Ticket" by his admirers, threw his screwball so many times that the palm of his left hand permanently faced outward. It's unfair to Hubbell that despite his marvelous years of pitching for the Giants, he often labored in the shadow of the Depression-era favorite Dizzy Dean. Dizzy always talked a better game than Hubbell ever did, but he was never as great a pitcher as Carl. From 1932 to 1937, Hubbell won 133 games, while losing only 61 times. But it took one Sunday afternoon in July 1933 to put him in the limelight that he deserved. On that day, he pitched an astounding eighteen-inning, 1–0 shutout against the Cardinals. For more

than four hours, Hubbell hypnotized the Cards, yielding *no* walks and striking out twelve. That certainly was the pitching highlight of his life—until a July day the next year. In the second annual All-Star Game ever played, Hubbell started for the National League before more than fifty thousand fans at his home field, the Polo Grounds. The prospect of facing one of the greatest array of sluggers of all time hardly fazed Hubbell, even after Charlie Gehringer singled and Heinie Manush walked to start the game for the American League. After a brief conference with his manager, Bill Terry (who was also playing first that day for the National League), Hubbell assured Terry he was okay. At that point he went to work in earnest. He started by fanning Babe Ruth on five pitches; then Lou Gehrig went down swinging. Jimmie Foxx struck out on three pitches to end the inning. "That was the greatest three-man concentration of power ever to appear in one lineup," Lawrence Ritter wrote. In the second inning, Hubbell picked up where he left off—striking out Al Simmons and Joe Cronin—before Bill Dickey broke the spell with a single. Those five strikeouts in a row against five Hall of Famers represent one of the most overwhelming demonstrations of pitching in history. When Hubbell finished the second inning by striking out pitcher Lefty Gomez, the notoriously weak-hitting hurler of the Yankees, he had gone from the sublime to the ridiculous. As Hubbell walked to the center-field clubhouse, his stint ended, the crowd roared its appreciation for a man who rarely smiled, weighed less than 171 pounds, and threw a pitch that acted like a ball dropping off a table.

# 6. *The* GREATEST WORLD SERIES

An eagerly anticipated confrontation between Ty Cobb (left) and Honus Wagner in the 1909 World Series was limited to some banter from Cobb and a tag by Wagner that resulted in three stitches being taken in Cobb's upper lip. The night before the seventh game, played in Detroit, Tigers fans hired three bands to play in front of the Pirates' hotel to keep the team awake, but manager Fred Clarke, apprised of the scheme, foiled it by secretly moving his squad to an out-of-town hotel.

OPPOSITE
On September 1, 1951, a bizarre reenactment of the Fred Lindstrom 1924 World Series pebble incident took place at Griffith Stadium in Washington. In this case, the pebble has become a small boulder, and Lindstrom is good-naturedly watching a rubber ball soar over his outstretched arms. After the original event, teammate Heinie Groh said, "It wasn't Freddy's fault. It could have happened to anybody. . . . It was fate, that's all. Fate and a pebble."

PREVIOUS
Harry "the Cat" Brecheen is being carried off the field on the strength of his stout pitching in Game Seven of the 1946 World Series. Red Schoendienst and Stan Musial can be seen moving in from the right.

## 1909: Pittsburgh 4, Detroit 3

The World Series of 1909 turned out to be the first Series to be won in the ultimate seventh game. But it was also known chiefly as the battleground for the two greatest players in the game at that time: Ty Cobb, twenty-two, of Detroit and Honus Wagner, thirty-five, of Pittsburgh. Both men had made it a habit of winning their league's batting titles, and each man had done it in 1909. But in this first post-season confrontation between them, they failed to dominate these games, as one might have expected. Wagner managed to do better than Cobb, as he got eight hits, stole six bases, and drove in six runs—not bad production for most mortals. On the other hand, Cobb batted only .231 and stole just two bases, one of which was a steal of home in the second game. Cobb did snarl at Wagner once or twice, but he didn't reach base often enough to intimidate the aging shortstop. However, it was a little-known pitcher, Charles "Babe" Adams, a twenty-seven-year-old rookie from Indiana, who became a household name by winning the first, fifth, and seventh games, the last on only two days' rest. During the season, Adams had been used only sparingly by manager Fred Clarke, but in the final game he stifled the Tigers, shutting them out on six hits, as Cobb wound up empty. The Series was the richest up to that point for the club owners. Each Pirates player received $1,825, while each of the Tigers took home $1,274, just to give you an idea of the kind of meal money players earned in those long-ago days.

## 1924: Washington 4, New York 3

Had there been television in 1924, there's little doubt that the ratings for the World Series would have broken all records. Not only did this weeklong drama go seven games, but it featured some of the tightest contests ever played in the Series. In addition, the "boy wonder" manager of the Senators, Bucky Harris, only twenty-seven years old, outthought and out-lucked the venerable John McGraw of the Giants. When it was all over, McGraw, a man who didn't take kindly to defeat, issued his grouchy summation: "The better team did *not*

win." Washington had never won anything before, in its twenty-three years in the American League—this despite the fact that for eighteen of those summers, Walter Johnson had been hurling fastballs for the team. Now at last in the Series, Johnson, nearly thirty-seven years old, lost his first two games against the Giants. That included a memorable opening game that went twelve innings, with New York on top, 4–3. Baseball fans everywhere still kept rooting for Johnson to win a Series game, and that moment finally arrived in the seventh game, played at Washington before a noisy crowd of thirty-two thousand. Going into the last of the eighth inning, the Giants led, 3–1, and it looked as if the Series would end with nothing more for Johnson than sympathy. But then the gremlins took charge in behalf of the Senators. With the bases loaded and two out, second baseman Harris, the playing pilot, hit an innocent-looking grounder in the direction of Freddy Lindstrom at third base. As Lindstrom prepared to make the play, a strategically placed pebble (of course, Harris had put it there) caused the ball to bounce over Freddy's head. Two runs scampered home, tying the game. At this point, Harris, fully aware of the difficulties Johnson had already suffered in the Series, nonetheless brought him in to pitch. The stouthearted Johnson grimly kept the Giants at bay, even as they continued to get men on base. In four innings of relief, Johnson fanned five. Finally, in the bottom of the twelfth inning, events took place that would haunt McGraw until the end of his life. When Muddy Ruel lifted a high foul pop behind the plate, catcher Hank Gowdy's foot became ensnarled in his mask. "It clung to his hoof like a bear-trap," wrote Fred Lieb, causing the ball to drop untouched at Gowdy's feet. Rewarded with new life, Ruel banged a double. Earl McNeely, the Washington center fielder, promptly hit another mischievous grounder toward Lindstrom. Freddy again stooped to conquer the ball, again it hopped over his head (same pebble?), and Ruel scooted home with the run that won the Series for Washington. It also gave Johnson his first Series victory. All Washington seemed to go wild. Usually not

GROH SAID, *"It wasn't Freddy's fault. It was fate ... and a pebble."*

*When Ducky Medwick slid hard into Marv Owen, the fans, believing Ducky had meant to injure Owen, proceeded to pelt Ducky with everything from bottles to rotten apples. Bob Hood wrote, "Ducky might have murdered one of those fans if he'd had a bat in his hands."*

much for lyricism, Judge Kenesaw Mountain
Landis, upon viewing the mobs marching joy-
ously down Pennsylvania Avenue, declared, "Are
we seeing the high point of this thing we love?"
Even the taciturn president, Calvin Coolidge,
was said to have chuckled all week long.

## 1934: St. Louis 4, Detroit 3

The ragtag, rough-and-tumble group known as
the Gashouse Gang of St. Louis probably does
not qualify as one of the all-time great teams.
But these Cardinals stirred up a fuss in the
World Series of 1934, with their derring-do and
grimy charm—so much so that many people
remember those games with relish. For sheer
excitement and feverish atmosphere in both St.
Louis and Detroit, few Series, before or after,
could compete with that of 1934. Even when
Dizzy Dean was inexplicably sent in as a pinch
runner by his manager, Frankie Frisch, in the
fourth game, something out of the ordinary
immediately occurred. As Dizzy slid into second,
shortstop Billy Rogell of Detroit threw a ball
that hit Dean squarely in the head. The next
day, the newspapers reported, possibly with
tongue in cheek, "X-rays of Dean's Head Show
Nothing." The Tigers led, three games to two,
going into the sixth game, but Paul "Daffy"
Dean, Dizzy's younger brother, stopped the
Tigers, 4–3. Daffy did it with the unexpected
batting help of the "All-America out," Leo
Durocher, who came up with three hits. The
night before the crucial seventh game in Detroit,
a sound truck circled the Book-Cadillac Hotel,
where the Cards were staying. Out of the truck's
loudspeaker came an insistent, loud message:
"Hold them, Tigers! Hold them, Tigers!" But
the Cards players responded by throwing waste-
baskets and bags of water out of the window at
the truck. So much for competitive civility.

    Everyone was looking for an explosion the
next day as the teams took the field, with Dizzy
on the mound for St. Louis, pitching with only
one day of rest, and Eldon Auker working for
Detroit. Before the game started, Dizzy shouted
over at Tigers manager Mickey Cochrane,
"That guy [meaning Auker] jes' won't do,
Mickey." And how right Dizzy was. By the third

Left fielder Joe Medwick stands in the debris that rained down on him from Tigers fans
in the sixth inning of Game Seven. In an effort to restore order, Commissioner Landis
removed Medwick from the game. Cardinals manager Frankie Frisch protested the
action, but Landis pointed to the scoreboard, reminding Frisch that his team was ahead
9–0. "If you can lose this one, your team needs a new manager," the judge said.

OPPOSITE
Detroit's Charlie Gehringer, "the Mechanical Man," posing with the Cardinals' Joe
"Ducky" Medwick before the third game of the 1934 World Series. The two men each
had eleven hits and batted .379 in the seven-game set, but Medwick drove in five runs to
Gehringer's two, and he was a major irritant in the Gashouse Gang's eventual victory.

inning, the Cards had trampled on Auker, as they took a 7–0 lead. Needless to say, Detroit's fans were in no mood for jollity. So when Ducky Medwick of the Cards, normally a pretty angry guy himself, slid hard into Marv Owen at third base in the sixth inning, the fans, believing Ducky had meant to injure Owen, erupted. Actually, Owen had inadvertently brought his foot down hard on Ducky's leg, causing Ducky to retaliate with a kick of his spiked shoe. Whatever the precise scenario, the fans proceeded to pelt Ducky out in left field with everything they could get their hands on, from bottles to rotten apples, in effect turning Ducky into a human garbage can. Observing this unseemly spectacle, Commissioner Landis, who had been sitting in a box on the third-base line, held court with Medwick, Frisch, Owen, and the umpire. He then decided to remove Ducky from the game, to avoid having the Series end in a forfeit. Ducky was enraged by the decision, saying that by putting him out, it made him look as if he were to blame. As Bob Hood wrote in a book on the Gashouse Gang, "Ducky might have murdered one of those fans if he'd had a bat in his hands." At the conclusion of this unprecedented game, won by St. Louis, 11–0, Dizzy had his second win of the Series. Between them, the Dean brothers won all four Series games. The new world champs became the darlings not only of St. Louis, but of most of the rest of the baseball-worshipping nation.

## 1946: St. Louis 4, Boston 3

For the first six games of the 1946 World Series, the Cardinals and the Red Sox alternated, from one game to the next, in winning. So when the crucial seventh game arrived in St. Louis on Tuesday, October 15, it seemed as if the long-striving Sox were finally destined to win a deciding contest. The sixth game had been won by St. Louis on Sunday, behind the slick pitching of a skinny southpaw, Harry Brecheen, from Broken Bow, Oklahoma. But it didn't work out for the Red Sox in the seventh game, due to the kinetic energy of Enos "Country" Slaughter, who had been hustling and bustling for the Cards since 1938, with time out for the military.

When the bottom of the eighth inning arrived, after the Sox had tied the score at 3–3 with two runs, Slaughter led off with a single against pitcher Bob Klinger, whom manager Joe Cronin was using for the first time in the Series. But when Whitey Kurowski failed to sacrifice successfully and Del Rice flied out meekly to Ted Williams in left field, it appeared the game would remain deadlocked. However, Harry "the Hat" Walker then hit the ball to left-center, where Leon Culberson—subbing for Dom DiMaggio, who had been injured earlier—was somewhat slow in making a play on the ball. Most in the park concluded that Walker had hit a routine single. But Slaughter rounded second base, as if he were being chased by the devil, and continued on his way to third. Still refusing to stop, he headed for home, running right through coach Mike Gonzales's stop sign at third. Culberson, meanwhile, threw to shortstop Johnny Pesky, who had his back to the play. For the slightest fraction of a second, Pesky hesitated before he threw home. That hesitation proved fatal: Slaughter slid across home plate with the go-ahead run, as catcher Roy Partee had moved slightly up the line to receive Pesky's tardy throw. Slaughter always had played that way—reckless abandon, some called it—and this time it paid off. The Red Sox tried hard to respond in the ninth inning, as Rudy York and Bobby Doerr opened with singles, but Brecheen, having won two days before as a starter, subdued the Sox in relief to win his third game of the Series. He became the first southpaw ever to win three Series games and the first pitcher to take three since Stan Coveleski of Cleveland beat Brooklyn three times in 1920. This Slaughter-induced defeat meant that the Sox had still not won a Series since 1918. Long after the dispirited Red Sox had departed from their clubhouse after the loss, Ted Williams, a .200 hitter with only one RBI in the Series, sat in front of his locker, a man obviously in misery. His iconic counterpart on the Cards, Stan Musial, didn't fare much better than Ted, with a .222 Series average. The difference was that Stan the Man was on the winning team.

A view of the St. Louis Cardinals deployed in the "Williams shift" during the second game of the 1946 World Series. Marty Marion is the shortstop, third baseman Whitey Kurowski is positioned just to the right of second base, and Red Schoendienst and Stan Musial are in their more or less usual spots. The shift may have had something to do with Williams's .200 average for the Series; the rest of the blame can be leveled at a sore right elbow suffered in a pre-Series workout.

Harry "Cookie" Lavagetto in the Dodgers' clubhouse, after his double in the ninth inning of the fourth game of the 1947 World Series ruined Yankee Bill Bevens's bid for a no-hitter and won the game for Brooklyn. The next day, Lavagetto again appeared as a pinch hitter in the ninth, but he was struck out by Frank Shea. "That three and two ball to Lavagetto was a belt-high fast one," Shea said. "He never saw it. Boy, that revenge was sweet!"

BELOW
Bill Bevens (left) is understandably deflated by Lavagetto's game breaker, as is Joe DiMaggio. To his credit, Bevens blamed himself as he endured the postgame interviews in the clubhouse. He acknowledged that any pitcher who gives up ten walks and a wild pitch in one game is living on borrowed time.

## 1947: Yankees 4, Dodgers 3

In 1947, Floyd Clifford "Bill" Bevens won only seven games, while losing thirteen, for the pennant-winning Yankees. He was also a fellow not known for saying very much. But as he went into the last inning of the fourth game of the 1947 Series against the Brooklyn Dodgers—the team of Jackie Robinson, Pee Wee Reese, Dixie Walker, and Pete Reiser—he was more quiet than usual, for he was nursing a no-hit (one-run) game. The dugout rule is not to talk about such an impending event. The curious aspect of Bevens's game was that he had walked eight men up to that point. Then odd things began to happen, as Bevens perched on the rim of the first no-hitter in Series history. Trailing by 2–1, down to their last licks, the Dodgers wrapped two outs around Bevens's ninth walk of the game, to Carl Furillo. At this juncture, manager Burt Shotton, the bespectacled old buddy of Branch Rickey, sent up the oft-injured Reiser to bat for pitcher Hugh Casey, as little Al Gionfriddo ran for Furillo. At once, Al lit out for second on a steal. He made it, helped by catcher Yogi Berra's poor throw. With first base open, Bucky Harris, the Yankees' manager, ordered Reiser to be walked. This defied baseball convention, which said you shouldn't ever put the winning run on base. Shotton put Eddie Miksis in as a pinch runner for Reiser. Then he sent right-handed batter Cookie Lavagetto up to bat for Eddie Stanky, also a righty hitter. It was a weird hunch that had the second-guessers in the stands shaking their heads. But within seconds, Cookie pounded a double off the right-field wall in Ebbets Field, as right fielder Tommy Henrich went chasing after the ball. Both Dodgers runners sped around the bases like frightened rabbits, and by the time Henrich retrieved the ball, Gionfriddo and Miksis were across the plate. A riotous scene then transpired as Dodgers fans, eluding the police, mobbed Lavagetto. Not only had Bevens lost his no-hitter, but the Dodgers had won, evening up the Series at two games all. It was Cookie's only hit of the Series, and some people with long memories insisted it was the only ball he'd hit to right field all year.

With their hopes high, the Dodgers went into the fifth game thinking that at last they had the Yankees on the run. But that wasn't to be their fate. On Saturday, October 4, Frank Shea pitched the Yankees to a 2–1 victory. Refusing to be pronounced dead, the Dodgers rallied to win the sixth game at Yankee Stadium before a mob of almost seventy-five thousand. After a long, grueling afternoon, the Dodgers emerged with an 8–6 victory. But it was scary for the Brooklyn team and fans, for in the sixth inning, with the Yankees trailing, 8–5, and two men on base, Joe DiMaggio hit a long fly to left field. It looked as if it was going to tie the score. But again it was the ubiquitous Gionfriddo, playing in left field, who raced and stumbled to the 415-foot mark and grabbed the ball as it was about to depart the premises. DiMaggio, who rarely showed any emotion on the field, kicked the dirt near second base, for once a victim of the same kind of defensive brilliance that he usually supplied. The next day, the Yankees defeated the Dodgers, 5–2, to take the Series, as Shotton employed five pitchers to no avail. DiMaggio hit two homers in the Series, although he batted only .231. But it was Bobby Brown, later to become a cardiologist, who wrote the most fascinating chapter. In four appearances as a pinch hitter, he never made out; he had two doubles, a single, and a walk. Only minutes after the Series ended, Larry MacPhail, president of the champion Yankees, retired from the game, induced, no doubt, by a few too many victory drinks.

## 1955: Dodgers 4, Yankees 3

It took a long time, but the Dodgers went to seven games with the Yankees again in 1955, and this time they beat them! It took a brilliant seventh-game pitching job by Johnny Podres to do the job. Although Podres gave up eight hits to a team that, by the way, was playing without the services of Mickey Mantle, he was tough when he needed to be. The end result was a 2–0 shutout, helped along by two runs batted in by Gil Hodges. (Remember, in the 1952 World Series against the Yankees, Hodges had gone to the plate twenty-one times without a hit!)

When it was all over, the New York press joined in the mass exultation in Brooklyn by headlining: "Next Year Is Here!" For years, the faithful in Brooklyn had had to salve their constant wounds by telling everybody, "Wait 'til next year." Now it had happened. However, only a few days before, it had looked as if the Dodgers would go down to defeat again, for the Yankees won the first two games at Yankee Stadium— and the record books stated that no team had ever rebounded in the Series under such circumstances. The Dodgers had watched their big twenty-game winner, Don Newcombe, falter in the opening game, and manager Walter Alston never brought him back. Instead, he relied on Podres, who won two games in the Series, and Clem Labine, who appeared in four games. In the fifth game, Roger Craig, a rookie, held the Yankees at bay to send the Dodgers ahead, three games to two. But the next afternoon, the great Yankee southpaw Whitey Ford tied the Series at three games all. That left it up to Podres, the twenty-three-year-old from Witherbee, New York, to turn back the Yankees in the climactic game.

In that seventh game, however, it was left up to Alston to make one of those last-second decisions that turned out to be the difference between success and failure. As the Dodgers nursed a 2–0 lead going into the last of the sixth inning, Alston moved Junior Gilliam from left field to second base and sent Sandy Amoros, a five-foot-seven, non-English-speaking Cuban, into left. There was then a prominent featherweight boxer named Sandy Saddler, and for some reason Amoros had inherited that nickname. At the time, nobody paid much attention to the fact that Amoros wore his glove on his right hand, since he threw with his left. There were two Yankees on base, and Amoros was pulled far toward center field, with southpaw hitter Yogi Berra coming to the plate. Yogi then picked on an outside pitch from Podres and sent the ball close to the left-field foul line. No way was Amoros going to catch that ball. But with his speed and his outstretched glove on his right hand, he seized the ball just inside fair territory. Both Yankee runners were tearing

around the bases. Gil McDougald, who had been on first base, had to reverse direction. A fine throw from Amoros to Pee Wee Reese, who then threw to Hodges at first base, doubled up McDougald. The astounding play by Amoros ended the Yankee hopes, for Podres kept them in check the rest of the way. To this day, Yogi doesn't see how Amoros caught that ball. Amoros, whose name has become etched in World Series lore, could only say, "I just run like hell." He might have added that he never would have caught the drive if his glove had been on his left hand.

## 1986: Mets 4, Red Sox 3

Bad things sometimes do happen to good people. Baseball is no exception. Take Bill Buckner of the Red Sox, for example. A good hitter, a good fielder, a good guy. But in a few seconds in the tenth inning of the sixth game of the 1986 Series, a ball slithered between Buckner's legs at first base. Thus, Buckner became a member of the Hall of Infamy, as he joined the Fred Merkles, Freddy Lindstroms, and Tony Kubeks of the world, all of them players victimized by balls that refused to be caught, or by a moment of forgetfulness. As the Red Sox were on the verge of finally winning a World Series, the world turned upside down again for them. And Buckner was forever the culprit. Mind you, Buckner had had a long and honorable baseball career. In 1980, he had led the National League in hitting, and he had played 162 games at first base for Boston in 1985, proving that even as a former outfielder, he had more than a little familiarity with that position. But when Mookie Wilson's grounder eluded Buckner's glove, the Mets scored the winning run, thus sending the unpredictable Series into a seventh game. Until that incident, the Mets had appeared to be doomed, for they entered the tenth inning two runs behind the Red Sox. When the first two Mets in that inning were retired, the fans started to pack up and go home. Even when Gary Carter singled, after two strikes, followed by pinch hitter Kevin Mitchell's single, it didn't look too promising for the fifty-five thousand fans in Shea Stadium. But when Ray Knight

Winning pitcher Johnny Podres said,
*"That catch by Amoros probably saved the game."*

The usually sure-handed Bill Buckner has just fumbled away the sixth game of the 1986 World Series. "I saw the ball well," he said. "It bounced and bounced, and then it didn't bounce. It just skipped. I can't remember the last time I missed a ball like that."

OPPOSITE
The Most Valuable Player of the 1986 World Series, Ray Knight (left), celebrating the last out of the seventh game with catcher Gary Carter. The Mets' victory was almost a foregone conclusion. Few teams would have recovered from the sort of calamity suffered by the Red Sox the night before.

singled, also with two strikes on him, the crowd got to its feet. The Red Sox then reached into their bull pen for Bob Stanley, to replace Calvin Schiraldi on the mound. All season long, Stanley had unleashed only one wild pitch. But as he faced Wilson, Stanley made it number two in that bleak department, allowing Mitchell to prance home with the tying run and moving Knight to second base. On the next pitch, Mookie, that most popular of all Mets, sent a ball in the direction of Buckner. Need we say more? Knight came home with the winning run, sending the Series to Game Seven. Boston commissioned Bruce Hurst to seek his third victory of the Series in the climactic game, trying to emulate such hurlers as Christy Mathewson, Lew Burdette, Mickey Lolich, Bob Gibson, and Harry Brecheen. Hurst's team even gave him an early three-run lead. But, haunted as always by the Curse of the Bambino, or by whatever strange chemistry it was that used to pervade Fenway Park, the Sox blew the lead by the end of the seventh inning. Knight, a key player in these games, and Darryl Strawberry hit homers to pace the winning Mets.

All of these events occurred after the Mets had opened the Series with two straight losses—the opener was a 1–0 defeat—and then had to travel to Fenway. But the Mets stayed alive by taking two out of three in Boston, setting the stage for the Buckner Bobble and then their victory in Game Seven. In commenting on this tumultuous Series, Tim McCarver, the Mets broadcaster, said he had never seen so many "crazed people pacing around," a reference to the near-hysterical Mets fans, as well as those watching in the broadcast booth and in the Nelson Doubleday Suite. When NBC's Joe Garagiola took his camera into the Red Sox locker room after the defeat, he said wisely, "Losing feels worse than winning feels good." The day after the Series ended, New York threw a ticker-tape parade for the Mets, a team that refused to die—thanks, in part, to the distressed Buckner.

*When NBC's Joe Garagiola took his camera into the Red Sox locker room after the defeat, he said wisely, "Losing feels worse than winning feels good."* THE DAY AFTER, NEW YORK THREW A TICKER-TAPE PARADE FOR THE METS, *a team that refused to die*.

# 7. *The* GREATEST TEAMS

# "These Yankees," SAID MCGRAW,
## "would have wiped the streets with us."

Before the first game of the 1927 World Series, Babe Ruth and Lou Gehrig posed with
Lloyd "Little Poison" Waner and his brother Paul, who was nicknamed "Big Poison."
Neither was poisonous enough to deter the Yankees. The Bombers flattened the
Pirates in four straight games. "They'd murder you with a smile," a New York reporter
wrote, summarizing the 1927 season.

## New York Yankees: 1927

They were the team that dominated the Roaring Twenties, a time that some chose to call the Era of Wonderful Nonsense. They were admiringly called many flattering names. But one rude name, Murderers' Row, seems to have stuck like glue to them. It appears that several killers at Sing Sing were awaiting execution at the time, so the team of Babe Ruth, Lou Gehrig, Bob Meusel, Tony Lazzeri, and Earle Combs was named after them. They were also the team of "the Window-Breakers," and since they had a penchant for late-inning rallies, just as the sun went down, they also became known as the team of "Five O'Clock Lightning." They were also the team generally voted, by one generation of baseball fans after another, as the greatest collection of baseball talent ever assembled. It didn't matter that these voters had not seen these Yankees play; they had heard and read of their exploits, and that was enough for such anointment. They were also the first baseball team that I ever saw, as a little boy. I was much taken with the shy and dogged Lou Gehrig and with the slender and aristocratic southpaw Herb Pennock. I gloried in Ruth's cloud-high home runs, though, I must confess, I preferred the introverted Lou to the flamboyant Babe. In 1927, the Yankees leapfrogged over second-place Philadelphia, a team so loaded with .300 hitters it even had three of them on the bench. At the end, the Yankees won by 19 games, with 110 wins, an American League record at the time. Ruth's sixty homers that year were more than any other *team* in the American League had, while Gehrig's forty-seven homers were more than four other teams achieved. Ruth, Gehrig, Meusel, Lazzeri—the heart of the lineup—each batted in more than 100 runs, with Gehrig having 175. Even today the words "1927 Yankees" evoke frissons of delight from those who know of this team only from the storybooks. Were they overrated? Hell, no! They had everything—sluggers, contact hitters, splendid defense, pitchers with chintzy ERAs, a wily midget-sized manager, Miller Huggins, and the best leadoff hitter in the game in Combs.

PAGE 177

It takes more than home-run brawn to create a championship team; a reliable defense is also required. Pictured here from left to right are first baseman Lou Gehrig, second baseman Tony Lazzeri, shortstop Mark Koenig, and Joe Dugan, who played third base. They were joined by a pitching staff that numbered six hurlers with ten or more wins each. The Yanks won the 1927 pennant by nineteen games.

Perhaps their only weakness was the catching staff, with three guys nobody ever remembers. One of them was Benny Bengough, whom Ruth playfully called "Barney Google," after the comic strip of the time. In 1927, as Waite Hoyt, a wonderful right-handed pitcher on that team, recalled, "we took first place on the second day of the season and held it for the rest of the way. There was no mystic force working. It was simply a perfect, dynamic machine. . . . Occasionally one team becomes sort of a freak outfit, or is able to perform beyond all conception of normal thinking. The '27 Yankees were like that." Take it from an old grouch like John McGraw, who grew up in the Baltimore Orioles tradition, and who happens to agree with Hoyt. "These Yankees," said McGraw, "would have wiped the streets with us." They probably would have done the same thing against any other team in history, including many Yankee teams that came after 1927.

## Philadelphia Athletics: 1911

Of all the teams—good and bad—that Connie Mack managed, it was said that he favored his 1911 crew over all the others. They were world champions that year, defeating John McGraw's Giants in six games, despite the presence in the Giants lineup of Christy Mathewson. In the 1905 Series, Matty had beaten the Athletics three times in six days, shutting them out each time. But the 1911 A's were a totally different ball club. For one thing, they featured their heralded "$100,000 Infield," embracing the skills of Stuffy McInnis at first base, Eddie Collins at second base, Jack Barry at shortstop, and Frank "Home Run" Baker at third base. Mr. Mack had often said about this foursome that "I wouldn't sell them for $100,000." Thus, they were known far and wide by Connie's financial estimate. In those simpler times, of course, $100,000 was indeed a bundle of bucks. Within a few years, however, the Athletics sold off all of that prized infield, except McInnis, for sums as high as $50,000 (for Collins), thus supporting Connie's estimate.

This 1911 club was truly the first great team in American League history, comparing

[MR. MACK] HAD THE SHREWDNESS AND ENERGY TO PUT TOGETHER, AS HE SAID, *"a team that had everything, including pitching, hitting, brains, defense, speed, desire."*

favorably with several of Mr. Mack's future aggregations. In that year, Mr. Mack (he was always known as Mr. Mack to his players, a singular mark of respect in that era) was nearly fifty, and in the prime of his managerial life. He had the shrewdness and energy to put together, as he said, "a team that had everything, including pitching, hitting, brains, defense, speed, desire." Always partial to players with an ability to think, Connie had recruited many collegians. Collins had played quarterback at Columbia University, and the pitching staff was led by Jack Coombs, a right-hander who had gone to Colby College. In 1911, Coombs won 28 games, after winning 31 in 1910. Eddie Plank, a southpaw out of Gettysburg College, had a record of 23–8 in 1911. The other part of Connie's pitching brain trust was Charles "Chief" Bender, a Chippewa Indian, who had attended the Carlisle Indian School. Jack Barry had gone to Holy Cross, and some lesser members of the team had also been exposed to higher education, certifying that this was the best-educated team in the pre–World War I era. In 1911, Home Run Baker matched the year with eleven homers, enough to lead the league. Imagine that! One of the remarkable feats of this club was that this was the first American League outfit to beat another team—the St. Louis Browns—twenty times during the season. Ultimately, Collins, Plank, Bender, and Baker made it to the Hall of Fame, joining their mentor, Mr. Mack. This team was also effective in another respect: it led the league in attendance, playing in a new stadium, Shibe Park.

## New York Yankees: 1998

If the 1927 Yankees topped all other Yankee teams, the Yankee club of 1998 still must be rated close to them. Daniel Okrent, the artful creator of the Rotisserie League, has asserted that the 1998 bunch "came as close to baseball perfection as anyone under 70 has seen." After the disappointment of 1997, when the Yankees were eliminated by Cleveland, still another omnipotent Yankee team emerged in the following season. This time, manager Joe Torre

Charles Albert "Chief" Bender won seventeen games for the Athletics in 1911, and he recorded a 2.16 earned run average, which was something of a letdown after three consecutive years in which his ERA never rose above 1.75. Teammates and opposing players alike regarded Bender as an unyielding competitor—as well as one of the nicest men in the game.

OPPOSITE
Seen here are three members of the Philadelphia Athletics' "$100,000 Infield": Frank "Home Run" Baker (left), the third baseman; Stuffy McInnis, who played first base; and shortstop Jack Barry (right). Between Barry and McInnis is Danny Murphy, the right fielder. Eddie Collins, the star second baseman, is not present. Baker earned his nickname on the strength of two home runs hit against the New York Giants in the 1911 World Series: one off Rube Marquard, and the other at the expense of Christy Mathewson.

On opening day at home in 1998, the Yankees were matched against the Oakland Athletics in an untidy slugfest eventually won by the New Yorkers, 17–13. First baseman
Tino Martinez is seen here crossing the plate after hitting a three-run homer in the
third inning. Darryl Strawberry is congratulating Tino, while Paul O'Neill (left) and
Bernie Williams, the base runners who scored on the home run, join the parade.

OPPOSITE
Unlikely heroes often emerge in World Series play, and Scott Brosius, a solid but
unspectacular player, added his name to the list in the 1998 Series against the San
Diego Padres. He is seen here celebrating his eighth-inning home run in the third game
of the set, hit off the Padres' superb reliever Trevor Hoffman. Brosius was named the
Series MVP after the Yankees' sweep.

led the 1998 team to a runaway flag and a World Series triumph, followed by similar victories in 1999 and 2000. In those three Series victories, Torre's men beat San Diego (in 1998), Atlanta, and the New York Mets, losing only one game in the process. It was the type of total demolition that had been previously matched only by the teams of Babe and Lou, and DiMaggio and Mickey. By the start of 1998, the youthful Brian Cashman was named general manager, following in the footsteps of such worthies as Ed Barrow and George Weiss. Cashman made some fine pickups, including third baseman Scott Brosius (whom Oakland was happy to part with) and second baseman Chuck Knoblauch of Minnesota. A further stabilizing influence was the signing of the popular veteran Chili Davis. However, the most touted addition was Orlando "El Duque" Hernandez, who had boated over from Cuba. These men supplemented a lineup that already boasted future Hall of Fame shortstop Derek Jeter; clutch right fielder Paul O'Neill; dependable center fielder Bernie Williams; first baseman Tino Martinez; and catching star of the future Jorge Posada. All of these hitters paid close attention at the plate, running into long counts, tiring out enemy pitchers, and intelligently choosing the right pitch to hit. As for hurling, David Cone, owner of the Laredo pitch, had a fine season (possibly his best) but it was the bulky southpaw David Wells—who worshipped at the altar of Babe Ruth—who threw the second perfect game in Yankee history, against Minnesota on May 17 at Yankee Stadium. Oddly, this magic season began with three consecutive Yankee defeats, giving Mr. Steinbrenner early tremors. But from then on, the team was close to unbeatable. By season's end, the Yankees had won 114 games, the runners-up only to the Chicago Cubs of 1906, who won 116 games. The Yankees finished 66 games over .500 and 22 games ahead of the usual suspects from Boston. This was the widest margin in Yankee history. In the postseason, the Yankees won seven straight games, with the surprising Brosius being acclaimed as World Series Most Valuable Player.

George Livingston "Moose" Earnshaw, at six-foot-four and 210 pounds, was aptly nicknamed. His 24–8 record in 1929 was the best in the majors, and in the World Series he recorded a win and struck out seventeen Cubs in thirteen-plus innings. When Bob Feller introduced himself seven years later, many compared his rocketing fastball with Earnshaw's.

OPPOSITE
The middle of the Athletics' 1929 lineup featured these smiling sluggers (left to right): Jimmie Foxx, Al Simmons, and Mickey Cochrane. Together they accounted for 370 runs batted in that season. Francis Stann, a writer for the *Washington Star*, thought Foxx was the most powerful slugger in baseball history. "A baseball never came off anybody's bat like it did off Jimmie's," he wrote. "Foxx put 'em into the seats like they'd been shot out of a cannon."

FRANCIS STANN *thought*
*Foxx was the most powerful slugger:*
*"[He] put 'em into the seats like*
*they'd been shot out of a cannon."*

### Philadelphia Athletics: 1929

It shouldn't surprise anyone to learn that many observers would place their money on the Athletics of 1929 as the world-class team of all time. From the muscled slugger Jimmie Foxx, who has remained something of a forgotten man among home-run hitters, to southpaw Robert Moses "Lefty" Grove, the choice of many as the best lefty of all time, this was a team that seemed to have everything. Yes, they had a journeyman shortstop, Joe Boley. But Boley teamed up with Max Bishop, the second baseman, who led the league in bases on balls in 1929, with 128. At every other position, they could compete with anyone in the universe. As a matter of fact, they had already competed successfully with the great Yankees of the late 1920s. For instance, in 1928, going up against a Yankee team that was essentially a carbon copy of the 1927 Yankees, they put on a late-season rush that brought them to within two and a half games of the New Yorkers. Manager Miller Huggins of the Yankees said at the time that he was happy the season ended when it did, for he feared that Mr. Mack's team might have caught his club. However, in 1929 the Athletics didn't wait until the end. They had momentum from the start and ended with 104 wins. By July, the A's were nine games in front of the Yankees. Ultimately, they beat Huggins's team in fourteen out of twenty-two games. That was proof positive that this was a great aggregation, one of the best ever to play the game. In addition to Foxx, the A's featured Al Simmons (real name: Szymanski), the man who batted with his foot in the bucket, and Gordon Stanley "Mickey" Cochrane, the sparkplug catcher, who handled the irascible Grove as well as the twenty-four-game winner, right-hander George Earnshaw. Left-hander Rube Walberg, who won eighteen games, rounded out the superb pitching corps. These pitchers helped to compile the stingiest number of runs yielded in the American League. And talking of stingy records, Bing Miller, the A's underrated outfielder, struck out only sixty-seven times in three seasons, starting in 1929. Mack, always partial to college-bred players (Cochrane came from Boston University and Earnshaw from Swarthmore), was also

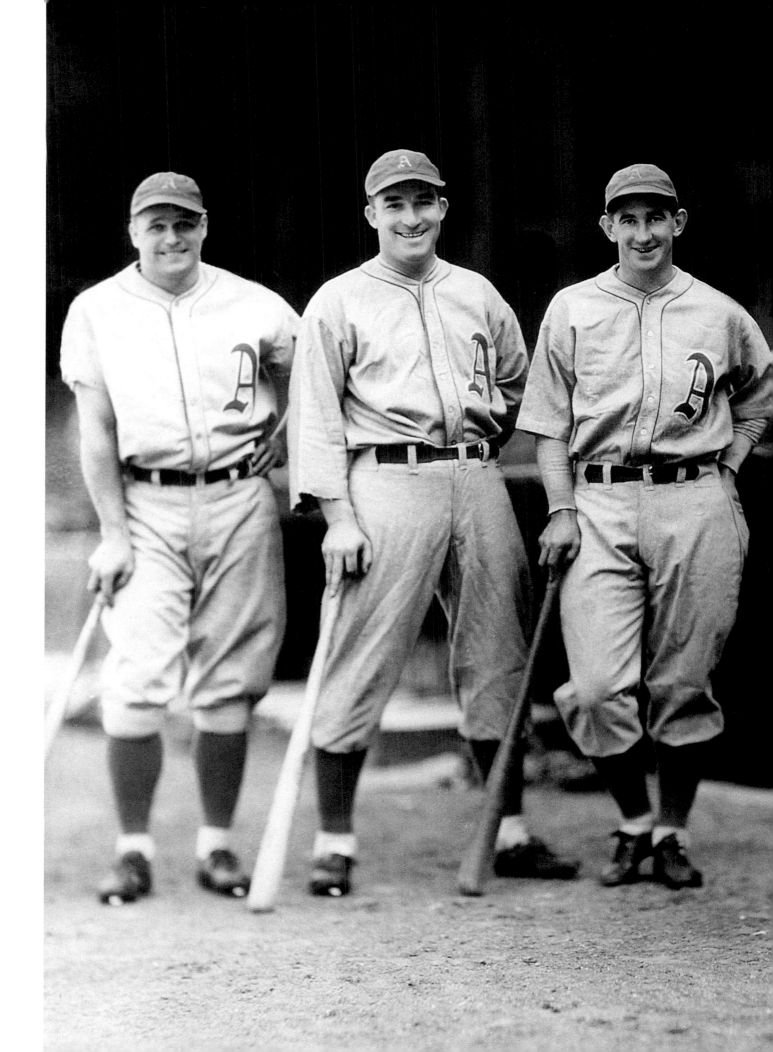

partial to large pitchers. Earnshaw was six-foot-four, Grove was not much smaller, and Walberg measured six-foot-one. In those days, those were surprisingly high numbers. Even while showing a preference for tall pitchers, Mr. Mack still had trouble remembering their names correctly. When this truly awesome A's team broke open the 1929 World Series with their onslaught in the fourth game, Jimmie Dykes, who played third base for that club and succeeded Mack as manager in 1951, said that with the lineup the A's had, "we were never out of a game." But the usually dour Grove was even more quotable about his fellow players. After they had clobbered the Cubs in 1929, he grunted, "Some team we got, huh?" And who could disagree with him?

### New York Yankees: 1939

As the 1939 season approached, it became evident that something was wrong with the Yankees' Iron Horse, Lou Gehrig. During the creeping mystery of the 1938 summer, Lou's production had fallen off. In the World Series that fall, he had hit only four singles. After going hitless five times in the first eight games of 1939, Lou went to manager Joe McCarthy and told him he was hurting the team and was going to bench himself. His consecutive game streak had reached 2,130 games—and that's the way it would end. By June, he discovered he was suffering from amyotrophic lateral sclerosis (ALS), an incurable disease (later it would also become known as Lou Gehrig's disease). A month later, on July 4, at Yankee Stadium, Lou made his famous farewell speech. Two years after that, not yet thirty-eight, he was dead. But even with Gehrig gone, the Yankees were a dynamic wrecking crew of a team. Babe Dahlgren had replaced Gehrig at first base—and he was certainly no Gehrig. But the others in the infield—Frankie Crosetti, leadoff batter and shortstop; Joe Gordon at second base; and Red Rolfe at third base—were all fine players and rarely needed to take a day off. The outfield, with the newcomer Charlie "King Kong" Keller joining George "Twinkletoes" Selkirk and Joe DiMaggio, was a tower of strength,

On September 21, 1939, the day this picture was taken, (left to right) Bill Dickey was hitting .304, Joe DiMaggio was at .389, Charlie Keller was at .331, and George Selkirk was batting .309. Keller, playing in his rookie season, ended his year at .334. He had been one of the standouts on the fabled 1937 Newark Bears team, which won the International League pennant by twenty-five and a half games.

"THEY WERE BETTER THAN THE '27 TEAM," *[Barrow] insisted.*
*Since he had also built the 1927 team, he should have known*
*what he was talking about.*

A duo of Hall of Famers: Lefty Gomez (left) and Red Ruffing. Gomez's best years were
behind him in 1939, but Ruffing won twenty-one games that season. Manager Joe
McCarthy said that Gomez and Ruffing were two of the three best pitchers he'd ever
managed. The third was Spud Chandler.

while Gehrig's former roommate Bill Dickey
was still the best catcher in the American
League. The pitchers, led by Red Ruffing (also
a premier pinch hitter), Lefty Gomez, Monte
Pearson, Bump Hadley, Atley Donald, and bull
pen master Johnny Murphy, rarely gave anything away. As the teams went into June, the
Yankees had amassed a long lead, and although
the Red Sox did later take five straight games
from them, the Yankees' supremacy was never
in doubt. They won 106 games at the finish.
The Yankees were first in runs scored, and
there was a compelling footnote to this fact: the
1939 team was the only team in the twentieth
century to outscore its opponents by more than
four hundred runs. 'Nuff said. When the
All-Star Game was played in July, at Yankee
Stadium, McCarthy was not shy about choosing
six of his men, including Ruffing, for the starting American League lineup. DiMaggio hit a
homer, and the American League—or you
might choose to call them the Yankees—won,
3–1. It was an augury of things to come in the
World Series, when the Yankees thrashed the
Cincinnati Reds in four straight, even though
the Reds had two pitchers, Bucky Walters and
Paul Derringer, who had won 52 games between
them. Keller, who bashed three home runs, was
especially annoying to the Reds. By taking the
Reds into camp, the Yankees became the first
team ever to win four straight world titles. Ed
Barrow, the general manager who presided over
the building of this team, made no bones about
how he rated this club. "They were better than
the '27 team," he insisted. Since he had also
built the 1927 team, he should have known
what he was talking about. However, one might
point to one major difference between the two
teams: the 1927 team had Earle Combs as leadoff batter. In that year, Combs had 231 hits and
23 triples, leading the league in each department. Crosetti didn't compare with him.

## St. Louis Cardinals: 1942
They weren't the Cardinals of Pepper Martin
and the Dean brothers. But they may have been
far better than the colorful Gashouse Gang of
1934. In assessing the Cardinals of 1942, the

first wartime baseball champs, author Tom
Meany wrote that "this group was a typical
Branch Rickey team—young, fast and well-
behaved." But Meany seemed to overlook
another facet of this club: they could play
like the devil, and they never gave up. That
year, the Brooklyn Dodgers, fresh off their
pennant victory of 1941, fought this Cards team
down to the wire in one of the most fascinating
National League races for the storybooks. In
early August, the Dodgers were ten and a half
games up on the Cards, causing "the Peepul's
Cherce," Dodgers outfielder Dixie Walker, to
bet Dodgers general manager Larry MacPhail
that the "Brooks" were going to win by at least
eight games. But MacPhail was an astute judge
of pennant races. Sniffing the air, he sensed
that something was up in St. Louis, something
relentless and defiant. As the final weeks of the
flag battle went by, the Cards inched up on the
Dodgers, aided by five wins in six games against
Brooklyn. Finally, by winning 43 of their last
51 games, the onrushing Cards nosed out the
disbelieving Dodgers. They had won 106 games,
while runner-up Brooklyn won 104 times. Both
totals were highly unusual. In 1909, Pittsburgh
won 110 games, which remains the highest
in the National League, despite the challenge
from St. Louis. However, the distraught Dodgers'
victory total was the highest ever for a second-
place team. Oddly, these Cards were not a
bunch of long-distance hitters. Long-distance
runners they were, but there were no Ruths or
Mel Otts among them. Country Slaughter's
thirteen home runs was the top figure on the
Cards. Slaughter was one-third of one of the
most versatile outfields in history. He played
with Stan "the Man" Musial and Terry Moore,
who ranks up there with Willie Mays as one of
the best defensive center fielders of all time.
Musial was then in the second year of his Hall
of Fame career. The Cards shortstop, Marty
Marion, at six-foot-three, defied the shortstop
stereotype; you were supposed to be no bigger
than the five-foot-five Rabbit Maranville. Marion
led the league with thirty-eight doubles. At first
base, Johnny Hopp shared time with Ray
Sanders. They replaced moon-faced Johnny

*In assessing the Cardinals of 1942, the first wartime baseball champs, author* TOM MEANY WROTE *that "this group was a typical Branch Rickey team—young, fast and well-behaved."*

Mize, who had taken his home-run bat to the Giants. Walker Cooper, the catcher, formed a battery of brothers with right-hander Mort Cooper. Mort's associates on the mound were Johnny Beazley, who won twenty-one games, and southpaw Max Lanier. At twenty-one, Howie Pollet was just getting started. Later he became the typical "stylish southpaw." As a group, the Cards pitchers turned in fourteen shutouts and were almost invincible in one-run games. What was the secret of this most under-rated team of all time? No joke about it, but it probably thrived on hunger, desire, and a need to win. As a whole, the team probably didn't earn more than $225,000 a year, with players like Slaughter receiving about $600 a month for playing baseball as if his life depended on it. In the World Series that fall, the Cards took four out of five from the astonished Yankees, as third baseman Whitey Kurowski locked it up in the ninth inning of Game Five at Yankee Sta-dium with a two-run homer off Red Ruffing. The Yankees, considered unbeatable, were astounded at manager Bill Southworth's upstart Cards. They shouldn't have been. The Cards had led their league in practically every-thing in 1942, including the lowest pay.

## Chicago Cubs: 1906

Who was Harry Steinfeldt? He was the third baseman who missed getting into Franklin P. Adams's little poetic vision of Tinker-to-Evers-to-Chance. The funny part about it is that Harry batted higher than all of the other Cubs in the poem. In 1906, as the Chicago Cubs rolled up 116 victories against 36 defeats (a mark that has been the target of every pennant winner since that year), Harry batted .327, trailing only Honus Wagner, who led the league. Yes, Unknown Harry was plenty good. On the other hand, the Joe Tinker–Johnny Evers–Frank Chance trio may also have been deserving of FPA's tribute, even if in recent times the revi-sionists have been at work trying to diminish their reputations. However, there has been no need to diminish the reputation of the 1906 Cubs, for they were one of the first grand teams. The fact that they lost the World

Series in 1906 to Charles Comiskey's "Hitless Wonders"—the across-the-road Chicago White Sox—doesn't really detract from the greatness of that Cubs club. The Cubs led the league in batting, and their pitching staff, featuring Mordecai "Three-Finger" Brown, Ed Reulbach, Orvie Overall, and Jack Pfiester, was so skilled that it was able to knock off Christy Mathewson and his New York Giants. These Cubs hurlers also had the good fortune to throw into the mitt of catcher Johnny Kling, who was often said to be the biggest brain in Chicago. The outfield was also first-rate, including Frank Schulte, Jimmy Sheckard, Jimmy Slagle, and Solly Hof-man. Coming back to the immortalized Tinker-Evers-Chance, it happens to be the case that they did *not* lead the league in double plays— but that may have had something to do with the pitching staff, which produced its share of strikeouts. That the trio did operate with marvelous precision is beyond dispute. But it becomes even more remarkable when we learn that the more composed Tinker rarely spoke to the gabby, querulous Evers off the field. The best batter of the three men was Chance, who was also the manager of the team. One doesn't get to be called "the Peerless Leader" for noth-ing. That's the way Chance was constantly referred to by friend and foe alike. Chance's guidance helped the Cubs to go 56–21 at home and 60–15 on the road. By continuing to win in 1907 and 1908, the Cubs supported the theory that Chance was indispensable to the fortunes of this team. A fine defensive first baseman, Chance also stole a league-leading fifty-seven bases in 1906. Seven Cubs that year followed Chance's example by stealing more than twenty-five bases each. However, it was the pitching that made the Cubs almost unbeatable. Since relief pitching was basically unknown in those days, the Cubs pitchers finished what they started. Brown, the man who had lost a section of his index finger on his right hand, won 26, while losing 6. Many believed he was the pre-mier pitcher of the decade. In face-to-face confrontations with Matty, he usually came out on top. Reulbach posted a 19–4 mark, and Pfiester was 20–8. Those eight losses were the

The 1906 Cubs. Harry Steinfeldt is the third player in from the left in the middle row. Joe Tinker is on the ground on the far right, Johnny Evers is sitting one player away, and Frank Chance is placed right behind Evers. Before the World Series began, Chance said to a reporter, "We expect to win easy, for we took four out of five from the White Sox last fall, and we are stronger this year by far than we were last fall."

*One doesn't get to be called "the Peerless Leader" for nothing. That's the way* CHANCE *was constantly referred to by friend and foe alike.*

most of any pitcher on the team! Many future Yankee teams spread-eagled the field, but these Cubs won 55 games and lost only 10 from July 22 to the end of the season. No Yankee team had ever done as well in crushing the opposition. Would the performance of the 1906 Cubs have been any different if the team had played in Wrigley Field (which opened in 1916) instead of West Side Park? We'll never know.

## Baltimore Orioles: 1969

Earl Weaver, the feisty manager of the Baltimore Orioles in their halcyon years in the late 1960s and early 1970s, once told Jim Palmer, his handsome right-hander, that he didn't care what dirty names people called him. "But," he warned, "don't ever call me insecure!" Now, how could Weaver ever have been insecure with the talent around him on the 1969 Orioles? The Orioles of that year were so good that they finished 19 games ahead of runner-up Detroit as they won 109 games. The 1969 Orioles were the first of three consecutive winners that Weaver produced. Each time, the Orioles won more than 100 games, making Weaver look like a genius. What made him a genius was an assemblage of pitching talent and hitters, plus one of the truly great defensive third basemen of all time in Brooks Robinson. But, for a moment, let's look at the *other* Robinson on this team. That was Frank, who had come over to Baltimore in 1965 in a trade that must go down as one of the worst of all time for the Cincinnati Reds. The rumor at the time was that Robinson was "an old thirty." But others felt that the subtext was that Robinson was an "uppity black." This uppity black not only won the MVP and Triple Crown in his first year with Baltimore, but in 1969 he came up with 100 RBIs, thirty-two home runs, and a .308 average. One aspect of Frank's overall game was his striking ability to run bases and break up potential double plays. He played without fear, and that's the kind of competitor Weaver relished.

Another Oriole who contributed mightily in 1969 was the massive first baseman John "Boog" Powell, who, like so many others on the team, had emerged from the Orioles farm

Second baseman Johnny Evers, nicknamed "the Crab," more for his disposition than his locomotion, freely admitted his dislike for shortstop Joe Tinker. "Tinker and myself hated each other," he said, "but we loved the Cubs. We wouldn't fight for each other, but we'd come close to killing people for our team. That was one of the answers to the Cubs' success."

OVERLEAF ABOVE
Brooks and Frank Robinson, posing at Yankee Stadium in 1966, the year Frank won the Triple Crown and MVP Award. Brooks was a magician at third base, but he felt he was less accomplished as a hitter. "I could field as long as I can remember," he said, "but hitting has been a struggle all of my life." This was modest indeed coming from a man who averaged .330 over the course of thirty-nine postseason games.

OVERLEAF BELOW
The aces of the Orioles' 1969 pitching staff (left to right): Dave McNally, Jim Palmer, and Mike Cuellar. Their skills notwithstanding, the Orioles managed to lose the World Series that year to the New York Mets. Asked to explain the upset, Baltimore manager Earl Weaver said after the final game, "You got to give the other man his chance at bat. This is why this is the greatest game of them all."

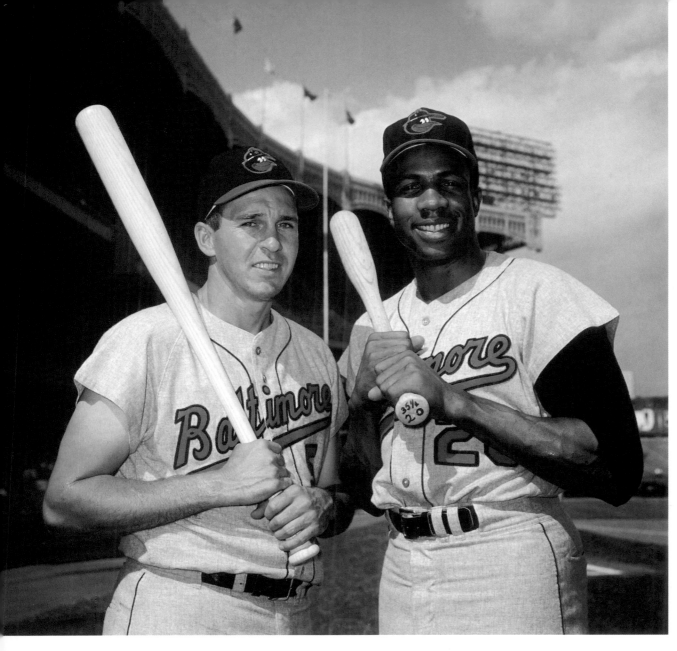

system. Batting behind Robinson, Boog, a perennial favorite in Baltimore, hit thirty-seven homers and knocked in 121 runs. Weaver had often said that his main strategy was "the three-run home run." He must have had Frank and Boog in mind. The other members of the Orioles cast—second baseman Davey Johnson (later the manager of the New York Mets) and shortstop Mark Belanger—rounded out a tight inner defense. Belanger invariably won the Gold Glove at his position. He also invariably batted in the low .200s. In 1969, however, he hit .287, a remarkable high for him. Teaming with Brooks Robinson on the left side of the infield, Belanger made certain that Oriole pitchers didn't suffer when ground balls were hit. Then there were those pitchers! Mark Cuellar, Dave McNally, and Jim Palmer, the latter returning from tendonitis in the shoulder and arm, were the best in the majors. Palmer won sixteen games—but lost only four times—while McNally was so effective that he didn't lose a game until the first week in August. Cuellar also won twenty-three games. In each of the pennant-winning seasons—1969, 1970, 1971—these three hurlers won twenty or more games (with Palmer the exception in 1969). Despite such a monopoly of batting and pitching talent, the Orioles lost to the "Miracle Mets" in the 1969 World Series, a shocking result that compared with the Cubs' 1906 loss to the Hitless Wonders. However, the next year, Baltimore beat Cincinnati in the Series. Which Baltimore club was better, the 1969 version or the 1970 version? Call Earl Weaver, and see what he thinks.

## Brooklyn Dodgers: 1955

Once upon a time, the Brooklyn Dodgers were regarded as clowns—they doubled into triple plays (so legend insists); they dropped third strikes that cost them World Series games; their outfielders fielded balls with the top of their heads (so legend also insists); they had a crazed player assault an airplane pilot and get himself murdered; and they had a pitcher with the unforgettably euphonious name of Van Lingle Mungo. But the Dodgers of 1955 were determined to erase that image of buffoonery

for all time. The '55ers were chock-full of stars—from the deft-fielding first baseman Gil Hodges to Pee Wee Reese (the team captain) at shortstop and Jackie Robinson at third base. Their outfield was headed by the smooth-swinging Duke Snider in center field (this fellow was always in the middle of every argument about which center fielder was better: Mays, Mantle, or the Duke?) and the hard-throwing right fielder Carl Furillo, a protector of the famous Abe Stark clothing sign. Behind the plate was the deceptively roly-poly Roy Campanella, who in 1955 had a year good enough to earn him the MVP. Campy's pitcher confederate, big Don Newcombe, went 20–5 with an ERA of 3.20. Often chastised for a supposed inability to win big games, Newk *was* a big-game pitcher. Fifty years ago, some mean-spirited and ignorant fans were still buying into the notion that black pitchers couldn't pitch in the clutch. Even today there are those, such as Rush Limbaugh, who have questioned the intestinal fortitude of black quarterbacks. So much for progress. Newk also qualified as one of the best-hitting pitchers in history, certainly as good as Red Ruffing, Red Lucas, Wes Ferrell, Bob Lemon, and Schoolboy Rowe. In fact, Newk even stole home in one game, proving that he was also alert underneath that enormous (six-foot-four, 230-pound) body. This team began the year with ten straight victories (a record at the time), then went to 22–2. The pennant race, such as it was, literally disappeared by July. Although the Dodgers ultimately won only ninety-eight games, they were never in trouble, and they remained in first place for 166 of 167 days. The Dodgers of the 1950s gained acclaim as the "Boys of Summer" club, but because the 1955 team scored the most runs, while giving up the fewest (and also banged out the most home runs), it must rate as the best of those Dodgers teams.

Ironically, although Jackie Robinson was once again an integral part of this team, by 1955 he was no longer the hard-charging, relentless performer that he'd been only a couple of years before. Now he was thirty-six years old, and the added weight on his body

hampered his speed. He had also been switched to third base, once the province of Billy Cox, leaving second base to Junior Gilliam and Don Zimmer (who didn't have Joe Torre sitting next to him in the dugout in those days). But if Jackie had retreated into baseball "old age," he was still a force on that wonderful Dodgers team. What made these Dodgers even more beloved in Brooklyn, just two years before they pulled up stakes and departed for the West Coast, was that they knocked off the hated Yankees in the World Series, with the help of a lefty named Johnny Podres. Incidentally, another lefty, the nineteen-year-old Sandy Koufax, still wild as a hornet, was on that Dodgers team. He contributed little that season—two wins—but soon he became great—in California. By that time, however, most of these '55ers had gone the way of all baseball flesh.

### Cincinnati Reds: 1976

When I was growing up in New York City, for some unfathomable reason I loved the Cincinnati Reds of 1939 and 1940. It's not easy to know why a kid becomes infatuated with a team, especially when that team is from out of town. But I did love that Reds team of Paul Derringer, Bucky Walters, Ival Goodman, Wally Berger, and Ernie "Schnozzola" Lombardi. I think that Lombardi could hit a baseball harder than any man that ever lived, so maybe that was one of the reasons I was so attracted to the Reds. Many years later—in the 1970s—Cincinnati developed a far better team than those Reds of 1939 and 1940. But by this time I had learned where Cincinnati was, and I stopped rooting for them. Go figure such preposterous reactions. That's what makes baseball such an idiosyncratic pastime. But let me tell you, that Reds team of 1976, which is more easily identified as "the Big Red Machine," was worthy of anyone's support. It may even have been one of the most efficient baseball juggernauts ever put together, and that includes the widely hailed Yankees of 1927. In 1976, the Reds finished ten games ahead of the Los Angeles Dodgers in the Western Division of the National League. Then they

*The Dodgers* OF THE 1950s *gained acclaim as the* "Boys of Summer" *club.*

walloped the Phillies three straight in the Championship Series. When they followed up by belting the Yankees four straight in the World Series, you might say that they established their credentials most emphatically. Indeed, the reason one would pick the 1976 Reds over the 1975 version of the Reds is that they became the first National League team to win two straight World Series since the Giants did it back in 1921 and 1922. This Reds team was headed up by Johnny Bench, a crushing catcher, who belongs on any all-time squad of receivers. In the World Series, he was devastating, as he batted .533, with two homers, a triple, and a double. Many, including me, would argue that little (five-foot-seven) Joe Morgan, who has become a first-rate broadcaster, might have been one of the best all-around second basemen in history. In 1976, he won the Most Valuable Player Award for the second straight year, beating out a number of his own teammates who might have also had a claim on the award. Some have complained that Joe wasn't as competent in the field as some other greats. But his qualities of leadership and inspiration— yes, these intangibles do count in the mix— made up for any deficiencies. In 1976, Joe hit .320 and drew 114 walks, seeming to be on base eternally. Underrated Davey Concepcion was at shortstop; he had gone from being a mediocre hitter to having a .281 average in 1976. At third base was the prolific switch-hitting Pete Rose, who, like Morgan, was a master at reaching base. Even when he walked, Rose ran to first, which is another positive thing you can say about this embattled figure. Others in that lineup, which led both leagues in most phases of hitting, including runs, homers, triples, and doubles, included George Foster, the outfielder, who hit twenty-nine homers; Ken Griffey (more famous now for being the daddy of Ken Junior), who just missed winning the batting title with a .336 mark; Cesar Geronimo, a good defensive outfielder, who wound up batting .307; and first baseman Tony Perez, with his ninety-one runs batted in. If there was one department in which this team did not have a top star, it was the pitching staff. Manager Sparky Anderson had

Gary Nolan, Don Gullett (injuries hurt what could have been a brilliant career for him), and Pat Zachry as his main starters. None of them were big winners. But they had a hard time losing with such a powerful array of hitters working for them. Anderson relied heavily on his bull pen, and particularly on Rawly Eastwick, a right-hander, who responded to Sparky's quick-yank system. This was a team with its share of Hall of Famers, including Bench and Morgan and, of course, waiting in the wings, still running (as he always did) for the job, Pete Rose.

BENCH WAS THE CINCINNATI COLOSSUS IN THE FOUR-GAME SWEEP. *"I hadn't done it for the club all year,"* HE SAID. *"It was my time to help."*

"The Big Red Machine," lining up prior to the final game of the 1976 World Series against the Yankees. Manager Sparky Anderson is at the far left, and the players closest to him are (left to right) Pete Rose, Ken Griffey, Joe Morgan, Tony Perez, Dan Driessen, George Foster, Johnny Bench, Cesar Geronimo, and Dave Concepcion. Bench was the Cincinnati colossus in the four-game sweep. "I hadn't done it for the club all year," he said. "It was my time to help."

# 8. *The* BALLPARKS

*"You must remember the Stadium is something more than just a ballpark. It's a national monument."*

## Yankee Stadium

"The Big Ballpark," as the Yankees' announcer Mel Allen habitually called it, inspired hyperbole from the start. A Yankee spokesman said in 1922, a year before the stadium opened, that the new park would be made "impenetrable to all human eyes, save those of aviators, by towering embattlements." The day after the park's debut game, Thomas L. Cummiskey, the Universal Service sports editor, wrote, "Today baseball came into a glorious manhood." A team official said in 1956, "You must remember the Stadium is something more than just a ballpark. It's a national monument." And during the pregame ceremonies marking the opening of the redesigned Yankee Stadium on April 15, 1976, former Yankee second baseman Bobby Richardson's invocation included, "In God's eyes the elegant playground, magnificent edifice though it may be, ran second to the immortal souls it held."

The ballpark had to be impressive to compete with the Polo Grounds, New York's baseball showcase since the late nineteenth century. The Giants' playground stood beneath Coogan's Bluff, less than a mile from Yankee Stadium, on the opposite bank of the Harlem River. The Yankees had been tenants there since 1913, but when Babe Ruth hit his unheard-of total of fifty-four home runs in 1920, helping the Yanks draw more spectators than their arrogant landlords, they were then encouraged to leave. More than sixty thousand people crowded into Yankee Stadium when it opened on April 18, 1923. For more than forty years thereafter, the Polo Grounds stood almost literally in Yankee Stadium's shadow.

The soaring profile of the ballpark included a mezzanine that created the first triple-deck stadium. The Osborn Engineering Company's original design called for a fully enclosed arena, but escalating costs limited the grandstand to a point just beyond first and third bases. Uncovered bleachers extended around the rest of the field. The *American Architect*, a professional journal, objected to the "rather idiotic" frieze that decorated the edge of the grandstand roof, an embellishment that as much as anything else

The redesigned Yankee Stadium lacks the majesty of the original, at least in the memories of those fortunate enough to have visited the ballpark prior to 1975. But for millions more, there is still plenty of magic as well as precious memories, thanks to new dynasties and deep bows to the old ones.

**OPPOSITE**

Yankee Stadium (foreground) is lit up in this picture taken in the mid-1950s, as is the Polo Grounds, on the west side of the Harlem River. It was unusual for the teams to play home games at the same time, and in this instance it appears that the Yankees have won the attendance competition.

**PAGE 204**

"The Friendly Confines" have been welcoming Cubs fans for more than three-quarters of a century. Before the Wrigley family moved in, it was called North Side Park, and it was built on land formerly occupied by the Chicago Lutheran Theological Seminary. Phil Wrigley thought that most newspaper advertising was a waste of money. For many years, the only announcement he provided was often included in the entertainment section: "Major League Baseball Today, at 3 PM, at Wrigley Field."

GLADYS GOODDING PLAYED
*"California, Here I Come," "After You've Gone," and*
*"Thanks for the Memories."* The park survived until February 1960.

Ebbets Field in 1913, several weeks before it opened for the first time. It was located in
a section of Brooklyn called Pigtown, which in the early 1900s was considered a slum,
but team owner Charles Hercules Ebbets thought that a "suburban" location would be
ideal. He turned out to be right. The area developed quickly, and it was soon reached
by IRT and BMT subways.

became the ballpark's signature. There were, however, many more admirers that day than detractors. Describing Babe Ruth's fourth-inning, three-run home run, the first hit in the new ballpark, Grantland Rice wrote in the *New York Tribune*, "On a low line it sailed, like a silver flame, through the gray, bleak April shadows and into the rightfield bleachers. And as the crash sounded and the white flash followed, fans arose en masse . . . in the greatest vocal cataclysm baseball has ever known."

In 1999, *Sports Illustrated* ranked Yankee Stadium as its favorite venue, ahead of the Augusta National links, West Point's Michie Stadium, the Saratoga Race Track, and sixteen other storied sites. "No sports arena in history, with the possible exception of the Roman Colosseum, has played host to a wider variety of memorable events," wrote Richard Hoffer, the author of the *SI* piece. Yankee Stadium was the setting for memorable prizefights, championship football games, traditional college football showdowns, historic baseball games, and papal masses. Joe Louis, Y. A. Tittle, Johnny Unitas, Doc Blanchard and Glenn Davis, Babe Ruth, Lou Gehrig, Joe DiMaggio, and Mickey Mantle all performed valiantly beneath the "towering embattlements."

Ruth, Gehrig, and Miller Huggins, the Yankees' manager during most of the Ruth years, had monuments faced with inscribed plaques dedicated to them, and for many years the three memorials stood on the field in the deepest center-field recess of the old Yankee Stadium. They were rarely in play, since they were more than 450 feet away, but once in a while a ball would reach them. On one occasion, an enemy player clouted a ball that bounced in front of the monuments, then behind them, prompting manager Casey Stengel to climb to the top step of the dugout and shout, "Huggins, Gehrig, Ruth: someone throw the damn ball back!" The tablets were moved behind the outfield wall after the renovation, forming the nucleus of Monument Park, an area that now includes more plaques and memorials honoring the accomplishments of players and managers, as well as the longtime

public-address announcer Bob Sheppard and Pete Sheehy, the man in charge of the Yankees' clubhouse for more than sixty years.

Since the mid-1980s, there has been much speculation about the future of Yankee Stadium and its location. Much of it is in response to the lamentations of "the Boss," Mr. Steinbrenner, who argued that the stadium was outmoded and in a dangerous neighborhood. His arguments were substantially deflated as attendance exceeded the three-million level in the late 1990s and early 2000s. Sooner or later, there will probably be a new Yankee Stadium, but it is unimaginable for it to reside anywhere but in the Bronx. Bob Sheppard asked, "Can you imagine moving the Statue of Liberty to Montauk Point?" How would anyone pledge allegiance to the Secaucus Bombers? Count on the new Yankee Stadium to rise, if not on the same site as the old, then within cheering distance. In the Bronx. Where it belongs.

## Ebbets Field

If you imagine, or, better yet, remember, Ebbets Field as a frequently eccentric venue, you're right, as a sample of the ground rules below, reprinted from a 1950 scorecard, testifies:

- Batted ball hitting wire on rightfield fence in fair territory and then dropping behind sign in foul territory (rightfield corner).... two bases
- Batted ball going through wire in rightfield fence....homerun; if ball sticks in wire.... in play
- Batted ball going through scoreboard.... homerun; if ball sticks in scoreboard.... in play
- Batted ball hitting above rail in extension of lower stand in extreme corner of centerfield marked with red lines....homerun
- Batted ball hitting parallel foul line in extreme leftfield, going into stands in either foul or fair territory....two bases; if ball comes back on field....in play

A ballpark conceived by Kafka? Umpires may have thought so as they struggled to interpret the code in the heat of action while Hilda Chester's cowbell, the Dodgers Sym-Phony, and the Flatbush Faithful clamored in the background. Umpires weren't the only victims. Dick "Rowdy Richard" Bartell of the despised New York Giants was smacked with a tomato on opening day of the 1935 season. Another Giants player, pinch-hitting demon Dusty Rhodes, said, "The ballpark is too hard to get to, and when you finally do get there you find out it wasn't worth the trip in the first place." After the Yankees lost three straight games at Ebbets Field in the 1955 World Series, the Bombers' Hank Bauer said, "I'll be glad to get out of this rat trap." Even Dodgers players joined the chorus. Cal Abrams growled, "I want to see the leftfielder who can last five years in Ebbets Field." He promised an award to whoever did, for "accepting the most abuse in the league." And Ivy Olson, Brooklyn's shortstop from 1915 through 1924, routinely stuffed cotton in his ears to drown out the invective directed at him.

Charles Hercules Ebbets, the owner of the Dodgers in 1913, when the park was built, supervised all construction details, taking special pride in the rotunda entrance situated beneath the grandstand behind home plate. Eighty feet in diameter and walled with marble, the entry featured a tile floor inlaid with a huge baseball design. Twelve brass-caged ticket booths and fourteen turnstiles admitted fans to their seats. A chandelier displayed twelve arms in the shape of baseball bats, from which light globes modeled after regulation-size baseballs hung.

In later years, the right-field wall and scoreboard provided additional character. The wall stretched fifty-five feet from the foul pole to the scoreboard and was divided into three horizontal sections: a padded, nine-foot slope, a ten-foot concrete segment, and a nineteen-foot wire fence on top. The edge of the scoreboard jutted out at a five-foot angle from the wall and screen, creating more opportunities for batted balls to carom crazily. Carl Furillo, for many years the Dodgers' virtuoso right fielder, described seventeen angles at which a batted ball could rebound from the various

configurations. He mastered them all—and he also protected Brooklyn clothier Abe Stark's "Hit Sign—Win Suit" ad that ran along the bottom of the scoreboard.

All these curiosities only added to the joy of an afternoon or evening spent at Ebbets Field. Nothing matched the first glimpse of the park's interior: the proximity of the grandstands, the green grass, the white baselines, and the bright red, blue, and yellow colors of the billboards decorating the outfield walls. Happy Felton and his Knot Hole Gang could be seen in the Dodgers' bull pen inside the right-field corner, and organist Gladys Goodding serenaded the faithful from her perch near the press box. After public-address announcer Tex Rickards intoned the starting lineups, the Dodgers bounded onto the field; white uniforms and blue caps are etched in our memory forever.

In 1957, Ebbets Field succumbed to its limited capacity, demographics, and, of course, the Dodgers' announced move to California. The last game, a 2–0 victory over the Pirates, was attended by less than seven thousand spectators. As the fans filed slowly out, Gladys Goodding played a medley of tunes that included "California, Here I Come," "After You've Gone," and "Thanks for the Memories." The park survived until February 1960, when demolition began on a chilly, overcast morning. Two months later, souvenirs were auctioned off to benefit Brooklyn Little League teams.

Eighteen dollars was the winning bid for the ballpark's blueprints, and Pee Wee Reese's clubhouse stool went for three dollars.

## Fenway Park

No one loved Fenway Park more than its longtime owner Tom Yawkey. After he bought the Red Sox in 1933, he spent more than a million Depression-era dollars rebuilding the ballpark. He also spent lavishly on players he hoped would enable him to fly championship flags above the park. But between 1933 and 1960, only one pennant was won, prompting Yawkey to say at the time, "It's awfully hard to win in this ballpark. I'm not sure we can ever do so. It

Johnny Podres, pitching against the Milwaukee Braves in the summer of 1957. Roger Kahn wrote about the old ballpark's intimacy: "In thousands of seats fans could hear a ballplayer's chatter, notice details of a ballplayer's gait . . . and you could actually see the actual expression on the actual face of an actual major leaguer as he played." Red Barber said, "When you had a box seat you were practically playing the infield."

BELOW
Fenway Park has inspired countless writers to flourish their pens, perhaps no one more so than Joe Falls, who wrote for the *Detroit News*. "I have often said that if I could have my choice of where I could die," he wrote, "it would be in the press box at Fenway Park on a fresh afternoon in June."

Much of the neighborhood surrounding Fenway Park would have to be razed to make room for a new ballpark, and so far the reconstruction efforts have been stymied. Historian Doris Kearns Goodwin campaigned for a new Fenway Park when she wrote, "After all, history proves that the Red Sox have won World Series championships each time they've moved to a new ballpark." History was rewritten by the Red Sox's stunning accomplishments in 2004.

OVERLEAF
Due to Wrigley's small scale, the bleachers are an excellent place to watch a game, and they are usually sold out. Bill Veeck said, "It doesn't matter if customers of customers, or friends of friends of NBC's advertisers crowd into boxes. It's the bleachers that count. Modestly put, bleacher fans are inspirational and irreplaceable."

kills the young pitchers, and you can't win without pitching."

The ballpark was built on a mudflat that the landscape architect Frederick Law Olmsted transformed into parkland at the turn of the century. Fenway's first game took place on April 9, 1912, when the Red Sox beat the Harvard University nine in a snowstorm. The first league game was played on April 20, against the New York Highlanders (later renamed the Yankees), a contest the Red Sox won 7–6, with Tris Speaker driving in the winning run. The original structure included a single-deck grandstand, a bleacher section between the grandstand and the left-field corner, more bleachers in center and right, and a pavilion in the right-field corner. A steep incline below the left-field wall was named "Duffy's Cliff," in honor of Red Sox left fielder Duffy Lewis, who traversed the hill with the surefootedness of a mountain goat.

Yawkey's rebuilt ballpark opened in 1934. The grandstands were by now connected, and everything was painted a bright green. Duffy's Cliff and the original wall were replaced by a high wall later dubbed "the Green Monster." It became Fenway's identifying feature. Outfield dimensions were 315 feet to the left-field foul pole, 420 feet to center field, and 334 feet down the right-field line. Except for right field, the distances have changed very little in succeeding years. Sky-view seats were added on either side of the press box in 1946, and lights were installed the following year. In 1958, the city rejected a proposal to annex Landsdowne Street and move the left-field wall back to accommodate additional seating. In recent years, the press box has been remodeled and expanded, and seats have been installed at the top edge of the Green Monster and above the top of the right-field grandstand. Despite such tinkerings, Fenway retains its charm.

The ballpark has achieved almost mythic status over the years, thanks to the many prose and poetry rhapsodies celebrating it, and the numerous calamities suffered by the Red Sox in the years between their World Championships in 1918 and 2004. For the present,

Fenway is safe from the abandonment ambitions of its new owners. Squabbles with the city and with neighboring residences and businesses seem eternal. And the notorious left-field wall still stands, a symbol of frustration and failure.

"Ah Hell, it's all in people's minds. It's the same everywhere. You have to throw the ball. I never worry about the park." These words were spoken by Red Sox pitcher Mike Torrez late in the 1978 season, just a few days before he threw a ball to a singles hitter named Bucky Dent—who lofted the ball into the net above the Green Monster, winning the pennant for the Yankees, and thereby denying the Red Sox on the last day of another star-crossed season.

### Wrigley Field

The Chicago Cubs have been competitive so infrequently since they began playing at Wrigley Field, almost ninety years ago, that some find it difficult to understand why fans turn out in such impressive numbers year after year. Anyone attending a game at Wrigley understands immediately. The ballpark often transcends the game. Affection for Wrigley Field at times exceeds loyalty to the team. The Cubs frequently disappoint; Wrigley Field never does.

Located on Chicago's North Side, the ballpark is part of a neighborhood of residences, taverns, and small businesses. Elevated trains clatter over tracks just a block from the bleacher entrance, the Chicago skyline rises to the south, and Lake Michigan shimmers to the east. Inside, the green field is bounded by a cozy, double-deck grandstand and pyramid-shaped bleachers topped by an antique scoreboard. The red-brick outfield wall is stitched with ivy and bittersweet. Writing in *Sports Illustrated*, E. M. Swift called Wrigley Field a "Peter Pan of a ballpark. It has never grown up and it has never grown old."

The ivy was planted in 1937 by Bill Veeck, whose father ran the Cubs for the Wrigley family. The growth lent aesthetic appeal, as well as occasional comic relief. In the early 1940s, a part-time Cubs outfielder named Dom Dallesandro, sometimes described as "the fireplug

who walked like a man," got snarled in the vines while attempting a leaping catch. During the 1945 World Series, a ball hit by the Tigers' Roy Cullenbine got lost in the thicket, and while Andy Pafko thrashed about madly in search of it, Cullenbine circled the bases and scored. Lou Novikoff, "the Mad Russian," another 1940s outfielder, was convinced that the wall was bristling with poison ivy, and he rarely ventured beyond the front edge of the warning track. And left fielder Hank Sauer, a devotee of chewing tobacco, used to stash bags of the stuff in the ivy vines, transforming the bush into a leafy humidor.

The park was built in 1914 for the Chicago Whales, a member of the short-lived Federal League, and originally named Weeghman Park for team owner Charlie Weeghman. The Cubs moved in two years later and renamed the stadium Cubs Park. At that point, the ballpark provided only about fourteen thousand seats. More seats were added in 1922 and 1923 with the enlargement of the grandstand and the construction of temporary bleachers. A second deck was added in 1927, increasing the seating capacity to nearly thirty-eight thousand. That year, a million paid admissions were counted for the first time in baseball history. By then, the Wrigley chewing-gum family owned the team, and the ballpark had been rechristened Wrigley Field. In 1937, the bleachers were expanded and raised above field level, the brick wall was constructed, and a new scoreboard, still in use, was put up.

Phil Wrigley was praised for preserving daytime baseball long after every other ball club installed lights, but in fact he began work on a lighting system late in 1941. Following the attack on Pearl Harbor, he donated the towers, cables, and lights to a naval construction facility. Throughout the 1940s and 1950s, portable lights were used for boxing and wrestling matches, rodeos, Harlem Globetrotter exhibitions, political rallies, and conventions. But until 1988, major-league baseball was played there only in the daytime.

Ernie Banks played in Wrigley Field for eighteen seasons, and he has returned regularly ever since. "People remember their days at Wrigley Field," he said. "It's the same there; it never changes. And when you leave, you're still there."

## Camden Yards

Oriole Park at Camden Yards is the ballpark's official name, but it is known now and forever as Camden Yards. The short version links the park immediately to its historic neighborhood, and history plays a major role in the stadium's character. The day before its debut, after an exhibition game between the Orioles and the New York Mets, Cal Ripken said, "You get the feeling this wasn't the first game played here." There may well have been friendly ghosts haunting the grounds. A house where Babe Ruth once lived stood in what is now right-center field.

One of the ballpark's charms is its rooted aspect. Even when it was new, it didn't seem to be, since it blended so naturally with the buildings adjacent to it. A reporter attending the first league game wrote that "it's as if this ballpark comes equipped with memories." That contest, against the Cleveland Indians, was won by the Orioles 2–0 in two hours and two minutes, another nod to tradition. Winning pitcher Rick Sutcliffe said the park was "a combination of many old friends put together."

A lot of people put together, friendly or not, were responsible for the masterpiece. Dismissing the new Comiskey Park in Chicago, which opened in 1991, a year before Camden Yards, the Orioles' playground was the first in a wave of retro ballparks, and it is still the best example. In addition to the architect, graphic designer, and club owner, other, less titled people contributed. The groundskeeper suggested a slight alteration to place the foul lines a bit closer to the spectators. A fan wrote to the club recommending field-level signage such as he'd seen at Ebbets Field, and another fan suggested designs on the ends of seat rows, reminiscent of those at the Polo Grounds. All were adopted.

In addition to Ebbets Field and the Polo Grounds, Fenway Park, Wrigley Field, and the departed Forbes Field in Pittsburgh served as

A decorative wrought-iron fence runs above the rear of the left-field grandstand, through which pedestrians can catch a tantalizing glimpse of Camden Yards' interior. The field is set sixteen feet below street level, allowing the park's exterior to loom less obtrusively. It also means that many fans walk down to their seats, as did New York Giants fans who entered the Polo Grounds from an elevated ramp behind home plate.

RICK SUTCLIFFE SAID THE PARK WAS

*"a combination of many old friends put together."*

The refurbished Camden Station stands at the left end of the warehouse and is the
terminal for commuter trains, as well as special trains carrying fans to the game.
William E. Thoms, assigned to describe the railroad setting for *Trains* magazine, wrote,
"Thus the Monumental City has again embraced downtown baseball and railroading
with the fervor once reserved for sailing ships and blue crabs."

inspirations. The degree of success achieved from such a blend was affirmed by Paul Goldberger, the architecture critic for the *New York Times*, who wrote, "This is a design that enriches baseball, the city, and the region . . . and makes every sprawling concrete dome sitting in a sea of parked cars look bloated, fat, and tired." David Ashton, the graphic designer whose passion contributed so much to the ballpark's appeal, had the concrete ovals very much in mind as he crafted details that celebrated baseball, not gimmickry. He wrote, "We were very cognizant of the fact that it could easily have been made cute and become a theme park. It's not a place that you go to ride the rides, you go there to be entertained by the ballgame."

To be sure, there are attractions and diversions outside the park. What's important is that the ballpark was built with these in mind, not the other way around. One such is the Baltimore & Ohio warehouse that looms above the right-field fence. It dates from 1898, and at more than one thousand feet long, it is the largest building of its type in the East. The red-brick structure is as much a signature of Camden Yards as the frieze that decorated the top of the old Yankee Stadium grandstand. Close by is the restored Camden Station, built in 1865 and renovated in 1912. It once stood along the double-track, B&O Royal Blue line between Washington, D.C., Philadelphia, and points north, and now it serves commuter traffic as well as trains to the ballpark from Washington. The trains, operated by the Maryland Rail Commuter service, are affectionately called "MARC to the park." The Maryland Stadium Authority, the organization that raised more than $100 million to build the ballpark, also raised $12 million to renovate the B&O warehouse, along with another $2.2 million to repair Camden Station. Baltimore Heritage President Fred Shoken asked, "Who would have thought a major league franchise would be interested in preservation?"

The only thing missing is a championship team, but through many lean years Orioles fans have supported the team loyally. Such unrequited affections are substantially

OVERLEAF
In the midst of all the raptures expressed about the new park's debut, Ray Ratto, a columnist for the *San Francisco Examiner,* issued a wet-blanket piece: "What we have here, you see, is not a miracle, but a bal park. . . . A nice ballpark, true, with all the quaint touches the architects could steal from all the other ballparks, but still just a ballpark."

rewarded by a trip to Camden Yards. The accomplished essayist Roger Angell wrote, "This is a fan's park. . . . They've done it at last."

## SBC Park

Like Camden Yards, SBC Park in San Francisco celebrates its city's roots and character. It is just a brisk twenty-minute walk from the downtown area, a short stroll from the Caltrain railroad station and BART stop, and accessible by ferry from various points around the Bay Area. It is an authentic neighborhood ballpark, tucked into a comparatively small thirteen-acre parcel. Neighbors include apartment buildings, restaurants, and small businesses. It displaced a decaying warehouse district, and it has brought to the China Basin area a new vitality. And like Camden Yards, it seems to have been there for a long time. After the park's first game in April 2000, a longtime resident of San Francisco told TV announcer Mike Krukow, "This park has an old soul."

Its ancestor was the infamous oval on Candlestick Point, a ballpark so vulnerable to gale-force winds that a slightly built Giants pitcher named Stu Miller was actually blown off the pitcher's mound on one occasion. Pop flies, routine in most ballparks, were adventures at Candlestick. Catcher Bob Uecker said, "The Stick could make you look like a Little Leaguer." Lefty O'Doul, a legendary Bay Area ballplayer, grew up in the hills of Hunter's Point, not far from Candlestick Point He often said that he should have been consulted as to the wisdom of locating a ballpark there. He would have told planners that he used to herd his father's sheep in the area, and that the animals were frequently blown down the hill by gusts of wind. It was later learned that some good old-fashioned municipal graft was primarily responsible for the location.

A more enlightened mentality guided the planning of the new park. A professor of aeronautical science and engineering from the University of California at Davis was hired to study wind patterns and prevailing temperatures at China Basin. He built a scale model of the planned park and simulated wind conditions

in a lab, assisted by sophisticated computer calculations. He concluded that the location would be significantly less windy—but no warmer. Spectators are happily living with that combination.

Fans are equally content with the ballpark's features and attractions. Most important is the magnificent setting. From most seats, the city skyline and adjoining bay are visible, and as the sun sets, the golden hue on the Berkeley and Oakland Hills is breathtaking. Inside the park, some imaginative touches include an eighty-foot-long wooden Coke bottle, tilted next to the center-field scoreboard, with a huge, four-fingered baseball glove next to it, an antique cable car resting near a picnic plaza, a promenade behind the right-field wall that offers pedestrians a view of the field at no charge, and of course the wall itself, placed at the edge of McCovey Cove, into which slugger Barry Bonds has plunked many of his towering home runs. They have become known as splash hits.

In addition to the heroes romping on the green field, another hero can be found in the owners' box. Peter Magowan, the senior partner of the Giants' ownership group, played a major role in arranging the financing for the ballpark in 1996. He recalled living in New York during the 1950s, and how heartbroken he had been when the Giants and Dodgers decamped for California. He was determined that the Giants would stay in San Francisco. The financing was accomplished with no taxpayer involvement, the first time a ballpark had been privately bankrolled since Dodger Stadium in 1962. Some of the costs were offset by naming rights, secured for $50 million by Pacific Bell. Pac Bell Park became SBC Park early in 2004, when the communications giant bought Pacific Bell. In 1998, Magowan briefly considered naming the park the Polo Grounds. He approached Ralph Lauren with the idea, thinking Lauren would agree that his polo logo would tie in nicely. Lauren responded eagerly, and he reportedly asked if a million dollars or so would be involved. Magowan remembers taking a deep breath and telling Lauren, "I was thinking somewhere north of that."

The ballpark opened on April 11, 2000. The Dodgers, an ancient foe, provided the opposition. The visitors spoiled the party by winning 6–5. The Giants went on to lose their next five games at home, and it was almost May before they won their first home contest. There was, of course, a happy ending to the ballpark's maiden voyage when the Giants won the National League West title after speeding through the last three months of the season at a .686 pace. After the division-winning victory, Giants players cavorted happily around the grounds, waving champagne bottles at their adoring fans.

McCovey Cove is in the foreground, where many of Barry Bonds's home runs splash down, some of which are retrieved by a team of black Portuguese water dogs. They are more or less officially known as the Baseball Aquatic Retriever Korps, or BARK, and their duties inspired the Dodgers' announcer Vin Scully to remark, "It's the only park where they can have a seventh-inning fetch."

# Index

## Credits

The authors and publisher would like to thank the following for granting permission to use photos from their collections:

AP/Wide World Photos (7, 13, 25, 35, 46 bottom, 54, 70, 78, 84, 95, 104, 107, 117 top, 118, 131, 132, 136, 142, 143, 144, 148, 156, 159, 160, 165, 166, 169, 170 bottom, 175, 180, 182, 183, 188, 219)

Bettman/CORBIS (147, 151, 178, 187, 194 both, 199, 216)

Brown Brothers (14, 15, 39, 50, 59, 101)

Getty Images (2, 53, 141)

Andy Jurinko (201, 203, 207 bottom, 208, 210, 213)

Library of Congress (11, 18, 19, 22, 23, 29 left, 30, 32, 40, 41, 44, 45, 48, 49, 56, 57, 61, 62, 64, 65, 66, 69, 76, 81, 85, 92, 97, 103, 121, 122, 133, 134, 137, 138, 181, 184, 193)

Sport Media Enterprises, Inc. (21, 29 right, 33, 36, 43, 73, 196)

Transcendental Graphics (38, 46 top, 51, 55, 58, 75, 79, 86, 87, 88, 98, 100, 111, 129, 164, 173 top, 177, 185)